Netscape Navigator® 4 Browsing and Beyond

Netscape Navigator® 4 Browsing and Beyond

Barbara Kasser

IDG Books Worldwide, Inc.

An International Data Group Company

Foster City, CA · Chicago, IL · Indianapolis, IN · Southlake, TX

Netscape Navigator® 4 Browsing and Beyond

Published by
IDG Books Worldwide, Inc.
An International Data Group Company
919 E. Hillsdale Blvd., Suite 400
Foster City, CA 94404

http://www.idgbooks.com (IDG Books Worldwide Web site)

Library of Congress Catalog Card No.: 97-71285

ISBN: 0-7645-3090-9

Printed in the United States of America

10 9 8 7 6 5 4 3 2 1

1DD/RQ/RQ/ZX/FC

Distributed in the United States by IDG Books Worldwide, Inc.

Distributed by Macmillan Canada for Canada; by Contemporanea de Ediciones for Venezuela; by Distribuidora Cuspide for Argentina; by CITEC for Brazil; by Ediciones ZETA S.C.R. Ltda. for Peru; by Editorial Limusa SA for Mexico; by Transworld Publishers Limited in the United Kingdom and Europe; by Academic Bookshop for Egypt; by Levant Distributors S.A.R.L. for Lebanon; by Al Jassim for Saudi Arabia; by Simron Pty. Ltd. for South Africa; by Pustak Mahal for India; by The Computer Bookshop for India; by Toppan Company Ltd. for Japan; by Addison Wesley Publishing Company for Korea; by Longman Singapore Publishers Ltd. for Singapore, Malaysia, Thailand, and Indonesia; by Unalis Corporation for Taiwan; by WS Computer Publishing Company, Inc. for the Philippines; by WoodsLane Pty. Ltd. for Australia; by WoodsLane Enterprises Ltd. for New Zealand. Authorized Sales Agent: Anthony Rudkin Associates for the Middle East and North Africa.

For general information on IDG Books Worldwide's books in the U.S., please call our Consumer Customer Service department at 800-762-2974. For reseller information, including discounts and premium sales, please call our Reseller Customer Service department at 800-434-3422.

For information on where to purchase IDG Books Worldwide's books outside the U.S., please contact our International Sales department at 415-655-3023 or fax 415-655-3299.

For information on foreign language translations, please contact our Foreign & Subsidiary Rights department at 415-655-3021 or fax 415-655-3281.

For sales inquiries and special prices for bulk quantities, please contact our Sales department at 415-655-3200 or write to the address above.

For information on using IDG Books Worldwide's books in the classroom or for ordering examination copies, please contact our Educational Sales department at 800-434-2086 or fax 817-251-8174.

For press review copies, author interviews, or other publicity information, please contact our Public Relations department at 415-655-3000 or fax 415-655-3299.

For authorization to photocopy items for corporate, personal, or educational use, please contact Copyright Clearance Center, 222 Rosewood Drive, Danvers, MA 01923, or fax 508-750-4470.

The IDG Books Worldwide logo is a trademark under exclusive license to IDG Books Worldwide, Inc., from International Data Group, Inc.

ABOUT IDG BOOKS WORLDWIDE

Welcome to the world of IDG Books Worldwide.

IDG Books Worldwide, Inc., is a subsidiary of International Data Group, the world's largest publisher of computer-related information and the leading global provider of information services on information technology. IDG was founded more than 25 years ago and now employs more than 8,500 people worldwide. IDG publishes more than 275 computer publications in over 75 countries (see listing below). More than 60 million people read one or more IDG publications each month.

Launched in 1990, IDG Books Worldwide is today the #1 publisher of best-selling computer books in the United States. We are proud to have received eight awards from the Computer Press Association in recognition of editorial excellence and three from *Computer Currents'* First Annual Readers' Choice Awards. Our best-selling *...For Dummies*® series has more than 30 million copies in print with translations in 30 languages. IDG Books Worldwide, through a joint venture with IDG's Hi-Tech Beijing, became the first U.S. publisher to publish a computer book in the People's Republic of China. In record time, IDG Books Worldwide has become the first choice for millions of readers around the world who want to learn how to better manage their businesses.

Our mission is simple: Every one of our books is designed to bring extra value and skill-building instructions to the reader. Our books are written by experts who understand and care about our readers. The knowledge base of our editorial staff comes from years of experience in publishing, education, and journalism — experience we use to produce books for the '90s. In short, we care about books, so we attract the best people. We devote special attention to details such as audience, interior design, use of icons, and illustrations. And because we use an efficient process of authoring, editing, and desktop publishing our books electronically, we can spend more time ensuring superior content and spend less time on the technicalities of making books.

You can count on our commitment to deliver high-quality books at competitive prices on topics you want to read about. At IDG Books Worldwide, we continue in the IDG tradition of delivering quality for more than 25 years. You'll find no better book on a subject than one from IDG Books Worldwide.

John Kilcullen
CEO
IDG Books Worldwide, Inc.

Steven Berkowitz
President and Publisher
IDG Books Worldwide, Inc.

Eighth Annual Computer Press Awards ≥1992

Ninth Annual Computer Press Awards ≥1993

Tenth Annual Computer Press Awards ≥1994

Eleventh Annual Computer Press Awards ≥1995

IDG Books Worldwide, Inc., is a subsidiary of International Data Group, the world's largest publisher of computer-related information and the leading global provider of information services on information technology. International Data Group publishes over 275 computer publications in over 75 countries. Sixty million people read one or more International Data Group publications each month. International Data Group's publications include: **ARGENTINA:** Buyer's Guide, Computerworld Argentina, PC World Argentina; **AUSTRALIA:** Australian Macworld, Australian Reseller News, Computerworld, IT Casebook, Network World, Publish, Webmaster; **AUSTRIA:** Computerwelt Osterreich, Networks Austria, PC Tip Austria; **BANGLADESH:** PC World Bangladesh; **BELARUS:** PC World Belarus; **BELGIUM:** Data News; **BRAZIL:** Annuario de Informatica, Computerworld, Connections, Macworld, PC Player, PC World, Publish, Reseller News, Supergamepower; **BULGARIA:** Computerworld Bulgaria, Network World Bulgaria, PC & MacWorld Bulgaria; **CANADA:** CIO Canada, Client/Server World, ComputerWorld Canada, InfoWorld Canada, NetworkWorld Canada, WebWorld; **CHILE:** Computerworld Chile, PC World Chile; **COLOMBIA:** Computerworld Colombia, PC World Colombia; **COSTA RICA:** PC World Centro America; **THE CZECH AND SLOVAK REPUBLICS:** Computerworld Czechoslovakia, Macworld Czech Republic, PC World Czechoslovakia; **DENMARK:** Communications World Danmark, Computerworld Danmark, Macworld Danmark, PC World Danmark, Techworld Denmark; **DOMINICAN REPUBLIC:** PC World Republica Dominicana; **ECUADOR:** PC World Ecuador; **EGYPT:** Computerworld Middle East, PC World Middle East; **EL SALVADOR:** PC World Centro America; **FINLAND:** MikroPC, Tietoverkko, Tietoviikko; **FRANCE:** Distributique, Hebdo, Info PC, Le Monde Informatique, Macworld, Reseaux & Telecoms, WebMaster France; **GERMANY:** Computer Partner, Computerwoche, Computerwoche Extra, Computerwoche FOCUS, Global Online, Macwelt, PC Welt; **GREECE:** Amiga Computing, GamePro Greece, Multimedia World; **GUATEMALA:** PC World Centro America; **HONDURAS:** PC World Centro America; **HONG KONG:** Computerworld Hong Kong, PC World Hong Kong, Publish in Asia; **HUNGARY:** ABCD CD-ROM, Computerworld Szamitastechnika, Internetto online Magazine, PC World Hungary, PC-X Magazin Hungary; **ICELAND:** Tolvuheimur PC World Island; **INDIA:** Information Communications World, Information Systems Computerworld, PC World India, Publish in Asia; **INDONESIA:** InfoKomputer PC World, Komputek Computerworld, Publish in Asia; **IRELAND:** ComputerScope, PC Live!; **ISRAEL:** Macworld Israel, People & Computers/Computerworld; **ITALY:** Computerworld Italia, Macworld Italia, Networking Italia, PC World Italia; **JAPAN:** DTP World, Macworld Japan, Nikkei Personal Computing, OS/2 World Japan, SunWorld Japan, Windows NT World, Windows World Japan; **KENYA:** PC World East African; **KOREA:** Hi-Tech Information, Macworld Korea, PC World Korea; **MACEDONIA:** PC World Macedonia; **MALAYSIA:** Computerworld Malaysia, PC World Malaysia, Publish in Asia; **MALTA:** PC World Malta; **MEXICO:** Computerworld Mexico, PC World Mexico; **MYANMAR:** PC World Myanmar; **NETHERLANDS:** Computer! Totaal, LAN Internetworking Magazine, LAN World Buyers Guide, Macworld Netherlands, Net, WebWereld; **NEW ZEALAND:** Absolute Beginners Guide and Plain & Simple Series, Computer Buyer, Computer Industry Directory, Computerworld New Zealand, MTB, Network World, PC World New Zealand; **NICARAGUA:** PC World Centro America; **NORWAY:** Computerworld Norge, CW Rapport, Datamagasinet, Financial Rapport, Kursguide Norge, Macworld Norge, Multimediaworld Norge, PC World Ekspress Norge, PC World Nettverk, PC World Norge, PC World ProduktGuide Norge; **PAKISTAN:** Computerworld Pakistan; **PANAMA:** PC World Panama; **PEOPLE'S REPUBLIC OF CHINA:** China Computer Users, China Computerworld, China InfoWorld, China Telecom World Weekly, Computer & Communication, Electronic Design China, Electronics Today, Electronics Weekly, Game Software, PC World China, Popular Computer Week, Software Weekly, Software World, Telecom World; **PERU:** Computerworld Peru, PC World Profesional Peru, PC World Profesional Peru, PC World SoHo Peru; **PHILIPPINES:** Click!, Computerworld Philippines, PC World Philippines, Publish in Asia; **POLAND:** Computerworld Poland, Computerworld Special Report Poland, Cyber, Macworld Poland, Networld Poland, PC World Komputer; **PORTUGAL:** Cerebro/PC World, Computerworld/Correio Informatico, Dealer World Portugal, Mac*In/PC*In Portugal, Multimedia World; **PUERTO RICO:** PC World Puerto Rico; **ROMANIA:** Computerworld Romania, PC World Romania, Telecom Romania; **RUSSIA:** Computerworld Russia, Mir PK, Publish, Seti; **SINGAPORE:** Computerworld Singapore, PC World Singapore, Publish in Asia; **SLOVENIA:** Monitor; **SOUTH AFRICA:** Computing SA, Network World SA, Software World SA; **SPAIN:** Communicaciones World España, Computerworld España, Dealer World España, Macworld España, PC World España; **SRI LANKA:** Infolink PC World; **SWEDEN:** CAP&Design, Computer Sweden, Corporate Computing Sweden, Internetworld Sweden, it.branschen, Macworld Sweden, MaxiData Sweden, MikroDatorn, Natverk & Kommunikation, PC World Sweden, PCaktiv, Windows World Sweden; **SWITZERLAND:** Computerworld Schweiz, Macworld Schweiz, PCtip; **TAIWAN:** Computerworld Taiwan, Macworld Taiwan, NEW ViSiON/Publish, PC World Taiwan, Windows World Taiwan; **THAILAND:** Publish in Asia, Thai Computerworld; **TURKEY:** Computerworld Turkiye, Macworld Turkiye, Network World Turkiye, PC World Turkiye; **UKRAINE:** Computerworld Kiev, Multimedia World Ukraine, PC World Ukraine; **UNITED KINGDOM:** Acorn User UK, Amiga Action UK, Amiga Computing UK, Apple Talk UK, Computing, Macworld, Parents and Computers UK, PC Advisor, PC Home, PSX Pro, The WEB; **UNITED STATES:** Cable in the Classroom, CIO Magazine, Computerworld, DOS World, Federal Computer Week, GamePro Magazine, InfoWorld, I-Way, Macworld, Network World, PC Games, PC World, Publish, Video Event, THE WEB Magazine, and WebMaster; online webzines: JavaWorld, NetscapeWorld, and SunWorld Online; **URUGUAY:** InfoWorld Uruguay; **VENEZUELA:** Computerworld Venezuela, PC World Venezuela; and **VIETNAM:** PC World Vietnam.   3/24/97

Credits

Acquisitions Editor	John Read
Development Editor	Susan Pines
Technical Editors	Paul Summitt
	Allen Wyatt
Copy Editor	Larisa North
Project Coordinator	Katy German
Book Designer	seventeenth street studios
Graphics and Production Specialists	Dina F Quan
	Elyse Kaplan-Steinberger
	Mario Amador
Proofreader	Arielle Carole Mennelle
Indexer	Ty Koontz

About the Author

Barbara Kasser is a network administrator and trainer for a Fortune 500 company. She also teaches classes and develops training manuals for Computer Coach, a private training facility in Boca Raton, Florida. Her favorite class involves teaching new users about the Internet. Barbara's friends and students call her an Internet junkie, because she logs in for a few hours every day.

When she's not working, writing, or teaching, Barbara loves to spend time with her husband, Bill, and her son, Richard. Barbara is learning to play golf, but her game has a long way to go. In her spare time (in the middle of the night), Barbara designs Web pages.

To the memory of my dad, Mort,
who was always proud of me.
He would have loved the Internet!
I miss you, Dad.

PREFACE

Everyone's talking about Netscape. As soon as people find out I'm a software trainer, they ask about Netscape and the Internet. I don't blame them! Even though I spend hours logged on to the Internet, I'm never bored. I always find something new, exciting, or informative to look at. My family uses it almost as much as I do — for research, messaging, games, and general information.

From seniors to students, everyone is eager to become part of the Internet explosion. And why not? Even if you don't have any Internet experience, Netscape Communicator enables you to surf the World Wide Web, send and receive
e-mail messages, join a discussion group, and conduct an Internet conference with someone around the world or just around the block.

Surveying Netscape Communicator

This book covers Netscape Communicator 4.0, Standard Edition, which is composed of several different software programs that work together, providing access to all of the Internet's components. If you want to search through the Web, Navigator can take you there. Sending and receiving e-mail is a breeze with Messenger. Conference enables you to speak and listen to other members of your organization, regardless of where they're located, and without incurring hefty long-distance charges. Collabra is designed to enable you to attend "virtual meetings" — online discussion groups that meet without the hassle of rounding up all the participants into one room. Netcaster sends information, such as headlines or the latest entertainment news or stock prices, from different channels to your computer, using the "push" technology. Finally, Composer enables you to create snazzy Internet pages for your personal or corporate use without having to learn HyperText Markup Language (HTML), the language with which Web pages are created.

Who Should Read This Book

If you have a busy schedule, have limited Internet knowledge or experience, and don't know much about Communicator, this book helps you become knowledgeable in a short time.

This book is designed for you to jump into Communicator immediately. Let's face it: you don't have time to wade through online manuals and technical journals filled with terms you can't comprehend. I understand you expect information and examples that make sense. Because I respect your time, I've provided you with exercises that help you learn by doing, instead of reading. For example, instead of learning about electronic mail in an abstract sense, you'll actually send and receive messages as you become proficient with e-mail.

You should have some elementary Windows knowledge, such as how to turn on your computer and how to perform simple Windows functions. You should also know a bit of information about your computer, such as whether it's equipped with a modem. I'll tell you where and when to click the mouse, and which mouse button to click.

How This Book Is Organized

This book is broken down into four parts that cover various components of Communicator. Each part includes a series of lessons, filled with exercises to help you learn by example. The parts of the book are described as follows:

Part I: Getting Starting with Navigator. This part provides the groundwork for visiting the Web with Navigator. As you move around the Web with Navigator, you learn Web basics, such as how a Web address is structured and how to visit and return to many Web sites. You print and save Web pages and customize Navigator for your own use.

Part II: Touring the World Wide Web. Once you've established Navigator basics, you're ready to move on to more advanced Web navigation. Whether you're using the Web for research or pleasure, you'll learn how to find the sites you want from over 17,000,000 existing Web pages. You'll have fun on the Web with a variety of exercises that will leave you feeling like a pro.

Part III: Communicating Electronically. In this part, you have the opportunity to communicate with others on the Internet. You use Messenger as you learn the ins and outs of e-mail; when you finish with this section, you'll be a master at sending and receiving e-mail messages. You set up both your Address Book and message folders. You also use Conference to speak (talk out loud) to another person running Conference. Finally, you learn how to join discussion groups—special interest groups that post messages about topics you find interesting. Over 15,000 discussion groups exist, so you're sure to find one you like.

Part IV: Composing Web Pages. In this section, you sample Web authoring techniques as you create Web pages using Netscape's Page Wizard and templates. Even if you have no experience designing Web documents, you'll find that you can put together a great-looking Web page. Once you have a little experience under your belt, you advance to using Composer, the component of Communicator that enables you to build custom Web pages, without knowing any special programming languages or code.

The accompanying CD-ROM. The CD-ROM included with this book contains the Netscape Communicator 4.02 and EarthLink Network TotalAccess software. See Appendix C for details and installation information.

How to Use This Book

You can read this book from cover to cover or simply open to the part that contains the material you want to learn. Once you've finished with the book, keep it next to your computer to use as a reference document. Here's a quick rundown of the elements you encounter in each lesson.

Stopwatch: Use the time shown next to the stopwatch as a guide for how long the exercises will take. Because the time shown is an estimate, don't be surprised if you take a few minutes more, or less, to complete the exercises.

Goals: Each lesson begins with a list of goals that you'll accomplish.

Get Ready: The Get Ready section tells you what you need to complete the lesson. For example, if you need to be connected to the Internet before you can complete the exercises, you find out in this section.

Exercises: Each lesson contains exercises with numbered steps that promote learning by example. Because this book is hands-on, you should perform each step. The steps are detailed so that you can easily follow along.

Visual Bonus: Use each lesson's Visual Bonus to explore a particular aspect of the material presented in the lesson. Think of the Visual Bonus as an extra reference card. Don't look for the Visual Bonus in the same place in each lesson; each bonus is placed where you'll get the most out of it.

Tips and Notes: Whenever you need just a little extra bit of insight, look for a tip. You'll find tips scattered throughout each lesson. A tip can give you additional ideas or may warn you against committing a common mistake. Notes provide added explanation or information.

Sidebars: Occasional sidebars discuss interesting, related material and give you a break from a lesson's main focus.

Skills Challenge: Take each lesson's Skills Challenge to make sure you've mastered that lesson's concepts. Each Skills Challenge contains numbered steps for you to perform. The Skills Challenge also contains Bonus Questions to make sure you've grasped the key points mentioned in the lesson. The answers for the Bonus Questions appear in Appendix A.

Troubleshooting: At the end of every lesson, a table lists unexpected problems and their easy solutions.

Wrap Up: The Wrap Up summarizes the current lesson's main points and leads you to the next lesson.

Let's Get Started

I know you're excited and ready to begin. It's time to start your Internet journey with Communicator. Grab this book and head for your computer. You're in for the time of your life!

Because the Web is always changing, the sites listed and shown in this book will probably look different when you connect to them. That's part of the Web's fun and excitement.

I love to hear from my readers. You'll find my e-mail address in the book, but in case you don't jot it down, please feel free to send me a message at bkasser@geocities.com. I'd enjoy hearing from you.

ACKNOWLEDGMENTS

Combining words, URLs, and many beta versions of software into a good book is a long and arduous process. It takes more than a few people to complete the job. Many folks are behind the scenes at IDG Books Worldwide. I thank each and every one of you. The Production department at IDG Books Worldwide deserves extra thanks for all the hard work.

   I thank David Fugate of Waterside Productions for always taking my phone calls. To John Read, Sue Pines, and Larisa North at IDG Books Worldwide, and technical reviewers Paul Summitt and Allen Wyatt — please accept my extra heartfelt thanks for making this book great! Dr. Andrew Ross, thanks for patching me back together on such short notice! And to my pals Lynn Luscher and Ken Shenkman, my deepest gratitude for helping me out when I needed you.

CONTENTS AT A GLANCE

TABLE OF CONTENTS

INTRODUCTION

You're about to jump into the most exciting aspect of computing today — the Internet. Most likely, you're a little nervous, a little excited, and more than a little confused. After all, you've probably heard stories about people who get so engrossed with the Internet that they let everything else slide. You may have heard people talking about the Internet like it's another planet. Well, relax. By choosing Netscape Communicator, you've made sure that your Internet journey will be fun and enlightening.

Getting Prepared

Read this introduction for a little background information — what the Internet is and how you get connected. You'll also learn a bit about Internet history. Aside from giving you some information that you can toss around with your friends, this material is designed to prepare you for your Internet journey.

What Is the Internet?

Ask five people, "What's the Internet?" and you'll probably get five different answers. The answer is simple. The Internet is a collection of millions of computers linked together to create one giant network. The linked computers contain special documents. Because the links occur through phone lines, the Internet has no physical location. (You can't go to the Internet like you can go to your local library.)

When you connect to the Internet, you can access all kinds of resources that are stored on the other computers. For example, you can read medical documents, shop, do research for a presentation, or read and send electronic messages (e-mail). It doesn't matter whether the *host* — the computer that contains the information — is located down the block or several continents away.

You'll visit three main elements of the Internet. The first of these is called the World Wide Web. The *Web* is made up of millions of *pages,* which are nothing more than small collections of text, pictures, and graphics. Web pages usually contain references to other pages with related material. A single Web site can include many of these pages.

Electronic mail, nicknamed *e-mail,* is the second element of the Internet. If you know the mailing address (and the proper postage is affixed to the envelope), you can send a letter to anyone by regular mail (called *snail mail* by Internet users). Instead of using snail mail, you can send an e-mail message to anyone on the Internet, if you know the correct e-mail address. You can also attach electronic files that contain text or pictures.

THE BIRTH OF THE INTERNET

In the 1960s, the Department of Defense in Washington, D.C., decided that in the event of a nuclear attack, they needed a way to maintain their computer messaging system. Their reasoning was easy to follow; after a catastrophic attack, the network could still operate as long as any two machines were functional and phone lines between them could carry data. Therefore, the new system had to be designed so that it did not contain a physical network hub, a need for centralized command, or dependence on any single part of the system.

When the new network was completed, it was called ARPANet, after the Department of Defense's Advanced Research Projects Agency. Over time, because the new messaging system was so easy to use, ARPANet connected research organizations in other government branches and the academic, commercial, and military fields. Over the next ten years, the number of locations connected to ARPANet grew.

The ARPANet system was so versatile that other networks hooked into its features. At the same time, computers became more powerful, less expensive, and easier to use. Soon, many universities discovered that they could share resources through their computers and ARPANet connections. Users at each network site increased dramatically. The idea of the "inter-network," or Internet, grew out of these academic connections.

The third element of the Internet is called newsgroups. *Newsgroups* consist of discussion groups, which are forums for specific interests. Everyone who shares a common interest corresponds through newsgroup messages. Think of newsgroups as huge electronic meeting rooms. As soon as you enter the Usenet meeting room, you are presented with a list of messages from other visitors to the room. You can read and respond to any of the messages or you can post a new message. When you return to the meeting room, you may find several responses to your message.

The History of Netscape

Although it's been around for decades, early users had to type complicated commands to get anywhere on the Internet. The popularity of Microsoft Windows sent developers scrambling to create new ways to use the graphical user interface (called GUI) that made Windows so easy to use. NCSA Mosaic, developed at the National Center for Supercomputing Applications at the University of Illinois, was the first browser to take advantage of some of the elements in Windows.

In April 1994, Marc Andreessen, who had been instrumental in the development of Mosaic, and Dr. James H. Clark, founder of Silicon Graphics, started a company called Mosaic Communications. The company changed its name to Netscape Communications in November 1994. In October 1994, Netscape introduced the first version of Netscape Navigator. Since then, Netscape has introduced several programs, all designed to make the Internet easy to search and understand. The latest Netscape program is the one you're using—Netscape Communicator 4.0. Netscape products remain the most popular Internet tools.

As of December 31, 1996, over 75 percent of Internet users were using Netscape software.

Making the Connection

To use Communicator, you need an IBM-compatible personal computer, a modem with a minimum speed of 9600, and a telephone line. The software will work on most 486 and Pentium computers running Windows 95 or Windows NT. If you're using an older computer or running an earlier version of Windows, there's no time like the present for upgrading. If you are running Windows 95 and you're comfortable with the speed at which it runs on your computer, then Netscape will run satisfactorily.

Before you can launch Communicator, you need to be connected to the Internet. If you are using Netscape from your office, check with your system administrator to find out what you need to do to establish the connection. If you are using Netscape from your home computer, you'll need to establish an account with an Internet service provider.

This book's CD-ROM contains EarthLink Network TotalAccess software, which enables you quickly to register EarthLink as your Internet service provider and to get connected to the Internet. Following are some considerations for choosing a provider.

How Do I Choose a Provider?

Choosing the right Internet service provider (ISP) is a key factor in making your Internet experience successful. It seems like just last year that only a handful of companies provided connections to the Internet. Now, new providers are emerging every day to compete for your business.

Before you select an ISP, make sure you know what you need. Take a few minutes and jot down your requirements. For example, if you travel and need to connect to the Internet from hotel rooms and offices far from your local area code, you need a provider with national or even international service. How many hours a month do you plan to be online? Do you need one account or separate accounts for other family members? Once you've listed your conditions, matching your needs to an ISP will be easier.

If you don't have a specific provider in mind, ask around. Most people who are connected will be happy to share their provider's name and telephone number. Look in the Yellow Pages and the business section of your local newspaper. Talk to the people at the computer store or computer training facility. Once you have a service in mind, call the Better Business Bureau to make sure that the provider is ethical and not an underequipped, understaffed operator. Next, call the ISPs. The answers to the following questions will be beneficial in determining which service is the best for you.

- How long have you been in business?

- How many other users subscribe to your service?

- How many users can be connected to the Internet at one time through your systems?

- How many high-speed connections does your service maintain?

- What is the cost of your service? (Are there hidden costs such as a setup fee or a charge to upgrade?)

- Is the charge based on unlimited or limited hours?

- Is there an extra charge if I want to set up my own Web site?

- Do you give discounts to students or other groups? (Am I entitled to the discount?)

- How long is my contract with you? (One year? Month to month?) How much lead time do you require if I want to cancel for any reason?

- Do you offer technical support? (At what hours?)

- Do you offer training?

- Do you support Netscape?

- Can you provide a list of references?

- During the last three months, how many hours was the service unavailable? (If there was down time, why?)

Use these questions as guidelines, and don't be shy about asking other questions or voicing your concerns. If the answers are not satisfactory or you're not comfortable with the company, call someone else. After all, choosing an ISP is your first step to getting on the Internet. Choose a reliable service so that you don't hear a busy signal every time you try to connect. Shop around so you can pick the ISP that's right for you.

When you establish your ISP account, your provider will give you detailed instructions on how to set up the connection on your computer. Follow each step carefully to create the Windows icon you'll click to connect.

Dialing In

Once you've established an account and followed the directions to create an Internet icon, you're ready to dial in to the Internet. For this section, you should be seated at your computer. The Windows desktop should be visible on your screen. Follow these steps to connect to the Internet:

1. Move your mouse pointer toward the bottom left corner of your screen.

2. Click the Start button on the Windows taskbar.

3. Move your mouse pointer to the Programs command in the Start menu.

4. Move your cursor to the submenu that appears and point to Accessories.

5. Position the mouse pointer on Dial-Up Networking and click your left mouse button once. (In this book, unless it says otherwise, always click your left mouse button.)

6. Double-click the icon you created for connecting to the Internet. The Connect to dialog box appears.

7. If you've set up your account so that you have to enter your log on name and password through a terminal window when you log on, don't enter them in the Connect to dialog box. Click Connect.

If you've set up your account so that you don't need to enter your log on information in a terminal window, enter your name and password in the appropriate text boxes and then click Connect. Skip to Step 10.

8. When the terminal window appears, type your name and press Enter. Type your password and press Enter. As you type your password, notice that it doesn't appear on the screen for security reasons.

9. (Optional) Depending on the type of connection you're establishing, at this point you may have special instructions from your ISP, such as typing **PPP** and then writing down the resulting IP number. Make sure you follow any instructions your ISP provided.

10. After a few seconds, the Connected to dialog box appears to let you know that you're connected, as shown in the following illustration.

Name of your ISP

Speed of connection

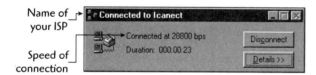

In the next section, called Jump Start, you learn how to open Communicator and move around a Web page.

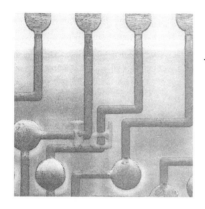

Jump Start

GOALS

In this section, you gain a basic understanding of the following:

- Opening Communicator
- Moving around in Navigator
- Using URLs
- Closing Navigator

30 MINUTES

1

GET READY

You should be seated at your computer, which is powered up and running Windows. Additionally, you should be dialed in to your ISP.

Don't worry about remembering all the features you're about to see. If there's something you need to know, I include the information in more detail in the lessons that follow. When you complete this section, you'll have taken a quick tour of Navigator and visited some Web pages, such as the IDG Books Worldwide site shown in the following illustration.

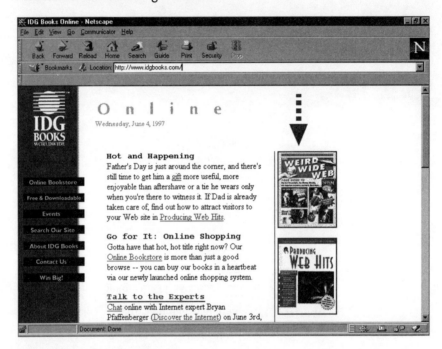

Opening Communicator

Opening Communicator is easy. When you installed Communicator, the installation procedure placed a shortcut icon on your desktop. Follow these steps:

1. Look on your Windows desktop for the Netscape Communicator shortcut icon with a small arrow. Text containing the words *Netscape Communicator* appears below the picture, as you see here.

A shortcut is a picture that appears on your Windows desktop and that starts programs quickly.

2. Place the tip of your mouse pointer in the Netscape Communicator shortcut icon.

3. Double-click the shortcut icon once with the left mouse button.

In a few moments, the Welcome to Netscape Web page appears on your screen. You're now viewing the Internet through the Navigator browser. Although Communicator includes several different components, most of the time you'll access them from within the Navigator program, as shown here.

If you're connecting from home, your telephone won't be available for incoming and outgoing calls while you're using Netscape. If you find that you're missing important calls, you may want to contact your local telephone company and ask about installing a modem-only line.

Moving Around in Navigator

When you start Navigator, your screen displays the Welcome to Netscape page. The folks at Netscape change this page several times a week to show the latest information and tips about Netscape, so don't be surprised if the page looks different each time you open Navigator. The page contains many *links* to other locations, both on the Netscape page and to other sites on the Web. In Lesson 1, you learn about the parts of the Netscape screen. For now, let's take a quick tour.

1. Place your mouse pointer in the top left corner of the screen and slowly move the pointer around the screen.

As you move the pointer down, you'll notice that as it passes over different areas of the screen, the shape of the pointer changes. The pointer may look like an arrow, a hand, or an I-beam as you move it.

2. Find some underlined text on the page that appears in a different color than the text around it.

Underlined, different-colored text indicates a hyperlink—a connection to another page or to a different section of the same page. When you click a link, you're whisked to the link's location. The pointer immediately changes to the shape of a hand (shown in the following illustration) whenever your mouse encounters a link on a Web page.

3. Point the mouse to the underlined text so that the mouse pointer's shape changes to a hand.

In the status bar located directly above the Windows taskbar, the words Document: Done are replaced by the location of the link, as you see in the following figure.

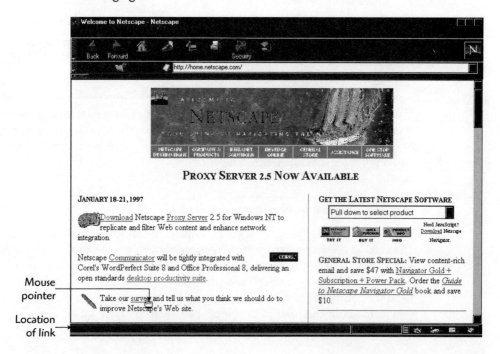

4. Click once with the left mouse button to connect to the Web page through the link.

In the top right corner of the screen, fireworks appear in the square box containing the image of a dark sky and the big (Netscape) N, shown below. In the status bar at the bottom of the screen, various messages flash as the linked page is contacted and then accessed. In a few moments, the new page replaces the one you were viewing previously.

5. Move your mouse over the new page. You'll see that this page, like the one that was on your screen before, also contains links.

As you move the mouse around the new page, make sure that you pass the mouse over some of the pictures that appear. The pictures are called *graphics*. Since pictures, as well as text, can contain links, your mouse assumes the shape of a hand as it passes over some of the graphics.

6. Move your mouse to one of the graphic links on the page.

7. Click once with the left mouse button to move to the link. In a few moments, the linked page appears.

8. Move your mouse pointer to the Back button at the top of the screen. The button shows an arrow pointing to the left.

As your mouse arrow rests on the button, the color of the word *Back* changes from black to blue. The title of the page you visited prior to the current page appears in a balloon.

9. Click once on the Back button with the left mouse button. In a few seconds, the previous page appears.

10. Click the Back button again. You return to the Welcome to Netscape page, the very first page you visited.

Using URLs

Now that you've discovered how to use links to move around, it's time to get a little more ambitious. Besides traveling through the Internet via links, you can specify which page you're going to visit next. The secret of traveling in this way is to know the URL, or address, of the page you'd like to visit. You're going to travel to the IDG Books Worldwide site.

1. Move your mouse pointer up to the box with the big N, located near the top right corner of the Navigator screen, and click once to reload the Welcome to Netscape page.

2. Move the mouse arrow over the box that contains the text `http://home.netscape.com/`, toward the top middle portion of the Navigator screen. The mouse arrow changes to the shape of an I-beam, as shown in the following illustration.

I-Beam ———— | http://home.netscape.com/ ⌶ | ▼ |

3. Click once with the left mouse button. All the text in the box becomes highlighted.

4. Type the following text carefully: **www.idgbooks.com/**

As soon as you start typing, the highlighted text disappears, so you don't need to delete it before you type the new text.

5. Press Enter on your keyboard. After a few seconds, the home page for IDG Books Worldwide appears.

6. Explore the IDG Books Worldwide page. Follow a link to a new location by positioning the mouse pointer on the link and clicking the left mouse button once.

7. Click the Back button to return to the IDG Books Worldwide home page.

8. Click the Back button again to return to the Netscape home page.

9. Click the Forward button (the button with the arrow pointing to the left, next to the Back button) to return to the IDG Books Worldwide page.

The Forward button works only if you've just used the Back button, and moves you to the page you saw when you last clicked Back.

10. Return to your home base, the Welcome to Netscape page, by clicking the Home button (next to the Forward button) on the toolbar.

Closing Navigator

When you've finished using Communicator, you need to close it and break the connection between your modem and your ISP.

1. Within Navigator, click File → Exit or click the Close button (the big X) located at the top right corner of the Navigator window.

2. Locate the Connected to icon on the Windows taskbar, and click it once to bring it up on your screen.

3. When the Connected to icon is visible, click the Disconnect button. In a moment, the connection will terminate.

Good work! You're ready to move on to more challenging tasks. In Lesson 1, you learn more about Navigator.

PART I

Getting Starting with Navigator

This part provides the background you need for using Navigator and starts you on your Web journey. It includes the following lessons:

- Lesson 1: Learning Navigator Basics
- Lesson 2: Keeping Track of Where You've Been
- Lesson 3: Navigating Through Frames, Forms, and Tables
- Lesson 4: Printing and Saving Web Pages
- Lesson 5: Personalizing Navigator

Learning Navigator Basics

1

35 MINUTES

GOALS

This lesson helps you master some Navigator basics. You work through the following exercises:

- Opening Navigator
- Working with Navigator's tools
- Viewing a Web page
- Entering URLs
- Using links to jump to different locations

GET READY

In this lesson, you work with Navigator, the component of Communicator that you will probably use most. To complete this lesson, connect to your Internet service provider.

When you finish this lesson, you will be familiar with Navigator's tools and will have learned how to view and move to a Web page, such as the one shown here.

UNDERSTANDING AND EXPLORING NAVIGATOR

Netscape Navigator is the element of Communicator that connects you to the World Wide Web (WWW), often simply called the Web. Think of the Web as a vast library filled with books about any topic you can imagine. Navigator is the program that opens the books and enables you to view any of their pages — in any order you choose. With Navigator, you can jump from page to page using links. You also can get, or *download,* files from many of the pages you visit (see Lesson 8).

A computer program that connects you to the WWW is called a Web browser. Navigator is the most widely used Web browser in the world.

Throughout this book, I refer to Netscape Navigator as "Navigator." You have probably noticed that when most people talk about the Navigator Web browser, they often call it "Netscape." This is not correct. The Navigator browser, although clearly the most popular of Netscape's products, is not their only product. Netscape Communications Corporation produces a number of software programs, including the Netscape Communicator suite of Internet tools. The next time you hear people talking about using Netscape, you'll know that they probably mean Navigator.

Exercise 1: Opening Navigator

In the Jump Start section, at the beginning of this book, you used a shortcut to open Navigator. You can also open Navigator from the Start menu, just as you would any other Windows program. Remember to connect to your Internet service provider before you open Navigator.

1. Click the Start button in the bottom left corner of the screen.

2. Move your mouse up to the Programs command and then slide across to Netscape Communicator. The Netscape Communicator submenu appears, as shown in the following illustration.

3. Slide the pointer over to Netscape Navigator 4.0 and click once. In a few moments, Navigator opens to the Netscape home page.

You're on the Web, ready to explore.

Before you open Navigator, look at the Windows taskbar to make sure the Connected icon is active. If you have forgotten to connect to your ISP, Navigator still opens; after a brief period, however, an error message appears, stating that Navigator cannot make a connection with your starting page. If that happens, just close Navigator by clicking the Close button in the upper right corner, connect to your provider, and then reopen Navigator.

Parts of the Netscape Screen

This Visual Bonus shows you the Netscape home page viewed in Navigator, and breaks down the elements of the screen.

Navigation Toolbar
Location Toolbar
Personal Toolbar
Link icon
Location/Netsite box
Menu bar
Netscape icon
Docked Component Bar
Links
Status bar
Security information

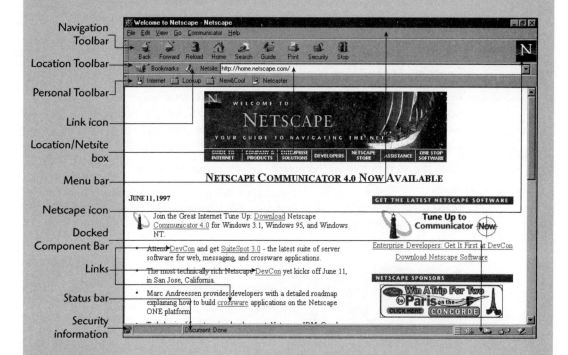

Examine the Netscape home page shown within the Navigator browser.

Menu bar. Like other Windows programs you've worked with, Navigator provides a menu from which you can choose commands.

Navigation Toolbar. The Navigation Toolbar provides speedy access to the commands you use most.

Location Toolbar. The Location Toolbar displays the address of the Web page that's currently on the screen, and also shows your bookmarks. You learn about bookmarks in Lesson 2.

Location/Netsite box. This box displays the *URL*, or address, of the Web page on the screen. You'll find more information about URLs later in this lesson.

Personal Toolbar. When displayed, the Personal Toolbar shows icons that enable you to return quickly to pages you want to revisit. (You can hide toolbars to provide more viewing space, as explained later in the lesson.)

Link icon. This icon provides drag-and-drop capabilities, including the capability to set a bookmark to the page that's currently displayed, so that you can return quickly to it at another time.

Netscape icon. The icon with the Netscape *N* (the logo of Netscape Communications Corporation) provides graphical information about what Navigator is doing. For example, when you are moving to another site on the Web, fireworks streak across the sky. Sometimes it takes a while for the other page to appear on your screen. When you see the fireworks light up the sky, you'll know that Navigator is still getting the other page and has not stalled or locked up your computer.

Links. When you clink a link, you're whisked to a new location — either on the same page or at a different site.

Security information. Click this lock icon to see information about the security of the page that's on the screen, including whether the page contains encryption or password protection.

Status bar. This bar is updated with messages about what's happening at the moment and about the security status of the current page.

Component Bar. This bar provides quick access to all programs in Netscape Communicator. You can *dock*, or anchor, this bar in one place on the screen, or you can "float" the bar so that you can move it around.

Exercise 2: Working with Navigator's tools

Navigator's screen tools make it easy to move around. Follow these steps to practice working with Navigator's tools:

1. Without clicking your mouse button, place your mouse pointer over any button on the Navigation Toolbar, which is shown in the following figure.

After a moment, a screen tip appears, showing you the name of the button and a brief description of what the button does. This is a great way to learn the function of each button.

2. Click the Reload button.

Fireworks appear in the Netscape icon, indicating that Netscape is processing your request to reload the site. On the status bar at the bottom of the screen, several messages flash across. When the page reloads, the status bar message reads Document:Done. Although nothing changed on the Netscape home page when you reloaded it, the Reload button is a useful way to update pages that contain quick-changing information, such as up-to-the-minute sports scores.

Buttons on the toolbar represent commands that you also find in Netscape Navigator's menu bar. Use the Navigator menu bar in the same way you use menus in most Windows programs: click the top menu command to open the menu, and then select a menu option from the list of commands.

3. Click File on the menu bar. The File menu opens, as shown in the following illustration. Depending on the Web page that's on the screen, some menu items may appear dim or "grayed out."

4. Click Print Preview to see how the current page will look when it's printed.

The preview opens in a separate window, as shown in the following figure. The entire page is visible, but the text is too small to read clearly. As you move the mouse over the preview, the mouse pointer takes the shape of a magnifying glass.

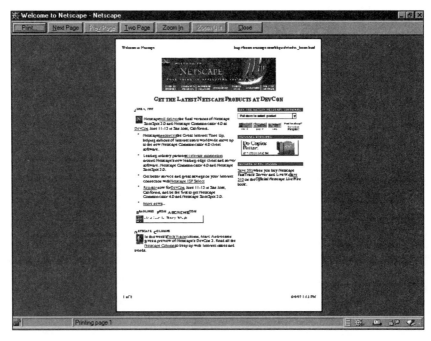

5. Click the button labeled Zoom In. (When you move the mouse up to the row of buttons, the pointer resumes its usual arrow shape.) The page enlarges on the screen. Click anywhere on the page to raise the magnification to a higher percentage.

6. You don't need to print the Netscape home page now, so click the Close button on the Print Preview window. You return to the full window.

7. To anchor the Component Bar (the bar that contains icons for other parts of Netscape Communicator, such as your Mailbox) to the bottom right of the screen, click Communicator → Dock Component Bar.

8. Click the down arrow at the edge of one of Navigator's toolbars to hide the toolbar from view. The toolbar closes, and all that's visible is a small arrow. To redisplay the toolbar, simply click the arrow.

When all the toolbars are displayed, portions of the Web page on the screen may be hidden. You can display or hide the Navigation, Location, and Personal Toolbars using the instructions in Step 8.

CHECKING OUT WEB PAGES

Web sites are the places that you visit as you travel through the Web. Every site consists of one or more documents, called *pages*. Unlike a page in a book, which has a predetermined length, Web pages do not have set boundaries. For example, when you print one Web page, your printer may spit out several sheets to print just that one page.

A Web page can consist of a few lines of plain text, or it can be a long, elaborate document filled with different typefaces, graphic images (some of which may be animated), and photographs. Some Web pages contain sound. A *home page* is the page at each site that serves as a sort of book cover or index that introduces and organizes the other pages and material at that site. As you move from site to site, you will visit many home pages. More and more home pages appear daily.

The next exercises show you how to view an entire Web page, enter a Web address to reach another page, and use links to jump to other pages.

Even if a site consists of only one page, it is still called a home page.

Exercise 3: Viewing a Web page

Most pages contain more information than can fit on your computer screen at one time. Fortunately, you can move to the parts of the page that you cannot see, using the following methods:

1. Position the mouse pointer on a word that's not underlined or colored on the Netscape home page.

2. Click once with the left mouse button.

3. Press the Page Down key on your keyboard a few times.

Each time you press Page Down, the view of the page changes on your screen. Once you reach the bottom of the page, nothing happens when you press Page Down.

4. To move to the top of the page, press the Page Up key until you're back at the top of the page.

By using the Page Down and Page Up keys to move through Web pages, you may miss a lot of the information that's on the page. Now, try moving more slowly.

5. Position your mouse pointer in the scroll box located on the right side of the page, as shown in the following illustration.

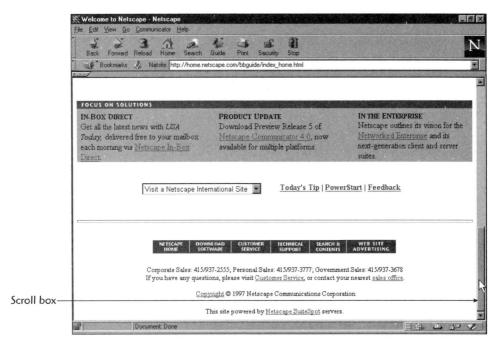

Scroll box

6. Click and hold down the left mouse button, and slowly drag the scroll box up and then down.

As you scroll through the page, additional lines and graphics move into view. If you pass something that you want to see, release the mouse button to stop scrolling and take a look at that portion of the page. When you've finished looking, drag the scroll box again until you want to stop. When the scroll box gets to the bottom of the bar, you're looking at the bottom of the page.

TIP

If you want to move a short distance, you can click the up or down arrows on the scroll bar, instead of dragging the scroll box.

Understanding URLs

Every page on the Web has its own address. The address, called a *Uniform Resource Locator,* or URL, consists of letters, slashes, and periods (usually called *dots*). Although the characters in a URL may look as if they're randomly placed, each letter and punctuation mark has a function.

URLs can sometimes look like alphabet soup, and typing them correctly is important. If you don't type the name exactly, with every slash, dot, and colon in the correct place, Navigator can't find the page you're seeking. When you break down a URL into distinct parts, however, it's a little easier to understand. Here's an example of a URL:

```
http://www.computercoach.com/
```

The http:// part is the *protocol* type, which specifies the type of page that's being accessed. Those letters tell Navigator that the Web site uses the HyperText Transfer Protocol (which is the standard for most Internet pages). Some pages you visit may start with other protocols such as ftp:// or telnet://. All you need to remember about protocol types is that the protocol is a series of internal rules that define how communication between computers takes place. Once it reads the protocol, Navigator takes care of the details!

The rest of the URL, `www.computercoach.com`, is the *domain name*. It identifies the name of the Web site's host computer and its particular Internet address. Every computer that's connected to the Internet has a unique domain name. Customized names, such as those mentioned on television and in magazines, are called virtual domain names and must be registered with a special Internet agency. (Most likely, your computer does not have its own virtual domain name, because you connect to the Internet through your ISP's connection.)

As you can see, the format of URLs is a well-defined addressing scheme. You may find that some URLs contain the name of a specific page after the domain name portion (for example, `www.computercoach.com/aboutframe.html`). If the name of a specific page isn't part of the address, you'll connect to that site's home page.

THE INTERNET NAME GAME

The domain names you are accustomed to seeing on the Internet are rapidly becoming overloaded. A conservative estimate indicates that the Internet doubles in size every 12 to 15 months. New domain names are needed to keep up the pace with new users.

The most crowded category of domain name is in the .com category. Thousands of new domain names are registered to this category each day. Courts are clogged with suits over domain names relating to copyright infringements and other similar concerns.

A committee was formed in October 1996 to find solutions for the problem. After several meetings, the committee announced in December 1996 that seven new domain name categories would be developed to accommodate the influx of new users. The committee appealed to the Internet community to help them design new names.

Internet users took the committee's plight seriously. At one point, the committee was receiving between 200 and 500 suggestions a day. Many people suggested that .biz should be adopted because it would denote a business connection similar to .com. Another popular choice for a new domain name was .sex.

In the near future (maybe even by the time you read this book), new domain names will be added. If you want to read more about the quest of the International Ad Hoc Committee of the Internet Society to find new domain names, go to `http://www.iahc.org`.

What's in a domain name?

If you've heard someone give an Internet address containing the words "dot com," you now know that they're referring to the domain name of the host computer that stores the page. The last portion of the domain name lets you know the primary use of the host computer. For example, in the URL `http://www.computercoach.com`, the ".com" indicates that the host is a commercial enterprise.

Although .com is the most common domain name extension, several others exist. If a name contains an .edu extension, the host is an educational institution such as a university or college; .net indicates a network-oriented domain, such as those used by many Internet service providers; .gov means a government facility; and .int stands for international. Additionally, .org (nonprofit organizations) and .mil (military) are valid domain name extensions.

To further identify a domain name, the three-letter extension may be followed by a country code. If no country code appears, the domain is probably in the United States. Here are some country codes:

Code	Country	Code	Country
uk	United Kingdom	cn	China
ca	Canada	jp	Japan
ch	Switzerland	br	Brazil
li	Liechtenstein		

Exercise 4: Entering URLs

If you have the correct URL, you can quickly view a Web page by following these steps:

1. Position the mouse in the Location box. The pointer takes the shape of an I-beam.

The label next to the box reads `Location:` after you have brought up a page, or `Netsite:` if the current page is from a Netscape server.

2. Click once. The URL that's already in the box becomes highlighted.

3. Without deleting the highlighted text, type **www.computercoach.com/** as shown in the following illustration.

You don't need to enter the http:// portion of the address because Navigator automatically uses the full URL.

URLs are case sensitive! The correct use of uppercase and lowercase letters is key to finding the page you want. Make sure you type the URL correctly; otherwise, you may see an error message or go to the wrong page.

4. Press Enter. In a few seconds, the page associated with the URL you typed (in this case, Computer Coach) appears as shown.

5. If you're more comfortable using menu commands, choose File → Open Page to bring up the Open Page dialog box, as shown in the following figure.

6. Type the URL of the page you want to view.

7. Click the Open button. In a few moments, the page appears.

Exercise 5: Using links to jump to different locations

Links are the vehicles that make it easy to travel from one location on the Web to another. A link can be highlighted text or a graphic object. When you click a link on one page, in seconds you go to a related page that may be located on a server just around the corner, or thousands of miles away.

Links that are placed in text are easy to spot. Most text links appear on Web pages as blue and underlined text. Once you click a link, the blue color changes to another distinctive color, such as red or purple. Netscape changes the color of links you've followed, so you can keep track of where you've already been if you return to the page later.

NOTE

The links you encounter as you visit Web sites have been placed there on purpose. It's up to the individual who set up the page to determine where to place the links, and assign what happens when the link is clicked. You learn how to design your own Web pages and add links later in this book.

To use links to jump to other Web pages, follow these steps:

1. Move your mouse pointer over Netscape's home page. The mouse pointer takes the shape of a hand whenever it passes over a link, as you see in the following illustration.

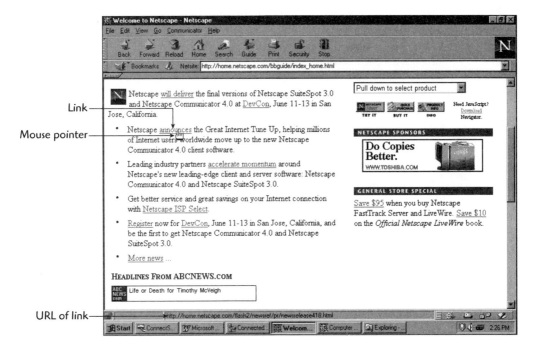

2. Click one of the links on the page.

The fireworks appear in the Netscape icon, and several messages regarding connection information appear briefly on the status bar. When the page is finished loading, the message Document:Done appears.

3. When the new page appears on the screen, find another link and click it.

TIP

Before you click a link, you can see where it will take you. Position your mouse pointer over the link. As long as your mouse pointer remains over the link, the URL of the Web page that's associated with the link appears in the status bar.

4. Click the Netscape icon to return to the Netscape home page.

5. Move the mouse over the *picture* at the top of Netscape's home page. When the mouse pointer becomes a hand, click the link.

Links can be graphics as well as text. It's harder to identify graphic links, because they don't have any special indicators. You'll always know that you're at a link when the mouse pointer's shape changes to a hand.

6. Look for another graphic link and follow it by clicking it.

7. Click the Home button on the toolbar to return to the Netscape home page.

NOTE

Clicking the Home button or the Netscape icon moves you to the Netscape home page, which is probably your default home page. Later in this book, you learn how to change your home page — the first page you see when you open Navigator. Clicking the Home button always takes you to your home page. On the other hand, clicking the Netscape icon always takes you to the Netscape home page, no matter which page you've designated as your own home page.

When links don't work

Eventually, you may click a link that doesn't work. When you click an invalid link, an error message appears on your screen after a brief period. Links become invalid for many reasons. As more people place pages on the Web, the occurrence of links that fail becomes increasingly common. The Web changes so rapidly that you may get an error message by trying to move to one of the pages referenced in this book. When you encounter a failed link, don't worry — it's probably not your fault. Table 1-1 contains a list of common error messages and what they mean.

TABLE 1-1	ERROR MESSAGES AND THEIR MEANINGS
Message	**What It Means**
File not found	The page has probably moved to a new location or has been removed from the Web.
Document contains no data	The address of the link is incomplete. If the address contains a specific file, try entering the URL manually, without the last part. For example, if the URL of the link is something like http://www.computercoach.com/barbara.html, enter it as **http://www.computercoach.com** and press Enter. You may be able to connect to the location and then navigate to the specific page.
Netscape is unable to locate the server (server name). The server does not have a DNS entry.	The most common reason for this message is that you were accidentally disconnected from your provider. Reconnect and then try the link again. If you are connected, the message may mean that the page to which the link refers doesn't exist anymore. If the error persists after you reconnect, the site is most likely having problems with its server.
Transfer interrupted	You may have clicked the Stop button on the Navigation Toolbar or hit a key on the keyboard. Click the Reload button to load the page again.
Too many users, try again later Connection refused by host	These messages are rare but occur if too many people try to connect to the page at the same time. Wait a few minutes and try the link again.

SKILLS CHALLENGE: MOVING AROUND THE WEB AND WEB PAGES

Now that you're familiar with the Navigator browser and basic navigation techniques, it's time to put together everything you've learned.

1. After you are connected to the Internet and Navigator is open, click the Home button on the toolbar.

2. Move to a new site by entering the URL **www.rv-coach.com/** in the Location box.

 *What does URL stand for?*

3. Move the mouse pointer over the page to find links.

2 *What happens when your mouse passes over a link?*

4. Click a link to move to the new page.

3 *How do links appear in Web pages?*

5. After a new page appears, follow a link on the new page.

6. Move to the bottom of the page using the keyboard.

7. Move to the top of the page using the scroll bar.

4 *How can you see more of the page than what's currently shown on the screen?*

8. Click the Back button to move back to the page you viewed previously.

9. Return to the Netscape home page.

TROUBLESHOOTING

You've finished your first Web journey. The following table can help with some common problems you may encounter as a new Navigator user.

Problem	Solution
Sometimes I see more than one Navigator button on the Windows taskbar. Why?	Navigator enables you to open several different Navigator sessions when you're connected to your Internet service provider. Because you may be looking at different pages in each session, it's sometimes hard to keep track of where you are! To see what's going on in each open session, place your mouse pointer in the first Navigator button on the taskbar. In a moment, you'll see a screen tip with the title of the page that's displayed. If you want to close the page, click the right mouse button once and choose Close. If you want to view one of the pages, just click its button on the taskbar to make it the active window.

Problem	Solution
I entered a URL in the Location box, but nothing happened	After you enter a URL, you need to press Enter to move to the new page.
After I clicked a link, I waited for a long time but the new page didn't apear.	The link is probably not valid. If you've waited for a while and nothing happens, press the Stop button (the Reload button changes to the Stop button when new pages are accessed). The message `Interrupt the current transfer` will appear in the status bar, and the page you were viewing when you clicked the link will become the active page again.

WRAP UP

You're now officially a member of the Internet community because you've spent some time on the Web! In this lesson, you learned many points, including the following:

■ How to use Navigator's tools

■ How to move around on Web pages

■ How URLs are structured and how to enter them

■ How to move around the Web by following links

If you want more practice with these skills, take another Internet journey and move to several different links. Remember, you can return quickly to the Netscape home page by clicking the Netscape icon.

In Lesson 2, you learn how to set bookmarks to keep track of places you'd like to visit again.

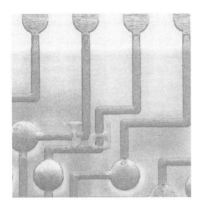

Keeping Track of Where You've Been

2

30 MINUTES

GOALS

This lesson advances your knowledge of Navigator's tools through the following exercises:

- Using link history
- Using Navigator history
- Resetting the cache
- Opening bookmarked sites
- Creating bookmarks
- Arranging bookmarks
- Searching for a bookmark
- Deleting bookmarks
- Enhancing your bookmarks

GET READY

In the last lesson, you learned basic Navigator maneuvers and explored a few sites on the Web. You are ready to extend your knowledge and venture out a little more. In this lesson, you learn some ways in which Navigator helps you keep track of sites you've visited. To complete this lesson, you need to be connected to your ISP with Navigator open.

When you finish this lesson, you will have learned how to use Navigator's history and bookmark features, including the windows shown in the following two figures.

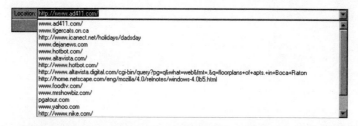

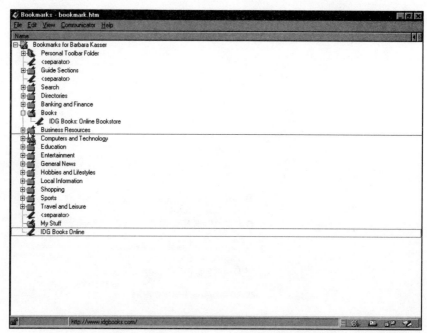

REVISITING PAGES: GOING BACK FOR A SECOND LOOK

The Web is a tourist's dream — spread out in every direction are virtual libraries, art galleries, movies, and video arcades. When you first begin your Web journey, you move quickly from site to site. Eventually, however, you may remember a spot that you would like to revisit. Unless you have recorded the exact URL or remember where the link to the page was located, it's hard to find your way back.

Does this mean you need to jot down the URL of every site you visit? Of course not! Navigator keeps tracks of the places you've visited in a few different ways, as you learn in the following exercises.

Exercise 1: Using link history

You have learned that any time you click a link, you move to the spot to which the link connects. The Webmaster who set up the referring page decides where the link takes you. The words in a text link can be as specific or general as the Webmaster wants them to be. For example, a link to the Hamilton Tiger-Cats on one page and a link to A Great Canadian Football Team on another page may both connect to the Hamilton Tiger-Cats home page.

Because the words in a text link don't always provide a clear reference to which page you'll see when you click the link, you may end up revisiting the page as you look for information. A Navigator feature called *link history* changes the appearance of text links in Web pages so that links to pages you've visited look different from links to sites you haven't seen. To see how link history works, follow these steps:

1. Click the mouse pointer inside the Location box. The URL currently in the box appears highlighted.

2. Type **www.tigercats.on.ca**, as shown in the following illustration, and then press Enter.

Remember, even though the address begins with http://, Navigator fills in the first part when it looks for the page.

Type URL here ———

3. When the Hamilton Tiger-Cats home page appears, move your mouse pointer down to the text links, which are called out in the next figure. The text links appear in blue and are underlined. Because the text links are located below the graphic (picture), you may need to use your scroll bar or press the Page Down key to move down.

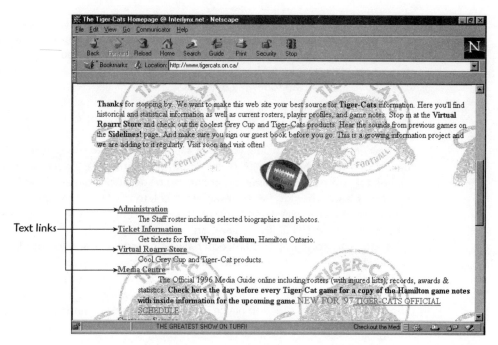

Text links—

4. Position the mouse pointer over the first text link (the pointer takes the shape of a hand) and click once. In a moment, the linked page appears.

Links, technically known as hyperlinks, connect two locations on the Web. The portion of the link that causes the mouse arrow to change shape is called an anchor.

5. After you have looked over the page, click the Back button on the toolbar. The Hamilton Tiger-Cats home page reappears on the screen.

6. Notice that the text links on the Hamilton Tiger-Cats home page now show up in two different colors. The *followed* link is one color (probably purple), while the *unfollowed* links are another color (most likely, blue).

Later, if you visit another site that contains a text link to the Hamilton Tiger-Cats home page that you visited, the text color of the link will tip you off to the fact that you saw that site before.

Navigator keeps track of the URL of a link, but not its content. A link pointing to a site that's updated frequently (such as a news service or stock quote listing) appears as followed even though you may not have seen the new information.

7. You can change the appearance of text links in Web pages. Click Edit → Preferences. The Preferences dialog box appears, as shown in the following illustration.

The minus (-) and plus (+) characters next to each category on the left indicate that the category is open (-) or closed (+). To expand a category to see all of its subcategories, click the plus sign. To collapse a category so that the subcategories are hidden, click the minus sign.

Expanded category

Collapsed category

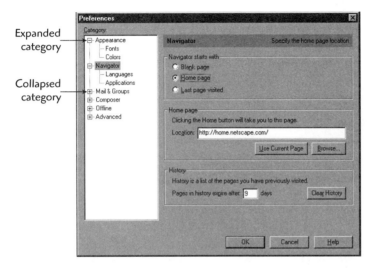

8. If the Appearance category is collapsed, click the + sign next to it to view the subcategories. When the subcategories are visible, click Colors. The Colors sheet appears, as shown here.

Color of unvisited links

Color of visited links

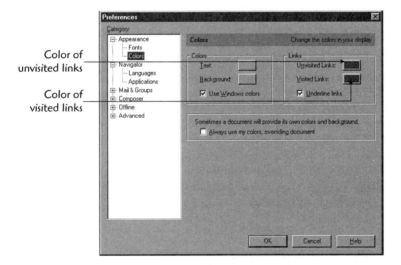

9. Click the button next to Visited Links. The Color dialog box appears.

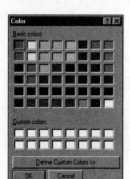

10. Click the color you want to use to indicate that a link's been followed, and then click OK. The Colors dialog box closes and you return to the Colors sheet.

11. If you want all the pages you visit to reflect your link colors, click the check box next to Always Use My Colors, Overriding Document.

Some Web pages (including Netscape's pages) are set to override the link colors you choose with preset colors, unless you specify otherwise.

12. Click OK to close the Preferences dialog box and return to the Web page.

The page disappears as it reloads. In a moment, the page reappears with the followed links displayed in your custom color. You can change the appearance of links as often as desired.

Exercise 2: Using Navigator history

Navigator maintains a running tally of the pages you visit as you move around the Web. Clicking the Back and Forward buttons is the easiest way to return to pages you've already viewed. However, these buttons have a limitation — they only work for your current Navigator session. If you closed Navigator right now and then reopened it, the Back and Forward buttons couldn't send you to the Hamilton Tiger-Cats home page.

Fortunately, Navigator also keeps track of the sites you visited when you followed links or typed in URLs. Follow these steps to use the Navigator history feature:

1. In the Location box, type **www.ad411.com/** and press Enter. In a few moments, the Ad411 page appears.

2. Click the down arrow next to the Location box. A drop-down list appears that shows the last 15 URLs you typed in the Location box. If necessary, use the scroll bar to view the oldest entries on your list, which appear at the bottom.

The URL list in the following illustration is taken from my computer. Your list will show some different URLs than mine. In fact, you may not have 15 URLs in your history list yet!

3. Move your mouse down to the **www.tigercats.on.ca/** entry on the list. The URL appears highlighted.

4. Click the mouse button one time. The Hamilton Tiger-Cats home page appears on the screen.

   The first time you opened the Hamilton Tiger-Cats page, it took a few seconds to load, but this time the page appears almost instantly.

5. Click Communicator → History or press Crtl+H to open the History window, as shown in the next illustration. A listing of the sites you've visited recently appears, regardless of whether you clicked a link or typed the URL.

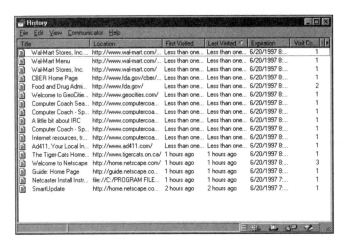

6. Hold the mouse pointer over a title to see the complete title of that page.

7. To return to a page that's displayed on the History list, double-click its title or URL location. The page opens in a new Netscape window. Notice that the History window and the page you were visiting previously appear on the Windows taskbar.

8. Close the History window by clicking the Close button (the big X) at the right of the History window title bar.

Exercise 3: Resetting the cache

After you open a Web page for the first time, Navigator stores the page in a *cache* (pronounced "cash") on your computer. When you return to that page, Navigator opens it from the cache instead of from the Web. Whenever you open a page, Navigator checks the *memory cache* first and the *disk cache* second to see if you've viewed the page before. If the page doesn't appear in either of your system's caches, Navigator gets the page from the Web.

Any time you revisit a page that may have changed or contains real-time information such as golf tournament scores, click the Reload button to get the latest information.

To reset the Navigator caches manually, follow these steps:

1. Click Edit → Preferences. The Preferences dialog box appears.

2. If a plus sign appears next to the Advanced category, click + once to expand the category and make the subcategories visible. When you can see the Advanced subcategories, click Cache to bring up the Cache sheet.

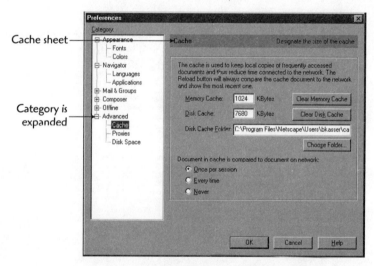

Cache sheet

Category is expanded

3. Click the button labeled Clear Memory Cache.

4. Click OK in response to the question, "This will clear all of the files in your memory cache. Continue?"

5. Click the button labeled Clear Disk Cache.

6. Click OK in response to the question, "This will clear all of the files in your disk cache. Continue?"

7. Click OK to close the Preferences dialog box and return to the Navigator screen. The current page reloads.

Every month or so, it's a good idea to clear the caches on your computer. In between, clear the cache when you notice that pages are consistently taking a long time to load.

USING BOOKMARKS

The Web is filled with millions of documents. As you look through more sites, you'll find that it becomes increasingly difficult to return to sites you want to see again. Navigator offers a great *bookmark* feature that keeps you from having to record the URL of each page you want to revisit.

Bookmarks are one of Navigator's most useful features. When you add a site to your bookmark list, Navigator notes the site's address and description. To return to a bookmarked site, select the item you want from the list. Navigator contacts the site and brings up the page. Because your bookmark list can grow quickly, Navigator enables you to organize your bookmarks into folders.

Think of bookmarks as Web shortcuts. They make it easy for you to navigate the Web without cluttering your mind (or your desk) with the addresses and descriptions of the pages you like.

Exercise 4: Opening bookmarked sites

Using a bookmark to open its related Web site is a snap! Follow these steps:

1. Click the Bookmark QuickFile icon (the picture of a book with a bookmark inserted) on the Location Toolbar. The list appears to the right.

2. If the bookmark is stored in a folder, click that folder to view the bookmarks it contains. For example, to use the preset bookmark for the *TV Guide* site, click the Entertainment folder first.

3. Click the bookmark you want to use. The list closes and Navigator opens the site. That's all there is to it!

Exercise 5: Creating bookmarks

Even though Navigator offers many preset bookmarks, you'll probably want to set your own for sites you visit frequently. Navigator makes it easy to create bookmarks. Follow these steps:

1. In the Location box, type **www.idgbooks.com/** and press Enter.

2. After the IDG Books Worldwide site appears on your screen, click Communicator → Bookmarks. The Bookmarks submenu appears.

2

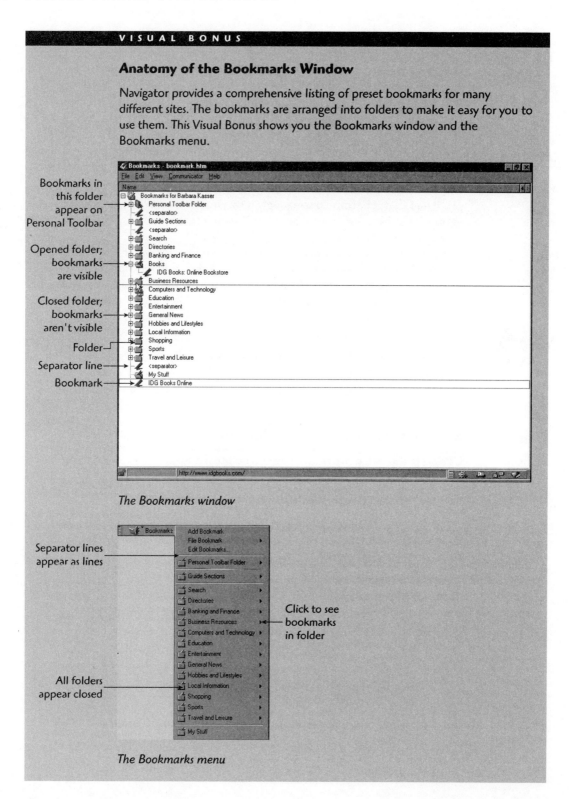

Anatomy of the Bookmarks Window

Navigator provides a comprehensive listing of preset bookmarks for many different sites. The bookmarks are arranged into folders to make it easy for you to use them. This Visual Bonus shows you the Bookmarks window and the Bookmarks menu.

Bookmarks in this folder appear on Personal Toolbar

Opened folder; bookmarks are visible

Closed folder; bookmarks aren't visible

Folder

Separator line

Bookmark

The Bookmarks window

Separator lines appear as lines

Click to see bookmarks in folder

All folders appear closed

The Bookmarks menu

3. Click Add Bookmark, as shown.

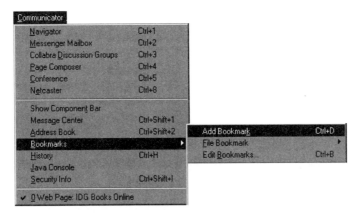

You have added the IDG Books Worldwide site to your bookmarks file. With a few clicks, you'll be able to return to the site anytime you want.

TIP

Take advantage of Windows 95 shortcut menus. When you're viewing a page for which you'd like to add a bookmark, click the right mouse button once. From the resulting shortcut menu, choose Add Bookmark and click the left mouse button. Like magic, the bookmark is added to your list.

4. Click the Online Bookstore link on the IDG Books page. From this site, you can find any book published by IDG Books, read sample chapters, and order books.

5. Place the mouse arrow on the Bookmark icon on the Location Toolbar.

6. Click once to open the Bookmark QuickFile. A drop-down list with your bookmarks opens.

7. Click the Add Bookmark command.

You've now set two bookmarks!

8. Type **www.rv-coach.com/** in the Location box and press Enter. The RV-Coach Online site appears on your screen.

9. To bookmark this site, position the mouse pointer on the Page Proxy icon next to the Location box. The picture of a page changes to a page with a bookmark on top of it, and the mouse pointer takes the shape of a hand, as you see in the following figure.

Page proxy icon ——

Mouse pointer ——

Status bar
message ——

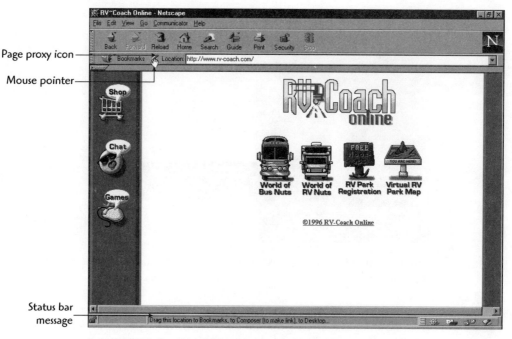

Design/CGI/HTML: Zane Good; CGI/Java Programming: Doug Breault

10. Click the mouse button once, drag the Page Proxy icon left to the Bookmark icon, and then release the mouse button. A bookmark for the current page is added to the bottom of the bookmark list.

If you hold the Page Proxy icon over the Bookmark icon for a second, the Bookmarks menu pops up, and you can then drag the Page Proxy icon to where you'd like the bookmark to appear in the list.

You have now set bookmarks using several different techniques.

Exercise 6: Arranging bookmarks

Once you have set several bookmarks, Navigator enables you to arrange them in any order you choose. You can use the existing folders or create new folders to keep similar bookmarks together. Follow these steps:

1. Click the Bookmark QuickFile icon on the Location Toolbar to open the Bookmarks list.

2. Click Edit Bookmarks. The Bookmarks window appears on top of the Web page that's currently displayed.

3. To move an existing bookmark up or down on the list, click the bookmark icon and drag it to the spot where you want it to appear. When you release the mouse button, the bookmark drops into its new spot. If you want the bookmark to appear in a folder, click the bookmark icon and drag it on top of the desired folder. When you release the mouse button, the bookmark is filed in the folder you chose.

4. If you have many bookmarks, you can either use Navigator's folders or create your own. You've been working with the Bookmarks window during this exercise, so the Bookmarks window should still be visible on your screen. If it's not, perform Steps 1 and 2.

5. To create a folder called Books, click the place in the Bookmarks list where you want the new folder to appear. The new folder will appear directly below the line you clicked.

6. To name the folder, select File → New Folder from the menu bar in the Bookmarks window. (Sometimes, when two windows are visible onscreen, it's easy to accidentally click the menu bar from the other window, so be careful!) The Bookmark Properties dialog box appears, as shown in the following illustration.

7. Replace the highlighted New Folder text with the name you want for the folder. If you want to add an optional description for the folder, click or tab to the Description text box and type it there.

8. When you've finished typing, click OK. The folder you created appears on the list of bookmarks with a picture of a file folder next to it.

9. Click a bookmark and drag it on top of the folder icon to place it inside the folder.

10. To add a separator line between folders or bookmarks, click Item → Insert Separator. A separator line appears.

11. Click the Close button on the Bookmarks title bar to close the Bookmarks window.

Exercise 7: Searching for a bookmark

When you look through all your bookmarks and folders, you may find that you still cannot locate the bookmarked page that you want. Because the title of the bookmark is actually the title of its linked Web page, sometimes the bookmark title may not provide clear information as to where it points. Navigator enables you to search for the exact bookmark you want. Follow these steps:

1. Click the Bookmark QuickFile icon on the Location Toolbar to open the Bookmarks list.

2. Click Edit Bookmarks.

3. Click Edit → Find. The Find Bookmark dialog box appears.

4. In the Find box, type the word or a few letters of the text you're looking for, as shown in the following figure.

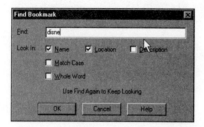

5. If you want to limit the search to items that match the text you typed exactly, click the box next to Match Case. If you want Navigator to find all occurrences of the text, leave Match Case unchecked.

6. Check the boxes next to Name, Location, or Description if you want to limit the search to any of these fields. (The Name and Location boxes are checked by default.)

7. Click OK.

   Navigator searches through all your bookmarks, and highlights the first bookmark that contains the text you typed.

8. To locate the next bookmark containing the text you typed, click Edit → Find Again or press Ctrl+G.

9. If no bookmarks contain the text you typed, a Not Found dialog box appears. You need to click OK to close the dialog box and return to the Bookmarks window.

10. When you've finished, click the Close button to close the Bookmarks window.

Exercise 8: Deleting bookmarks

Deleting bookmarks and bookmark folders is easy. Follow these steps:

1. Click the Bookmark QuickFile icon on the Location Toolbar to open the Bookmarks list.

2. Click Edit Bookmarks.

3. If the bookmark you want to delete is in a closed folder, open the folder by clicking the plus sign (+) to the left of the folder icon.

4. Click the bookmark or folder you want to erase and then press Delete.

5. Repeat Steps 3 and 4 to delete additional bookmarks.

Delete bookmark folders carefully! When you delete a bookmark folder, you eliminate the folder and all the bookmarks it contains.

6. When you've finished, click the Close button to close the Bookmarks window.

Exercise 9: Enhancing your bookmarks

Bookmarks are great helpers. Here are a few more tricks to make your bookmarks even more helpful! For example, if you use many folders to arrange your bookmarks, you may want to place the same bookmark in more than one folder. You can also change the description of a bookmark or folder to help you identify it later. Follow these steps:

1. Click the Bookmark QuickFile icon on the Location Toolbar to open the Bookmarks list.

2. Click Edit Bookmarks. The Bookmarks window opens.

3. Click the bookmark you want to copy to another folder with the right mouse button. (You may need to open the folder that contains the bookmark before you can select it.) A submenu appears.

4. Click Make Alias from the submenu. The *alias,* or copy of the bookmark, appears in italicized text below the original bookmark, as shown in the following illustration.

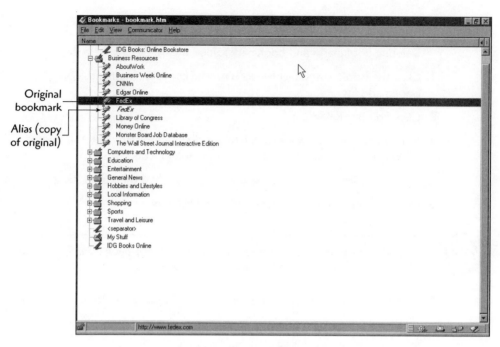

Original bookmark

Alias (copy of original)

5. Drag the alias to the new location or folder.

TIP

Both the original bookmark and its alias are linked. If you make changes to the original, such as adding an optional description or changing the title, the alias automatically changes, too.

6. Click a bookmark whose name or description you want to change. The selected bookmark appears highlighted.

7. Click Edit → Bookmark Properties. The Bookmark Properties dialog box appears, as shown.

8. If you want to change the name of a bookmark, replace the existing text in the Name box with a new name.

9. Click or tab to the Description text box and type an optional description.

10. If the URL of the related site has changed, carefully type the new URL in the Location (URL) box.

11. When you've made all the changes you want, click OK to close the Bookmark Properties dialog box.

12. Click the Close button to close the Bookmarks window.

SKILLS CHALLENGE: PUTTING NAVIGATOR'S MEMORY TO WORK

You're doing a great job. Look how far you've come! In this Skills Challenge, you'll practice what you learned in this lesson.

1. After you're connected to the Internet and Navigator is open, click the Home button on the toolbar.

2. Move to the following page on the Web:

`www.idgbooks.com/`

 Can you describe one way to move to a new Web site?

3. Find a link on the IDG Books Worldwide page and move to the new site.

4. Go back to the IDG Books Worldwide page.

 How do you return to a site you've viewed before?

5. Go to `www.foodtv.com`.

6. Create a bookmark to the Food TV page.

3 *What is the quickest way to create a bookmark to the site that is currently shown on the screen?*

7. Change the title of the bookmark you just created to Great Recipes.

8. Create a folder called Cool Sites.

9. Place the Great Recipes bookmark into the Cool Sites folder.

10. Close Navigator and disconnect from your Internet service provider.

TROUBLESHOOTING

You're learning to negotiate your way through the Web. The following table may help with some common problems that occur when using Navigator link history and bookmarks.

Problem	Solution
I clicked the Back and Forward buttons on the toolbar, but I couldn't get to the page I saw yesterday.	The Back and Forward buttons only work on sites you've visited during the current Navigator session.
Why does it take forever for the new page to load when I click a link?	You need to clear the caches on your computer. Click Edit → Preferences → Advanced → Cache and then, one at a time, click the buttons to clear the memory and disk caches. If the page still takes a long time to load, the telephone lines are clogged with other Internet users.
Help! Suddenly I can't see any toolbars.	No biggie. You closed all the toolbars. Each toolbar on the Navigator screen has a tab to open and close it. When you look at the screen under the menu bar, notice three tabs with triangles pointing to the right. Click each of the triangles to open the corresponding toolbars. (Notice that when the toolbar is open, the direction of the arrow changes.) You can close any of the toolbars anytime you want.

WRAP UP

Good work! In this lesson, you learned the following:

- How to use Navigator's history
- How to optimize Navigator's performance by resetting the caches
- How to work with Navigator's bookmarks

If you want more practice with these skills, you have many opportunities. Use Navigator's preset bookmarks to explore the Web. The next time you see a URL on television or in a newspaper, make a note of the Web address. When you have some free time, connect to the Web and explore the site. If you like it, bookmark the page so you can return to it.

In Lesson 3, you learn how to navigate your way through tables, frames, and forms.

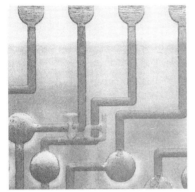

Navigating Through Frames, Forms, and Tables

20 MINUTES

GOALS

This lesson teaches you additional Navigator skills, including the following:

- Working with multiple Navigator windows
- Moving in a framed Web page
- Entering information in a search form
- Completing an e-mail form
- Filling in an information form
- Looking at Web tables

GET READY

In the last lesson, you covered a great deal of new ground as you learned how to keep track of where you've been on the Web. You're going to be looking at more Web pages in this next lesson, so you need to have Navigator open on the screen and be connected to your ISP.

When you finish this lesson, you will have learned how to move between multiple windows and how to move around Web pages that contain elements such as frames, online forms, and tables, including those shown in the following figures.

Boca Raton News is a registered trademark.

Please fill out the form below for more information

Name

Street Address

City   State   ZIP

Phone   Email- Required (use phone if no email)

What price range are you considering:

$100,000-$150,000   ▾   Click on the little triangle to show a list of choices.

What style property are you interested in?   What type of community would you like?

- □ single family home
- □ townhouse
- □ villa
- □ condominium
- □ vacant land
- □ multi-family/investment

- □ country club
- □ gated
- □ ocean front
- □ intracoastal/deep water
- □ other

How many bedrooms? 2 ▾   Bathrooms? 2 ▾

VIEWING MULTIPLE WINDOWS

You can open more than one page at a time during a Navigator session. Why would you want to? Well, perhaps you're looking for information about a certain topic on one page, and you want to check the latest golf scores on another page. Or, you may want to use one page like an index, as you visit its links to connecting pages. Opening multiple Navigator windows and switching between them serves many purposes.

Exercise 1: Working with multiple Navigator windows

In this exercise, you learn how to open two Navigator windows and navigate between them. Follow these steps:

1. With Navigator open and on the screen, click File → New → Navigator Window. A new Navigator window appears.

2. Click the Bookmark QuickFile icon. The Bookmarks menu appears.

3. Click a bookmark from the list. In a few seconds, the bookmarked site appears in the second window. (If you do not have the site bookmarked, type a URL in the Location box and press Enter.)

4. Position your mouse pointer on a blank spot on the Windows taskbar at the bottom of your screen, and click the right mouse button once. The Windows shortcut menu appears, as shown in the following figure.

5. Click Cascade with the left mouse button. Your open windows appear stacked on the screen, as shown in the following figure.

3

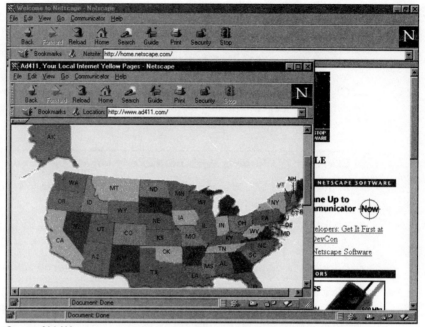

Courtesy of Ad 411

6. To switch between the open Navigator windows, click the Window menu. The titles of the open windows appear at the bottom of the menu.

7. Click the title of the window to which you want to move. (A check mark appears next to the Navigator window that's currently active.)

Buttons for both open Navigator windows appear on the Windows taskbar.

8. (Optional) Repeat Steps 1 through 3 to open additional Navigator windows.

9. Close any of the Navigator windows by clicking the Close button or clicking File → Close.

Other multiple window arrangements

You can arrange the windows on your screen in any way you want. Instead of choosing Cascade, as described in Step 5 in the previous section, you can select Tile Horizontally or Tile Vertically when you right-click the Windows taskbar.

When they are open on your desktop, you can minimize, maximize, or resize any window to suit your needs.

STEERING THROUGH FRAMES

As you cruise around the Web, you'll come across pages that are divided into two or more rectangular windows. Each separate window has the characteristics of a Web page. These windows within a page are called *frames*. A large amount of information can be divided into small compartments with frames. In a framed page, locating the information you're looking for is easy because you can jump from frame to frame.

Different pages use frames differently. Some Web pages contain only two frames, while other pages are divided into several frames. You can achieve many different effects with frames.

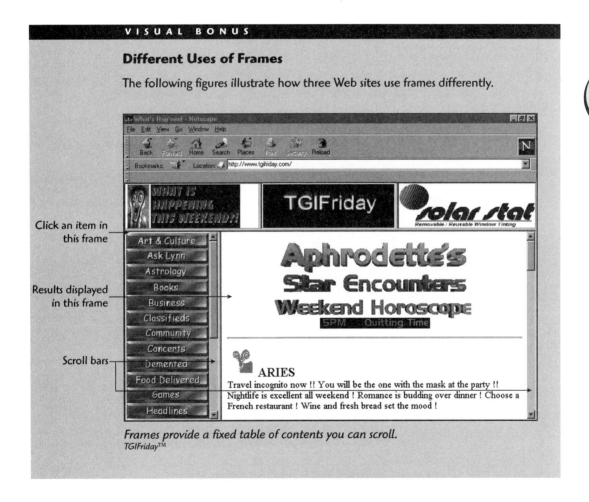

VISUAL BONUS

Different Uses of Frames

The following figures illustrate how three Web sites use frames differently.

Click an item in this frame

Results displayed in this frame

Scroll bars

Frames provide a fixed table of contents you can scroll.
TGIFriday™

3

This frame holds text

This frame holds a picture

Scroll bars

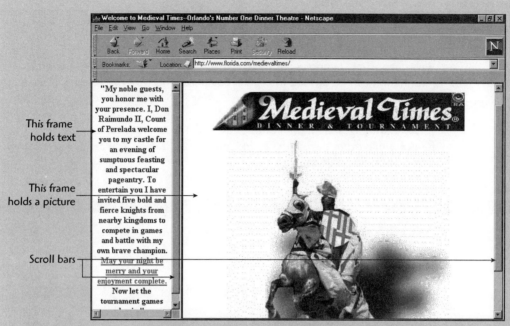

Frames provide two different windows on the same page.

Click frames to open related sites

Frames hold links to other sites.
Boca Raton News is a registered trademark.

Exercise 2: Moving in a framed Web page

Moving in a Web page with frames is easy — as long as you know the tricks. Follow these steps:

1. Click the mouse pointer inside the Location box. The URL currently in the box appears highlighted.

2. Type **www.florida.com/realestate/** and press Enter. The FloridaCom Real Estate Web Page appears, as shown in the following illustration.

Remember that it's not necessary to type the http:// portion of the address because Navigator fills it in for you.

Different frames —

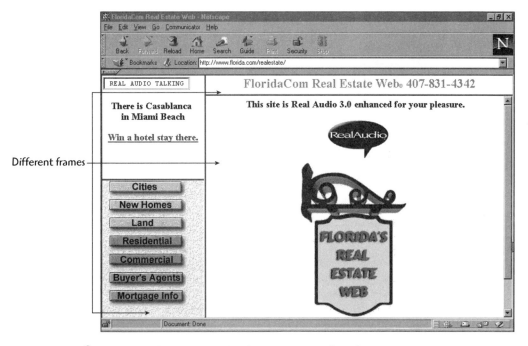

3. Click the Cities link in the frame on the left. Information about the cities appears in the frame on the right.

4. Use the scroll bars to look at parts of the page that don't fit on the screen, as shown in the following figure.

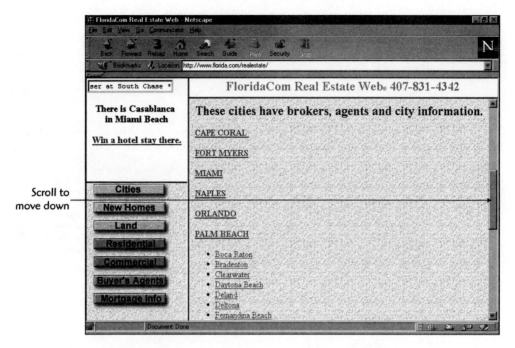

Scroll to
move down

5. Click one of the links to change the view in the frame again.

6. Click the Back button to return to the frame you viewed previously.

Using the Back and Forward buttons with frames

When you are moving through frames, the Back and Forward buttons work in a different way. Instead of moving you back to the *page* you visited last, you return to the *frame* you visited last.

If you feel as though you are hung up in a frame and the Back button isn't moving you to where you think it should, click the Back button with the right mouse button. Click the page you want to revisit from the resulting shortcut menu.

UNDERSTANDING AND COMPLETING WEB FORMS

We live in a forms-oriented society. During a normal day, forms intersect your life repeatedly. For example, the check you write for your groceries, the slip that the clerk at the dry cleaner's fills out when you bring in your shirts, and the card you complete to enter a million dollar magazine giveaway are all variations of forms. Small wonder, then, that you come across so many Web pages that contain forms.

Three main types of forms exist on the Web. The first is a form you submit to gain information, such as when you're searching for details about something specific. (In Lesson 6, you learn more about searching techniques.) The second is an e-mail form, which pops up on the screen when you click the appropriate link on some Web pages. The third type is a structured form that you fill out to provide information. You complete this type of form when you're shopping or subscribing to a service, for example. The common denominator of Web page forms is that each form requires your input.

Exercise 3: Entering information in a search form

In this exercise you enter information in Yahoo's search form to look for specific information on the Web. This exercise is an example of filling out a form to gain information. Follow these steps:

1. Type **www.yahoo.com/** in the Location box and press Enter. The Yahoo home page appears.

Keep in mind that the Webmasters, the people who design and maintain Web pages, change the pages often. Therefore, the pages you see onscreen as you complete the exercises may look different than those shown in the illustrations in this book.

2. Click in the text box next to the word Search and type **Old Glory**, as shown in the following illustration.

3. Click the Search button once with the left mouse button.

The fireworks appear in the Netscape icon and the status bar reflects the various stages of the search as Yahoo looks through Web pages to find references to Old Glory. When the search is complete, a page similar to the one shown in the following figure displays links to the sites that contain references to the words you typed.

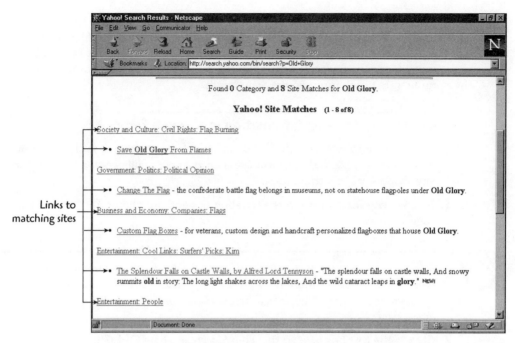

Links to matching sites

4. Use the scroll bar on the right side of the page to move down through the listed documents. Click one of the links to find information about Old Glory on the linked page. Depending on what you typed in the Search box, a message may appear in the status bar at the bottom of the Netscape screen.

5. The listed documents may be about or may contain references to Old Glory. Follow the links to read the documents that interest you, using the Back button on the toolbar to return to the Yahoo page that displays the Search results.

TIP

Unfortunately, you may find that some of the links refer to pages that no longer exist or that have moved to different locations. Most search engines cannot keep up with the volume of pages flooding the Web, and may be a bit out of date.

Exercise 4: Completing an e-mail form

An e-mail message form from within a Web page is another common type of form encountered on Web pages. Follow these steps to fill out an e-mail form:

1. Type **www.cameta.com/** in the Location box and press Enter. The Cameta Camera home page appears.

2. Drag the scroll box down the scroll bar to see more of the page and find the links to e-mail, as shown in the following figure.

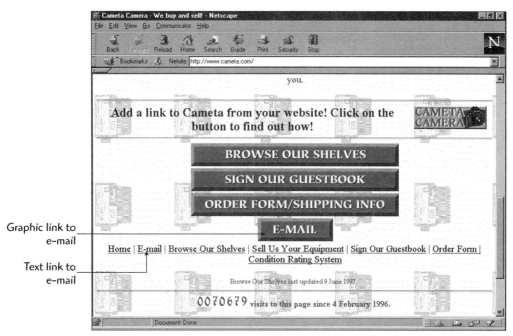

3. Click the left mouse button on either the text or graphic e-mail link. (Both the graphic and text e-mail link bring up the same window, so it doesn't matter which you choose.) The Netscape Composition window appears, as shown in the following illustration. You're ready to send a message to Cameta Camera.

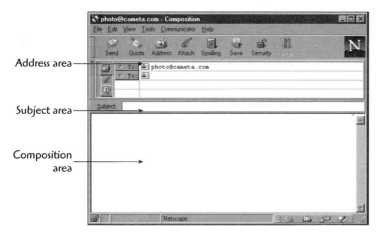

4. The e-mail address of Cameta Camera is already filled in for you in the address section of the window. If you want to include a subject line, click the left mouse button in the Subject text box and type a brief subject.

5. Click in the Composition area and type the message.

As you type the message, it's not necessary to press Enter at the end of each line to move to the next line. As with your word-processing program, the text is word-wrapped, or automatically advanced to the next line as each line is filled.

6. When you've finished typing the message, review it briefly. The following illustration is an example of a completed message.

Send button—

7. Click the Send button to send the message.

Your mail server is contacted and the message is sent over the Internet to the address shown in the address area. Your e-mail address is automatically recorded when the message is received, so a response to your message will be simple.

You must enter the correct information in the Netscape Communicator Mail Preferences section for the e-mail message to reach its destination. You learn all about e-mail in future lessons.

FORMING KNOWLEDGE ABOUT FORMS

Any time you enter unique information on a Web page, you complete a form. It doesn't matter if you click a check box or an option button, chose an item, type information, or enter a password — all of these are Web forms. Navigator passes your input through the phone line to the requesting server, which then sends the information to a program that processes the information you entered. All of this complicated routing takes just a few seconds — less time than it would take to get a glass of water.

Forms are like the Web version of Windows dialog boxes. In Windows, you type in text, choose a listed item, or make some other choices. Once you complete the dialog box and click OK or Close, you pass the information to the program that you're using. In most Web forms, you click Submit or Send after filling out the form.

Navigator is considered to be *forms-capable*. When you use Navigator, you can complete everything from simple, one-line forms to multipage, complex forms. If you see a statement on a Web page such as "Best viewed with Netscape Navigator," it's probably because another browser can't handle the forms on the page correctly. Some browsers don't enable the use of forms, and others can process only the most basic of user input requests.

After you complete a form, you may see some output on your screen. The type of output you can expect is based on the type of information you submitted. For example, when you submit a search to a search engine, you'll see a list of documents that match your query. On the other hand, after you complete a contest entry form, you may see a message thanking you for your participation. In the case of an e-mail form, after you send the message, you probably won't see any reference to the fact it was sent.

Exercise 5: Filling in an information form

In this exercise, you complete a fill-in-the-blanks form that contains several different form elements. Follow these steps:

1. Type **www.netrunner.net/~sjcohen/formpage.html** in the Location box and press Enter. The South Florida Real Estate Form Page appears.

This page contains a form that you can complete and submit to obtain information on distressed and foreclosed properties for sale in Florida. The form contains several elements, including text boxes, drop-down lists, and check boxes, as shown in the following illustration.

Toolbars
are hidden

Text boxes —

Drop-down list —

Check boxes —

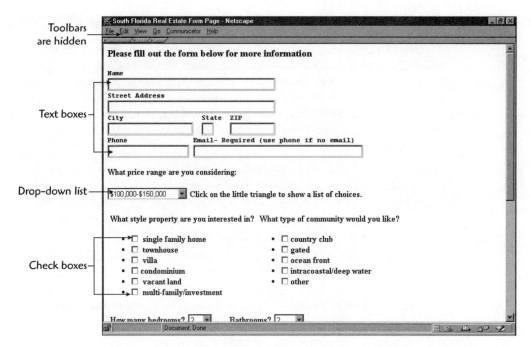

2. Click the mouse button in the first text box labeled Name and type your name.

3. Click in the next text field, labeled Street Address, and type your mailing address.

Instead of clicking the mouse to advance to each text field, you can move to each text box by pressing Tab on your keyboard.

Both the size and the typeface of text fields are determined by the settings you specified in your Navigator Preferences.

4. When you've entered information in each text field, choose a price range by clicking the triangle to open the price range drop-down list, and then selecting a price from the list, as shown in the following figure. As soon as you select a list item by clicking it, the list closes.

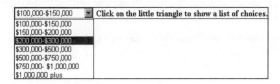

5. Click the boxes next to each of the property types that interest you. Because these are check boxes, you can select as many as you like.

6. Use the scroll bar to move down through the form and complete all the questions on the form.

7. When you reach the bottom of the form, click the button labeled either Click here to send your information, or Click here to start over.

Click here to send your information	Click here to start over

If you click the button to send your information, the information you typed is automatically routed to the real estate agents. In a moment, information appears on a separate page with the notation that you will be contacted shortly. Click the Back button on the toolbar to back up to the sites you were viewing previously.

If you click the button to start over, the form is cleared of the information you typed, and you can re-enter new data. If you do not wish to submit information, click the Back button to return to previously viewed pages.

You have now filled out three types of common forms you encounter as you look through the Web with Navigator.

UNDERSTANDING WEB TABLES

Tables are used to organize information in a grid form. All you can do with a table — unlike a frame or form — is appreciate how easy it is to read the information inside it. In the following exercise, you look at a typical Web table.

NOTE

Just like a spreadsheet, a table is arranged in horizontal rows and vertical columns. The intersection of each row and column is called a cell. You learn how to create your own Web tables later in this book.

Exercise 6: Looking at Web tables

1. Type **www.geocities.com/~stgregory** in the Location box and press Enter. The St. Gregory's Episcopal Church home page appears.

2. Using the scroll bar, move down the page to the section that displays text links to various places in the site, as shown in the following illustration.

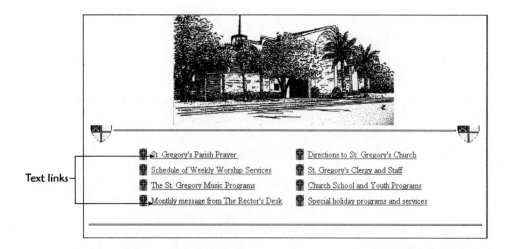

Text links

The text links are contained in a table with no grid lines. Notice how the text in each link is perfectly aligned. Even the tiny graphics next to each text link are lined up with each other, creating a chart that's easy to read.

3. Click the Schedule of Weekly Worship Services link. You're whisked to a set of tables that display both the daily and Sunday service schedule, as shown here.

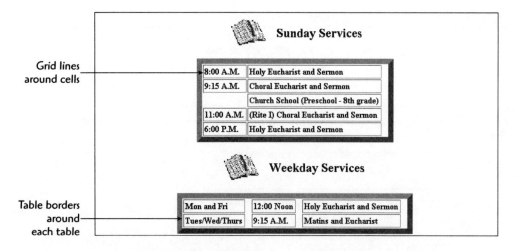

Grid lines around cells

Table borders around each table

Unlike the first table on the page, each of these tables is arranged with grid lines and a border around the whole table. Again, tables present the information so that it's easy to follow.

SKILLS CHALLENGE: WORKING WITH A FRAMED WEB PAGE

In this lesson, you increased your knowledge of how Web pages are arranged. You'll use the information you've learned about frames, forms, and tables to complete this Skills Challenge. Take a deep breath. Now you're ready!

1. After you connect to the Internet and open Navigator, move to the following page:

```
www.missamerica.org/
```

The Miss America Organization Home Page appears, as shown in the following figure.

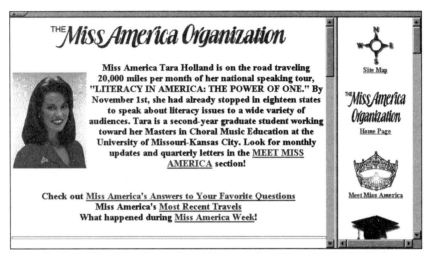

Courtesy Miss America Organization. Miss America and Miss America Pageant are trademarks of the Miss America Organization.

 Why does this page contain two separate windows?

2. Use the scroll bar in the frame on the left to look at the page. Click the first text link you see.

3. On the new page, again click the first visible link.

4. Click the Back button on the toolbar.

 Why didn't the Back button take you back to the site you were viewing before the Miss America site?

5. Click the Back button again.

6. Using the scroll bar on the frame on the right side of the window, move to the link to the Miss America Shopping Mall.

7. Click the Miss America Shopping Mall link.

8. When the Miss America Shopping Mall frame appears, click the link to Miss America Specialty Items to display an order form designed in a table.

 What are two ways to move from field to field in a fill-in form?

9. Pretend you're ordering merchandise and complete the form. You can leave any of the fields blank by not entering any information.

10. When you reach the bottom of the form, click the Clear Text button.

11. Move the mouse pointer to the frame on the right and click the Talk to Us button.

12. (Optional) Fill out the Talk to Us form and submit your information by clicking the Send button when you've typed all the information.

13. Click the Send E-Mail text link at the top of the Talk to Us frame.

14. In the table that appears on the screen, click the Other link from the Topic/Departments list.

15. Compose an e-mail message in the Composition form. In the body of the message, mention how you arrived at the site.

16. Send the message to the Miss America Organization.

17. Exit the Miss America Organization pages and return to the Netscape home page.

 What's the fastest way to return to the page that loads when you first open Navigator?

TROUBLESHOOTING

The following table can help with some common problems you may encounter when using frames, forms, and tables.

Problem	Solution
How can I get rid of the Composition window after I've accidentally clicked an e-mail link?	Click the Close button (the big X) on the Composition window to get rid of the window.
Why can't I get back to the pages I've viewed before, when I click the Forward and Back buttons?	If you're trying to use those buttons to return to sites you viewed in the current Navigator session, chances are you're in a page with frames. Click Go on the menu bar and choose the page from the list that appears.

Problem	Solution
I opened multiple pages, and now I see several Navigator icons on my Windows taskbar.	Place your mouse pointer in each Navigator button on the taskbar and hold it there for a second or two. A balloon that lists the site's name appears. If you want to close that site without returning to the page, click the right mouse button to bring up the shortcut menu. Click Close with the left mouse button.

WRAP UP

You're gaining some enduring Navigator skills. In this lesson, you learned the following:

- How to open multiple pages in Navigator
- How to work with frames
- How to work with different types of Navigator forms
- How to view tables

3

The Web is full of opportunities for you to practice these skills. Visit several pages and look for frames, forms, and tables. In Lesson 4, you learn how to print and save Web pages for future reference.

Printing and Saving Web Pages

20 MINUTES

GOALS

This lesson shows you how to keep a permanent record of Web pages by mastering the following skills:

- Previewing a page before you print
- Sending the page to print
- Creating a folder for saved pages
- Saving the text on a Web page
- Saving the HTML Web page
- Saving a Web page you haven't viewed yet
- Saving graphic images
- Opening a saved Web page

GET READY

In this lesson, you learn how to print and save Web pages. To complete this lesson, you need to connect to your ISP and have Navigator open on the screen. Make sure that your computer is connected to a printer.

When you finish this lesson, you will know how to print the pages you see on the screen (as shown in the following figure). You will also know how to save Web pages on your computer so you can look at them later. Navigator makes both options available with a few mouse clicks.

Barbara Kasser's Page   hup://www.geocines.com/Paris/Left2ank/4487/

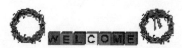

Hi! Welcome to my page. This page is a place for my friends and students to drop by and visit with me . I
try to provide some interesting links and things for you to take with you when you leave! Have fun!

Barbara Kasser's Page

 Here are a few recipes for a great evening!

Chocolate Praline Cheesecake

-----CRUST-----

* 1 1/3 cups Graham cracker crumbs
* 3 tablespoons Butter, or margarine -- melted
* 2 tablespoons Honey

-----FILLING-----

* 12 ounces Semisweet chocolate morsels
* 1/2 cup - Water -- boiling
* 2 teaspoons Instant coffee granules
* 2 packages 8-oz. cream cheese -- softened
* 1 cup Brown sugar -- packed
* 4 large Eggs
* 1 cup Pecans -- coarsely chopped

-----TOPPING-----

* 1/2 cup Brown sugar -- packed
* 1/4 cup Heavy cream
* 1 teaspoon Butter -- or margarine
* Pecan halves -- for garnish

Preheat oven to 350°. To prepare crust, combine crumbs, butter, and honey in a 9" springform pan.
Press mixture evenly onto bottom of pan. To prepare filling, in top of a double boiler set over simmering
(not boiling) water, combine chocolate morsels, water, and coffee. Stir mixture until smooth. Remove top
of double boiler from water. Set aside.
In a lg. mixing bowl, using an electric mixer set on high speed, beat cream cheese and brown sugar until
smooth and fluffy, about 2 mins. Add eggs, 1 at a time, beating after each addition. Add chocolate mixture,
beat until smooth. Beat in pecans. Pour filling over crust, bake cheesecake until center is set, about 1 hr.,
25 mins. Place cheesecake on a wire rack and cool completely.

1 of 2   6/11/97 4:14 PM

PRINTING WEB PAGES

Instead of dragging out research material, it's easy to turn to the Web when you want to find information. Do you need a recipe for vegetable soup? Want to learn how to remove rust stains from a white shirt? The Web can tell you. But there is one big problem with this volume of data: how can you remember it all? Fortunately, if your computer is connected to a printer, you can print any Web page you see on your screen. If you don't want to print the full page, you can print a portion of it.

Remember that Web "pages" are not pages at all — they're actually documents of varying lengths. On the Web, the page designer determines the size of the page you see on the screen. Therefore, one Web page, such as the Netscape home page, may translate to several printed sheets. Web pages don't have the same physical characteristics of pages in a book. The pages of a published book conform to a preset size, no matter how much information each page contains. (Think how funny this book would look if each page was a different height and width.)

Exercise 1: Previewing a page before you print

Using Print Preview before you print a Web page is always a good idea. Print Preview enables you to see how many printed sheets of paper the Web page on your screen will take. What if you want to print only a small section of a page? Print Preview enables you to identify the exact section you need to print, rather than printing the entire Web page and then throwing away most of the sheets. This exercise shows you how to use Navigator's Print Preview. Follow these steps:

1. Type **www.geocities.com/Paris/LeftBank/4487** in the Location box and press Enter. The Barbara Kasser home page appears on the screen.

2. Use the vertical scroll bar to move down to the bottom of the page. As you can see, the page is long.

3. Click File → Print Preview. The Print Preview window appears.

As the page loads in the Print Preview window, the status bar at the bottom of the screen may display several messages. When the page is fully loaded in the Print Preview window, the message Printing Page 1 appears. The following illustration shows the page in the Print Preview window.

4

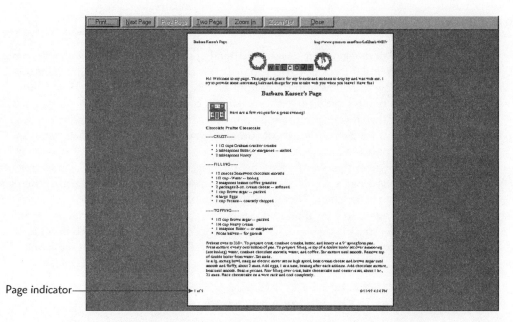

Page indicator————————————▶

4. To make the page easier to read, click the Zoom In button. The page is magnified.

Notice that as you move the mouse on the page, the mouse pointer takes the shape of a magnifying glass. When the mouse reaches the row of buttons at the top of the screen, it assumes its regular arrow shape.

The Print Preview window has its own menu bar and toolbar. Print Preview works the same way in many programs in the Netscape Communicator suite (and in most Windows programs).

5. To raise the magnification level again, position the mouse pointer (the magnifying glass) on the portion of the page you want to enlarge and click the left mouse button once.

Alternatively, you can click the Zoom In button again. Either way, you can raise the magnification level only twice.

6. Use the vertical scroll bar to move through the magnified text on the Print Preview window.

7. Move to the bottom left corner of the page to the page indicator, which shows the current page and the total number of printed pages.

8. Click the Next Page button to view the second page that will print when you print the Barbara Kasser home page. The second page appears.

The second page, as shown in the following figure, contains the information you want to print.

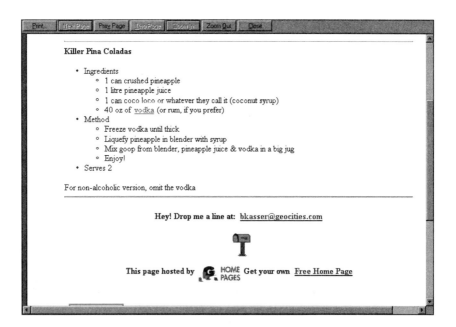

Remember that magnifying the text in the Print Preview window is for display purposes only. The text is not magnified when you print it.

9. To restore the screen to its nonmagnified view, click the Zoom Out button twice.

Each time you click the Zoom Out button, you reverse the previous level of magnification. Because you clicked Zoom In twice, you need to click Zoom Out twice as well.

10. You're not going to print the page yet, so click the Close button to close the Print Preview window and return to the page in normal view.

Exercise 2: Sending the page to print

In this exercise, you print the Web page that's on the screen. Follow these steps:

1. Barbara Kasser's home page should be on the Navigator screen. If it's not, click the Back and Forward buttons until the page appears. (Or, type **www. geocities.com/Paris/LeftBank/4487** in the Location box and press Enter.)

2. Click the Print button or click File → Print. The Print dialog box appears, as shown in the following figure.

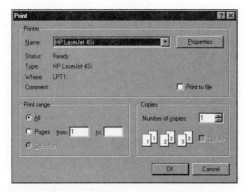

3. Make sure that the correct printer is selected in the Name box. If it's not, click the drop-down arrow to open the list of printers and choose the correct one from the list.

VISUAL BONUS

Getting Set Up to Print

This Visual Bonus explains the Print Setup dialog box and its options.

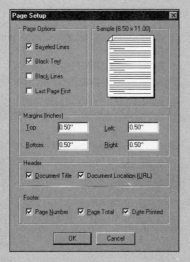

Print Setup provides many options for printing Web pages.

Page Options. (You can select more than one.)

- **Beveled Lines.** Check this option if you want your printed page to show the three-dimensional, dividing lines found on some Web pages.

- **Black Text.** Select this option to print all the text on the page in black. For example, you may not want the links in a document to show on the hard copy (although the links will probably appear as underlined). A color printer is a prerequisite for this option.

- **Black Lines.** Select this option to print all the lines in black. As with the Black Text option, a color printer is a prerequisite for this option.

- **Last Page First.** Select this to print the document from back to front, in reverse order.

Margins. Margins are the distance from the edge of the paper to the edge of the text. When you type a number in one of the margin boxes and then click the mouse pointer in another margin box, the Sample in the top right corner changes to reflect the new setting.

Header. (You can select more than one option.) The header is the line in small text that appears at the top of every page. You can print the Document Title (the text that appears in the Navigator title bar when the page is onscreen) and/or the Document Location (URL). The header of a printed Web page helps you identify where the document came from, long after you've forgotten the name and location of the site. If you don't want the header to appear, deselect both options. You can also deselect either option to keep it from appearing on the hard copy.

Footer. (You can select more than one option.) The footer is the line in small type that appears at the bottom of every page. You can print the Page Number, Page Total, and Date Printed. The footer of a printed Web page organizes the pages in case you plan to store them and look at them later. If you don't want a footer option to print, deselect it.

4

TIP

If you're using Microsoft Fax or a similar product to send faxes directly from your computer, make sure that the fax printer is not selected before you try to print. If it is, your computer will try to fax the Web page instead of sending it to the printer.

4. In the Print Range section of the dialog box, choose whether to print the entire page (All) or a range of pages (Pages).

If you chose the Pages option, enter the starting page number in the From box and the ending page number in the To box. For example, if you want to print only the page with the recipe, which you've identified in Print Preview as Page 2, enter 2 in both the From and To boxes.

5. Unless you tell Navigator otherwise, you'll get one printed copy. If you want more copies, type the new number in the Number of copies box.

6. If you're printing more than one copy of a very long page, you can choose whether the copies should be collated.

If you're printing three copies, for example, choosing to collate them means that your printer will produce three complete sets in page number order. If the print job is not collated, the printer will print three copies of Page 1, and then three copies of Page 2, and so on.

7. That's it — you're ready to print! Click OK. In a few seconds, your printer delivers a hard copy of the Web page.

Depending on the type of printer you're using, some options may be unavailable and appear dimmed out in the Print dialog box. If an option such as Collate is dim, your printer can't do it. Don't waste your time trying to activate a dimmed-out option.

SAVING WEB DOCUMENTS

Navigator provides the option of saving any page on the Web. You can save a page to the hard drive of your computer or to a diskette. Once the page is saved, it becomes a regular document. A saved Web page is like any other Windows document; text from the page can be copied or cut and then pasted into other documents. Saved Web pages can be opened later, stored indefinitely on the hard drive of your computer, or deleted after you read them.

It's important to understand that Web pages are created in HyperText Markup Language — or HTML, for short. (You learn about HTML in later lessons.) HTML documents contain text and formatting codes, called *tags,* that tell Navigator how to display the Web page on the screen. Some Web pages also contain graphics, sounds, and movies — elements that make the pages interesting and fun to browse. These extra elements must be saved individually, or they won't appear when you view the saved page later.

When you save Web pages, you can choose from several different formats. The next set of exercises help you understand the best way to save a page for your needs.

Although the Web may seem like a free-for-all, much of the material is copyrighted. Generally, you can take information on the Web for your own use, but not for publication or profit. Internet law is changing rapidly, so if you're not sure about using someone else's material, consult an attorney.

Exercise 3: Creating a folder for saved pages

In this exercise, you create a folder on your desktop to store the pages and graphics you save from the Web. If you're familiar with Windows and have another folder that you'd like to use, such as My Documents, feel free to use it instead. Although this exercise has more to do with Windows than with Navigator, following these steps helps you create a specific location for saved Web materials:

1. Close or minimize all open programs on your computer so that your Windows desktop is visible, as shown in the following example.

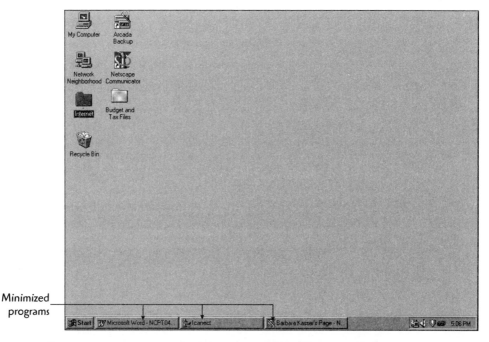

Minimized programs

2. Place the mouse pointer on a blank area of the desktop and click the right mouse button once. A pop-up shortcut menu appears.

3. From the shortcut menu, click New. The submenu appears.

4. Slide the mouse pointer to Folder, as shown here, and click once.

5. A new folder appears on the desktop, like the one in the following illustration.

6. Type **WebSave** to rename the folder.

The text *New Folder* is selected, so you needn't delete it before you begin typing. If the text becomes deselected accidentally, right-click the folder and choose Rename from the resulting pop-up shortcut menu.

Now, you have a folder that holds all the information you save from the Web.

Exercise 4: Saving the text on a Web page

In this exercise, you save only the text in a Web document. Once the page is saved as text, you can open it in Windows Notepad or WordPad, or any other word processing program. Follow these steps:

1. If necessary, reestablish your Internet connection and open Navigator.

2. Move to a page that contains text. You can either move to a site you've bookmarked in a previous lesson or use the Netscape home page, as I do here.

3. Click File → Save As. The Save As dialog box appears.

4. Click the drop-down arrow next to the Save in box to open the list of drives and folders. (Your list will look a bit different from mine.)

5. Click the folder named WebSave, as shown in the following illustration.

As soon as you click the WebSave folder, the list closes and the folder name appears in the Save in box.

6. Click the drop-down arrow next to the Save as type box to open the list of available file formats.

7. Choose Plain Text (*.txt).

8. Click in the File name box. The filename displayed in the box has the file extension HTML. (The file extension is composed of the letters following the period after the filename.)

9. Delete the letters html and replace them with **txt**, making sure you don't delete the **.** character.

Even though you specified that you wanted to save the file as a .txt file, Navigator won't change the file extension automatically.

10. Make sure that your Save As dialog box looks like the one shown in the following illustration before you proceed.

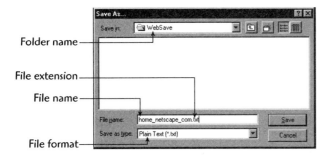

Folder name ─────

File extension ─────

File name ─────

File format ─────

11. Click the Save button. A box appears, telling you that the location is being saved. When the box disappears, the text portion of the Web page is saved.

TIP

When you save the text from a Web page, that's all you get! The formatting and text attributes, such as bold and underline, are not saved with the text.

Exercise 5: Saving the HTML Web page

If you need to review several Web pages for a research project, save the pages and examine them later, when you're not connected to your ISP. Saving a Web page as an HTML file ensures that the text and the accompanying formatting, such as italics or bold, will be intact when you look at the file later. Follow these steps:

1. Make sure that the same page whose text you saved in the previous exercise is onscreen.

2. Click File → Save As. The Save As dialog box appears.

3. If the WebSave folder is not showing in the Save in box, click the drop-down arrow next to the Save in box to open the list of drives and folders. Click the folder named WebSave.

NOTE

The last folder in which you opened or saved a file automatically appears when you choose the Save As command again during a Windows session. You can use the same folder or choose another one.

4. Make sure that HTML Files is specified in the Save as type box. If another file type is specified, open the drop-down list and choose HTML Files from the list of available file types.

5. Click the Save button. A box appears briefly, informing you that the location is being saved. When the box disappears, the text of the Web page is saved in HTML format.

Want to see what HTML code looks like? Anytime a page is completely loaded on the screen, click View → Source. The HTML version of the document appears in its own window. Close the window when you're finished.

Exercise 6: Saving a Web page you haven't viewed yet

In this exercise, you save a Web page before you look at it. Follow these steps:

1. Type **www.iahc.org/** in the Location box and press Enter. The IAHC home page appears, as shown in the following figure.

The Internet International Ad Hoc Committee is an important presence on the Web. At the time this book was written, the IAHC was making far-reaching decisions about the future of domain names, as discussed in Lesson 1.

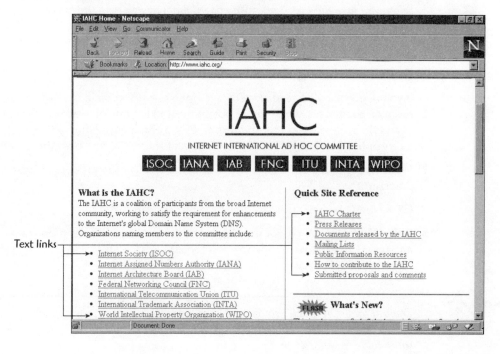

2. Position the mouse pointer (now in the shape of a hand) on the first text link and click the right mouse button. The pop-up shortcut menu appears.

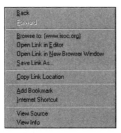

3. Choose Save Link As. The Save As dialog box appears.

4. Follow the steps detailed in Exercise 5 to save the link as an HTML file in the WebSave folder.

5. If you wish, save a few more links on the IAHC home page in the same manner.

Exercise 7: Saving graphic images

The pictures on a Web page, called *graphic images*, must be saved separately from the text. Saving graphics involves most of the same steps you use to save the text and formatting on Web pages. Follow these steps to save graphics:

1. Click the Home button on the toolbar to load the Netscape home page. Or, type **home.netscape.com/** in the Location box and press Enter.

2. Position the mouse pointer on the big boat at the top of the page and click the right mouse button. A shortcut menu appears.

3. Choose Save Image As, as shown in the following illustration. The Save As dialog box appears.

4. Just as you did previously, choose the WebSave folder to store the saved graphic. (If you need help with this step, review Steps 4 and 5 of Exercise 4 in this lesson.)

5. Click Save.

Because Navigator identifies the filename and file type of the graphic, it's not necessary to change the name and type shown in the Save As dialog box.

You need to save each graphic separately if you want to see it when you open the saved page. To quickly identify each graphic on a page, click View → Info. At the top portion of the resulting page, you'll see a list of all graphics contained on the page. Save each graphic file to your computer.

Exercise 8: Opening a saved Web page

You can open the Web page anytime. The only requirement is that Navigator be open and onscreen. You don't need to be connected to your ISP. Follow these steps:

1. From the Navigator menu bar, click File → Open Page. The Open Page dialog box appears.

2. Type **c:\windows\desktop\websave** in the Location box, as shown. Or, if you're comfortable with the arrangement of files and folders on your computer, you can click the Browse button and select the WebSave folder.

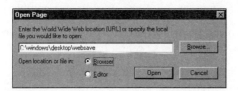

3. Make sure that the option button next to Browser is selected.

4. Click Open. The directory listing of the files in the WebSave folder appears in the Navigator window, as shown in the following figure.

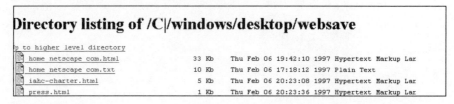

5. Position the mouse pointer, now in the shape of a hand, on one of the filenames and click the left mouse button once.

6. The saved Web page appears onscreen.

Most likely, the graphics won't appear when you open the page, even if you saved each one separately. If a graphic doesn't appear, you'll see a placeholder instead.

WHERE ARE THE GRAPHICS?

Where have all the graphics gone? You're probably asking yourself that question right now. The fact is that graphics and other elements on Web pages, including fancy backgrounds, scrolling banners, sounds, and movies, are separate from the text.

When you view a Web page in Navigator, you often see a visual feast. You don't see the careful planning that went into creating the page. Nor do you see the layering of all the effects needed to create the finished product. When you view a Web page's source code, you see just how many parts are needed to create the page.

When you save a Web page, then, you need to save all of its elements separately. Saving the text and its formatting is easy. Saving the graphics so that they appear when you open the saved page can be tricky. The graphics need to be saved in the same folder structure in which they were placed when the page was created. Sometimes it's easier to print a page with lots of graphics rather than trying to save each graphic file in a subfolder.

SKILLS CHALLENGE: CREATING A LASTING IMPRESSION

Put your Navigator savvy to the test. If you're stuck or unsure about how to complete one of the steps, review the information in this lesson. Ready?

1. Move to the IAHC home page. The address is **www.iahc.org/**.

2. Look at the page in Print Preview.

3. Move down to the footer on the page.

4. Magnify the page two times.

 Why does Print Preview show two pages, when there's only one page on the Navigator screen?

5. Reverse the magnification.

6. Close Print Preview.

 What determines whether headers and footers are included on printed Web pages?

7. Move to the Computer Coach page. If you don't have a bookmark for it, the address is **www.computercoach.com/**.

8. Click the link to visit the Boca Raton, FL, site.

9. Save the page in HTML format to your WebSave folder, making sure that you use the Save As menu selection.

What are the two file formats you can use to save Web pages?

10. Open the saved page in Navigator.

 Why can you see the text but not the graphics in a saved Web page?

11. Move to the Netscape home page.

TROUBLESHOOTING

You're acquiring additional Navigator skills. Don't be surprised if your friends and family ask you for help. Even with all you've learned in this lesson, however, you may run into a few roadblocks. The following table discusses a few problems you're likely to encounter.

Problem	Solution
I tried to print a page but the Print command reads Print Frame. Why?	Navigator is so smart that it recognized that you were on a frame within a page. Whenever you're in a framed page, Navigator substitutes "Frame" for "Page" when you try to print or save.
Help! I sent a page to print and nothing happened. Now, I can't seem to print anything.	Check the connection to the printer and the computer to make sure that both ends of the cable are secure. If they're plugged in properly, your printer probably doesn't have enough memory to print the page. Delete the print job by clicking Start and then Settings → Printers. Double-click your printer and then choose Printer → Purge Print Jobs. Once you've cleared all the jobs out of the queue, don't resubmit the page that caused the problem.

Problem	Solution
I saved a page as text but my word processor doesn't see the file in my WebSave folder.	The most likely answer is that your word processor is looking for specific file extensions, such as .DOC or .WPD. To enable your word processing program to see all files in the WebSave folder, click File → Open. Change the entry in the Files of type to All files by clicking the drop-down arrow and selecting All Files (*.*) from the list. The filename of the page you saved as text now appears.
Now that I've saved lots of pages and graphics, how can I get rid of them?	This question is a Windows question rather than a Navigator question. You need to use My Computer or Windows Explorer to delete the files. Follow the instructions shown in the Windows Help system to delete files. You can also refer to a book about Windows that provides information on this and other Windows topics, such as *Discover Windows 95*, published by IDG Books Worldwide, Inc.

4

WRAP UP

Good work! In this lesson, you learned many points, including the following:

- How to print a Web page
- How to save a Web page
- How to save graphics
- How to open a page you've saved

Practice these skills anytime you're looking around on the Web. In Lesson 5, you learn how to personalize Navigator to fit your style and needs.

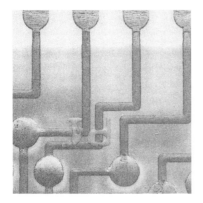

Personalizing Navigator

40 MINUTES

GOALS

This lesson teaches you how to customize Navigator for your use. You work through the following exercises:

- Specifying a different opening page
- Setting up a PowerStart page
- Customizing Navigator's appearance
- Editing the Personal Toolbar

5

GET READY

In this lesson, you change some of Navigator's settings to match your personal preferences. After all, you're going to spend a lot of time using Navigator, so why not set up the program the way you want it? As usual, Navigator should be open and your connection to the Internet should be established.

After you work through the entire lesson, you will have learned several customization techniques, including how to change the location of your start-up page, how to create a PowerStart page (as shown in the following example), how to modify toolbars, and how to set up user profiles for all the people who use Communicator on your computer.

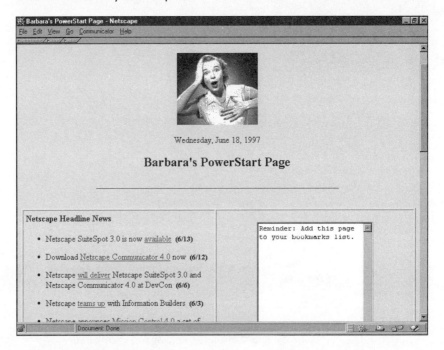

CHANGING YOUR OPENING PAGE

Your opening page is the first page you see when you start Navigator. If you are using Navigator on an intranet, you probably open to your company's page. Many users automatically begin their Web journey at the Netscape home page.

As you have traveled around the Web in the previous lessons, you've probably found some wonderful sites. Often, these are the first pages you visit every time you come on the Web. If you visit one particular page repeatedly, make it your opening page. That way, the page you look at most will be the page you look at first.

What type of page works best as an opening page? The answer is based simply on what you like. Maybe the IDG Books Worldwide site would be a good launch site for you. Or, if you find that you conduct many searches, the search engine you prefer would make a great starting place. (See the next lesson for more details on search engines.) One of the best parts of changing your opening page is that you can change it again whenever you like.

As an alternative to setting up a regular site as your launch pad to the Web, Navigator helps you set up a *PowerStart* page. Unlike the Web pages you usually see, PowerStart contains links both to the sites you like to visit and to special elements, such as a stock ticker with quotes of your favorite stocks.

Exercise 1: Specifying a different opening page

In this exercise, you set a new Web page to appear each time you open Navigator. Follow these steps:

1. Open Navigator (if it isn't already open and visible onscreen).

2. Select Edit → Preferences. The Preferences dialog box appears.

3. Under the Category section, click Navigator.

4. In the first section, make sure that the option button next to Home page is selected, as shown in the following figure.

Make sure this button is selected

Type URL of the page you want

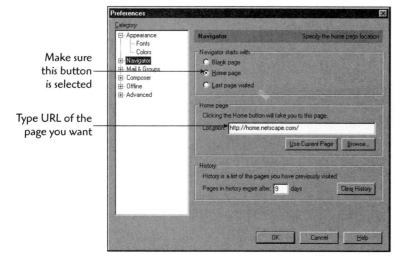

5. In the middle section, called Home page, change the URL that's currently displayed in the Location text box to the URL of the page you want.

6. Check the URL you typed for typing errors or other mistakes. As you learned in previous lessons, URLs are case-sensitive, so typing an uppercase letter instead of a lowercase letter will produce an error message the next time you start Navigator.

7. If you want to open to the page that's currently on the Navigator screen, click Use Current Page.

8. After the new URL appears in the Location text box, click OK. The Preferences dialog box closes and you return to the page you were viewing previously.

9. Click the Home button to move to the new home page you selected.

The next time you open Navigator, the page you entered will be the first to appear.

Exercise 2: Setting up a PowerStart page

In this exercise, you set up your own PowerStart page. The PowerStart page is a great way to organize and arrange all the links to sites you like. If you're in a rush, you can use the Quick Start option and let Netscape construct the page for you. With an investment of a few more seconds, however, you can design a customized PowerStart page. Follow these steps:

1. Type **home.netscape.com** in the Location/Netsite box and press Enter to move to the Netscape home page.

2. Scroll down the page to the section that contains information about the PowerStart feature.

3. Click the PowerStart link. The Netscape PowerStart Setup page appears, with text in the Preview frame.

The PowerStart Setup page is composed of three frames. The Options frame on the left side contains a list of instructions, links, and other selections. The Preview frame on the right displays the page as you build it. The bottom frame contains information and additional choices about the items you select from the Options frame.

4. Read the information about PowerStart and then click Continue to begin setting up your own PowerStart page. The second PowerStart Setup page appears.

Need help working with frames on the PowerStart Setup page? Go back to Lesson 3 for information about working with frames.

---

5. (Optional) If you're in a hurry, click the Quick Start button in the Options frame to set up a PowerStart page that contains Netscape's defaults.

6. If you're designing your own PowerStart page, scroll down through the Options frame and click the Contents link in the Contents Collections section.

As displayed in the following illustration, the bottom frame shows different content collections, such as Technology. Click the option button next to the one you want to include on your PowerStart page.

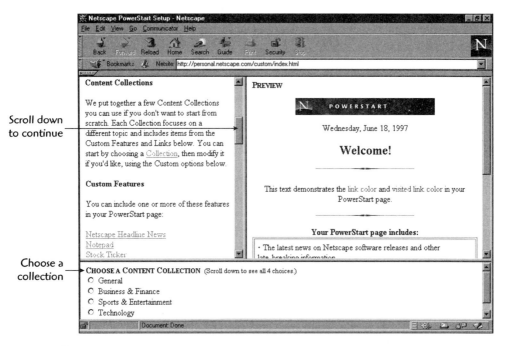

Scroll down
to continue

Choose a
collection

7. Use the scroll bar in the Options frame to move down to the Custom Features. Click a link to one of the features in the following table for inclusion on the PowerStart page. A confirmation frame appears at the bottom of the page.

Link	Description
Netscape Headline News	Shows the latest information on Netscape products and other late-breaking news.
Notepad	Enables you to type notes, reminders, and other helpful information to yourself.
Stock Ticker	Provides a stock ticker, updated every minute with the latest quote for stocks you've selected.

8. Confirm that you want to include the feature by clicking the option button next to Yes. If necessary, answer the onscreen prompts for additional information, such as a stock symbol.

9. To include another of the Custom Features, repeat Steps 7 and 8. You see the items you've selected in the Preview frame, as shown in the following figure.

5

Your PowerStart page includes:

· The latest news on Netscape software releases and other late-breaking information

· A Notepad, where you can type reminders, to-do lists, and other useful notes to yourself

· 7 Daily News links	· 1 Reference link
· 9 Business & Finance links	· 7 Entertainment links
· 2 Sports links	· 2 Shopping links
· 4 Technology News links	· 2 Netscape links

10. When you've finished selecting Custom Features, scroll down the Options frame to the Custom Links section, and select from the list a link that you'd like to include on your PowerStart page.

The links are taken from Netscape's Guides. (You learn about Guides later in this book.)

11. Each time you click a link from the Custom Links section, you're presented with a submenu of options from which to choose. For example, if you select the Technology News link, you must choose which of the available Technology News site links to feature on your PowerStart page, as shown in the following example.

Choose as many as you want

CHOOSE FROM THESE TECHNOLOGY NEWS SITES (Scroll down to see all 12 choices.)
☐ @ Computerworld
☑ CMP's TechWeb
☑ c|net
☑ IDG

12. Repeat Steps 10 and 11 for each Custom Link you want to include.

TIP

Don't be tempted to add too many custom features and links at first. A page with stock tickers, headlines from several sources, and fancy design elements makes it difficult for any one item to stand out. Start with just a few custom options and links. After you've viewed the page, you can add more.

13. Once you've added all the Custom Links you want, the fun begins! Scroll down to the Page Style section of the left frame and click the Style Sheets link. An array of colored sheets with different layouts appears, as shown in the following figure.

CHOOSE A STYLE SHEET (Scroll to the right to see all the choices.)

14. Click the style sheet that most closely matches the way you want your PowerStart page to look. (Don't worry if it isn't exactly right — you'll be able to change some of the elements in a few moments.) A sample of your PowerStart page appears in the right frame.

15. After you've looked at the sample, you can change the layout, add a greeting or headline, add a headline image, or add horizontal lines by clicking the corresponding link in the Custom Design Elements section and then following the instructions shown in the bottom frame.

As you add or change Custom Design Elements, the elements appear in the sample of your PowerStart page in the Preview frame.

16. In the Custom Colors section, the links offer the option of changing the background color or pattern and changing the color of text, links, or visited links. If you want to change any of these page elements, click the link and select the color or pattern you want.

17. Look over your selections in the Preview frame, where a sample of your page is displayed. If you want to change a PowerStart page element, scroll back to its section in the Options frame and make the changes.

18. When you're satisfied, click the Build button at the bottom of the Options frame. If you want to discard your choices and begin again, click Start Over.

19. In a moment, the message shown in the following figure appears on the screen. Click OK when you've read it.

20. Your PowerStart page appears onscreen, as shown in the following illustration. (Based on the options you chose, your page will look different from mine.) Along with the custom features and links you added, the page contains links to various sites; it even includes a Cool Sites Link. Scroll through the page to find the elements and features you inserted.

The completed
PowerStart page

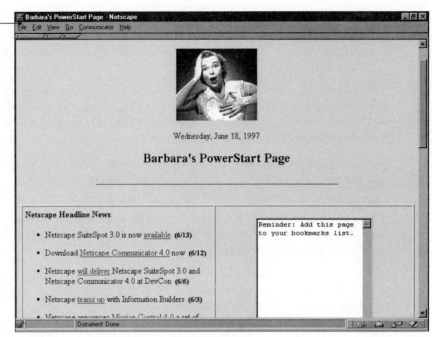

21. If you want to designate the PowerStart page that's on the screen as your opening page, click Edit → Preferences and choose Navigator from the list of categories. Click the Current Page button in the middle section. Or, bookmark the PowerStart page on the screen by dragging the Page Proxy icon over to the Bookmark QuickFile icon.

Anytime you want to make changes to the PowerStart page, open it first and then click the Change PowerStart link at the top of the page.

The PowerStart page you just created is stored on your computer's hard drive in a file called COOKIES.TXT. Although you can find and look at the COOKIES.TXT file, take care not to move or delete it.

Adding Profiles to Navigator

Navigator enables you to set up individual profiles for all the people who access the Internet from your computer. If you use Navigator for serious work, such as business or school research, and also for fun, you can set up two profiles that match all your online requirements. If two people share the same copy of Communicator on one computer, set up profiles for each one. Profiles hold your bookmarks, stored messages, settings, and preferences.

The command to set up a new user profile is in the Netscape Communicator section of the Windows Start menu. Click Start → Programs → Netscape Communicator → Utilities → User Profile Manager. When the Profile Manager dialog box appears, click New to begin. Anytime you set up a profile or change an existing one, none of Communicator's components can be open.

This Visual Bonus displays the dialog boxes you encounter as you set up a new user profile.

Click to continue

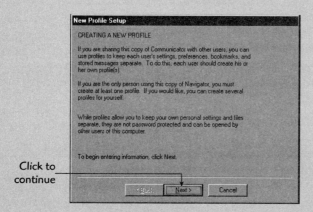

Start creating the profile.

Click to continue

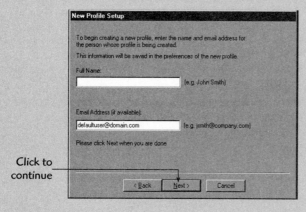

Type name and e-mail address (if available) for the new profile.

5

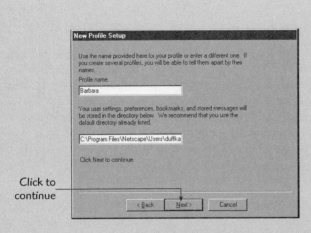

Click to continue

Type a name for profile and change folder if desired.

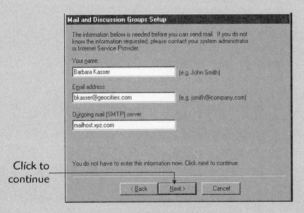

Click to continue

Options for outgoing mail.

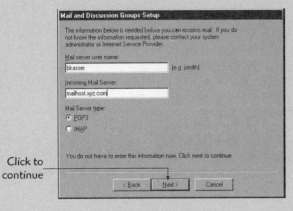

Click to continue

Options for incoming mail.

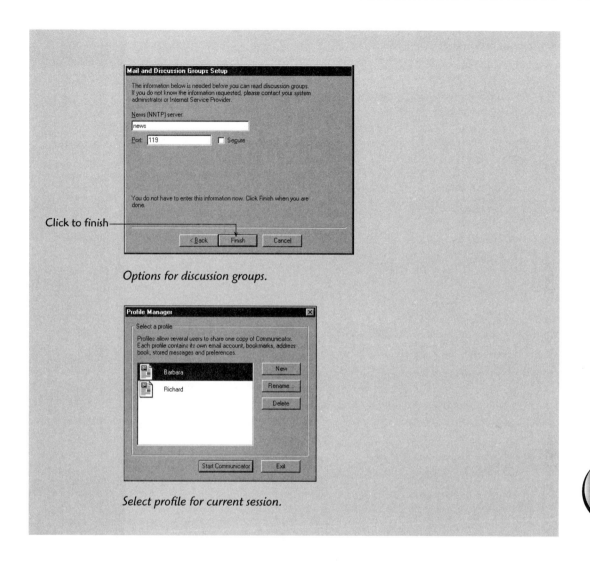

Click to finish

Options for discussion groups.

Select profile for current session.

5

TAILORING NAVIGATOR

After you use any program for a while, you find a few things you'd like to change. For example, maybe you'd like to add a button to a toolbar. Netscape makes it easy to tailor Navigator to your preferences.

Exercise 3: Customizing Navigator's appearance

In this exercise, you change Navigator's appearance in several ways. Follow these steps:

1. By default, the Navigation Toolbar shows both pictures and text. To change the appearance of the toolbar, from within Navigator, choose Edit → Preferences.

2. Select the Appearance category to access the Appearance sheet.

3. Click the option button next to Text Only, as shown in the following illustration.

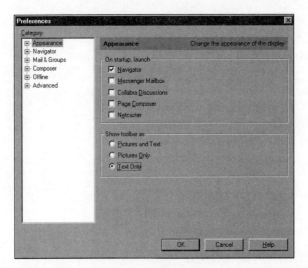

4. While you're changing Navigator preferences, you can change both the font and colors. If the Appearance tab is collapsed (you see a plus sign next to Appearance and you can't see the Appearance subcategories), click the plus sign. The sign changes to a minus, and items relating to Navigator's display appear below the Appearance heading. If the subcategories are visible, skip to the next step.

5. Click Fonts. The Fonts sheet opens, as shown in the following example.

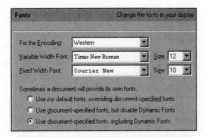

6. Click the drop-down arrow next to the font name that currently appears in the Variable Width Font box to open the list of font names. The fonts are listed alphabetically and correspond to the fonts installed on your computer.

Font is another word for typeface. Variable width fonts are proportionally spaced; each letter takes up precisely the amount of space that it needs. For example, the uppercase W takes up more space on a page than a lowercase i.

7. Scroll up the list and choose Arial.

8. Click the drop-down arrow next to the box labeled Size.

9. Choose the number 14 from the list. The list closes.

NOTE

Although you can change the display for three fonts, change only the Variable Width font. Changing the other two fonts can result in unreadable pages.

10. The Preferences dialog box is still open. Choose Colors from the Appearance category. The Colors sheet opens.

11. If a check mark appears in the box next to Use Windows color, click it to deselect the option. Click the box on the Background line that's currently displaying the default color. The color dialog box appears.

12. Click the color that you want to see in the background and then click OK. No matter how exciting some of the darker colors seem, pick a neutral color that's easy on your eyes.

13. Make sure that the box next to Always use my colors, overriding document is checked. If the box contains a check mark, you'll miss many of the design elements that Webmasters have added to their pages.

14. Click OK to close the Preferences dialog box and return to Navigator. The page reflects the changes you made.

Exercise 4: Editing the Personal Toolbar

In this exercise, you edit the Personal Toolbar by adding a new button and editing an existing one. Follow these steps:

1. If the Barbara Kasser Page does not appear on the Navigator screen, type **www.geocities.com/Paris/LeftBank/4487/** in the Location box and press Enter.

2. Carefully click the Page Proxy icon (the icon in between Bookmarks and Location on the Location Toolbar) and drag it to a blank spot on the Personal Toolbar. When you release the mouse, a button containing a bookmark to the site appears, as shown in the following figure.

Button you added to Personal Toolbar

Toolbar buttons display only text

Page Proxy icon

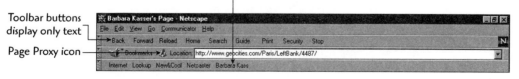

3. It's easy to edit the buttons on the Personal Toolbar because they appear in a folder on the Bookmark QuickFile. To edit the Personal Toolbar, click the

Bookmark QuickFile icon on the Location Toolbar. The list of your bookmark and bookmark folders appears.

4. Select Edit Bookmarks at the top of the list. The bookmarks file opens in its own window onscreen, on top of the Web page.

5. If it's collapsed, expand the Personal Toolbar folder in the Bookmarks window by clicking the plus sign next to it. All the buttons on the Personal Toolbar appear.

6. Click the bookmark named Internet. The Internet bookmark appears highlighted.

7. Click Edit → Bookmark Properties from the menu bar in the Bookmarks window. The Bookmarks Properties dialog box appears, with the word *Internet* highlighted in the Name text box.

8. Type **Guides**. Because Internet is selected, the new text you type replaces the selected text.

NETSCAPE NETCASTER — THE NEWEST NETSCAPE MILESTONE

Netcaster is a component of Communicator that delivers information directly to your desktop. It uses a new form of technology called *push*. With Netcaster, you subscribe to a channel, similar to a specialized television channel, that pushes the information to your computer. The information can be viewed immediately or stored and looked at later, when you're not connected to the Internet. Netcaster enables you to customize Communicator; you choose the channels, the update intervals, and where you want the information to appear.

Netcaster features Netscape Channel Finder, a centralized location for viewing all channels available to Netcaster users. Channel Finder enables you to preview and subscribe to all available channels, such as `ABC.com` and `CBS.SportsLine`. When you subscribe to a channel, you tell Netcaster how often you want the information from the channel to be updated on your computer. You also decide where you want the information to appear — anchored to your Windows desktop, for example.

Netcaster needs to be set up before you can subscribe to a channel. In fact, when Communicator was released in June 1997, Netcaster was still in Preview Release and was an additional component that needed to be downloaded separately from Communicator. Netcaster is becoming an important element of Netscape software, and promises to be a key component of Netscape Constellation.

If you're not sure how to set up Netcaster, click Communicator → Netcaster from any open component of Communicator, such as Navigator. You'll be walked though the channel selection process and setup options. Enjoy Netcaster; when you take advantage of Netcaster's push technology to have information delivered to your computer, you're using the latest technology. In fact, by using Netcaster, you're becoming a part of Internet history.

9. When you've finished typing, click OK to close the Bookmark Properties dialog box. You return to the Bookmarks window.

10. Click the Close button next to the Bookmarks window title bar to close the Bookmarks window and return to Navigator. The changes you made are reflected in the Personal Toolbar.

SKILLS CHALLENGE: MAKING NAVIGATOR YOUR OWN

In this Skills Challenge, you use the skills acquired from the exercises in this lesson to continue personalizing Navigator. You should complete all exercises in the lesson before you attempt the challenge.

1. Open Navigator and move to your new home page.

2. Change the home page to another site.

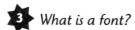 *How do you change the page you see when Navigator opens?*

3. Open your PowerStart page.

4. Click Change PowerStart at the top of the page.

5. Scroll down the Options Frame to the link for Personal Links.

6. Follow the instructions to add at least one link to a site you've enjoyed. (If you can't think of any, use `www.idgbooks.com/.`)

7. Click the Build button.

What's the difference between your PowerStart page and your home page?

8. Open the Navigator Preferences dialog box.

9. Change the display font you see in most pages to Times New Roman, 12 point. (This resets your Navigator default font back to its original setting.)

What is a font?

10. While the Preferences dialog box is open, change the way the toolbars are displayed to Pictures and Text. (This resets your Navigator default toolbar setting back to its original setting.)

11. Close the Preferences dialog box.

 *What kind of technology is used in Netcaster?*

5

TROUBLESHOOTING

All right, you! You should be very proud of the great work you're doing. You'll probably be able to relate to some of the problems and solutions that appear in the following table.

Problem	Solution
I entered the URL for a new home page but instead of seeing the page I expected, I got an error message. Why?	First, go back and check your typing to make sure that you typed the URL correctly. If you didn't make a typing mistake, the most likely cause of the error is that the page moved or was removed. Try another URL.
My husband and I load our own profiles when we enter Navigator. Can we each create a PowerStart page?	Not at this time. You can only have one PowerStart page per installation of Navigator. Work around the problem by building a PowerStart page that contains links and features on which you agree.
Why don't some of the pages I visit show the background color I selected as a default color?	Web pages are written in a language called HTML, which uses codes, called *tags*, to insert various design elements. The background color you selected as a default appears only when a page does not have a tag for a background color.

WRAP UP

In this lesson, you took control of Navigator. The following list shows some of the skills you mastered:

- How to change the page that opens when Navigator loads
- How to set up your own PowerStart page
- How to set up different user profiles
- How to change Navigator's appearance

Take a few minutes after the lesson and customize Navigator with the colors, fonts, and home page settings you want. Remember that you can change the defaults as often as you like, so don't be afraid to experiment. In Lesson 6, you learn some strategies for searching the Web.

PART II

Touring the World Wide Web

You're ready to learn advanced Web navigation and downloading techniques. This part includes the following lessons:

- Lesson 6: Designing a Game Plan for Searching the Web

- Lesson 7: Having Fun on the Web

- Lesson 8: Downloading from the Web

Designing a Game Plan for Searching the Web

45 MINUTES

GOALS

This lesson shows how to perfect your search techniques for the Web sites you want to find. Some of the skills you learn include the following:

- Working with Netscape's search page

- Customizing Netscape's search page

- Searching with HotBot

- Using advanced search techniques

- Harnessing the power of many search engines

- Searching through Yahoo's site directory

- Using telnet

6

GET READY

You have spent the last few lessons wandering the Web, jumping from link to link. While link-hopping is fun, you won't find a special topic that way, unless you accidentally land on a link that takes you where you want to go. In this lesson, you learn how to use various searching tools to look through the Web. You also learn some search techniques and tips. You need to be connected to the Internet with Navigator open before you begin. If you use Navigator through an intranet, make sure that you have access to the Web and not just your company's site.

When you complete this lesson, you will know how to use any search tool to find the information you need, as shown in the following figure. Although you can choose from many search tools, in these exercises you use HotBot, MetaCrawler, and Yahoo.

WHERE DO YOU START YOUR SEARCH?

Looking for Web pages about a specific topic can be maddening. Where do you start? Unlike your local library, the Web does not have a master catalog of every Web page. Thousands of new pages appear each day. How can you ever find the sites you want?

Fortunately, the Web has indexing tools to help you. These Web assistants lead you to the exact documents you want. With a little practice, you can find a page on just about every topic available on the Web. You tell the tool what you are looking for, and the tool retrieves links to matching sites. Whether you're performing serious research or looking around for dirt on your favorite soap star, you'll find that indexing tools make the Web seem a little smaller. The two main types of indexing tools are described as follows:

- **Search engines** send electronic *spiders, worms,* or *robots* to roam the Web looking for indexed pages. When the spider finds a site that is not in the index, it adds an entry to its database with the page's title, URL, and some of the text. (Different search engines use different sections of the text.) Because it could take spiders years to find a new site, Webmasters may give the search engines the URLs of their own sites and invite spiders to visit.

- **Site directories** sort sites into categories and may include comments or reviews. Each category is divided into subcategories, which can also have subcategories (almost like the folder structure of your computer). For example, the Entertainment category can be divided into Movies, Television, and so on. Site directories provide a catalog of sites. Webmasters generally register the URLs listed in site directories.

Every search tool indexes Web pages a little differently, so you may need to try a few different searches to get the results you want.

If you are interested in Web robots, The Web Robots FAQ by Martijn Koster is a page to visit. Cruise to `http://info.webcrawler.com/mak/projects/robots/faq.html`.

USING NETSCAPE NET SEARCH

The following two exercises show how to use the search page that Netscape presents.

Exercise 1: Working with Netscape's search page

In this exercise you use a search tool from the list that Netscape has assembled for you. Follow these steps:

6

1. Click the Search button on the Navigation toolbar. Alternatively, you can type **home.netscape.com/home/internet-search.html** in the Location box. The Netscape Net Search page appears.

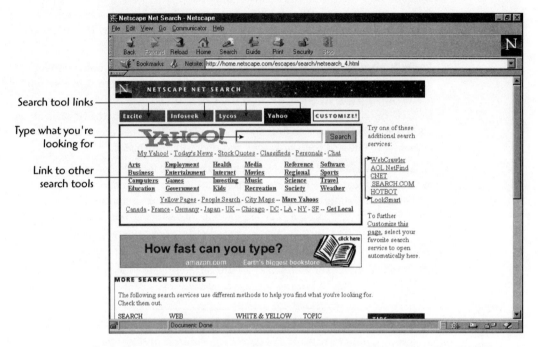

2. A row of links to popular Web search tools appears, with one link already selected. Click each link and look at the search tools.

Although every search tool has a different look, each one contains a box in which you can type what you're looking for and a button you can click to begin a search through the Web.

3. Click the Yahoo button if it's not already selected.

4. Type **cairn** in the text box. (You are looking for references to cairn terriers.)

5. Click the Search button.

6. In a few moments, a page like the one in the following example appears, showing the results of the search. Each site or category that matches *cairn* appears as a link. The matches are called *hits*.

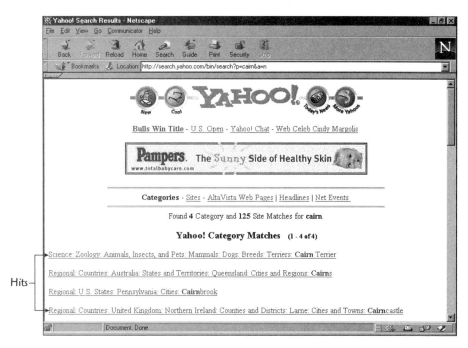

7. Scroll down the page and look at the hits. Although many of them link to Web pages about cairn terriers, some of the hits are linked to sites that contain the word *cairn* but have nothing to do with dogs.

Different search tools use the word documents on the results list. Don't get confused — document is another way of saying Web site or page.

8. Click the Back button on the Navigation Toolbar.

9. Click a button that shows the name of another search tool on the Net Search page.

10. Type the word **cairn** again and click the Search button.

11. When the results of the search appear, scroll through the hits.

12. Click the Back button on the Navigation Toolbar.

13. Choose a third search tool by clicking one of the buttons.

14. Again, type **cairn** in the text box and click the button that begins the search. Scroll through the resulting hits.

Because you used the term *cairn*, the search engines did not limit your search to cairn terriers. Instead, they found references to phrases and topics that contained the word *cairn*, such as a page with information about *Cairn*brook, PA.

NOTE

Different search engines produce different hits because they each reference the content of Web pages differently. Therefore, the sites that are listed first on the results list are the sites that contain the most hits or that best match the search criteria, as defined by the search engine.

Exercise 2: Customizing Netscape's search page

In this exercise, you customize the Netscape Net Search page by adding a search engine to the available tools and changing how the page appears. Follow these steps:

1. You already visited this site in the preceding exercise, so click the Back button on the Navigation Toolbar to return to the Netscape Net Search page. Or, click the Search button on the Navigation Toolbar.

2. Four search tools are listed on tabs across the top. Click the last tab labeled Customize. The Customize! - Netscape dialog box appears, with two questions for you to answer.

Click to choose a search service

Click to choose opening service

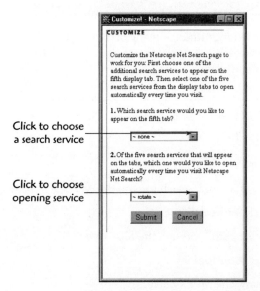

3. The first question asks which search service you'd like to appear on the fifth tab. Click the drop-down arrow to open the list.

4. Choose AOL Netfind from the list.

5. The second question asks which search service you'd like to see when the Netscape Net Search page appears. Click the drop-down arrow to open the list.

6. Choose Yahoo from the list.

7. Click Submit. A box appears, asking if you're sure you want the settings you selected.

8. Click OK. In a moment, the Netscape Net Search reloads. Your choices are now included in the Net Search page.

LEARNING WEB SEARCH RULES

Understanding a few search rules makes playing the Web search game fun. To play the game, you pick a search tool and then enter a *query* made up of *keywords*. The search tool responds with a *results list* containing links to Web sites that match your query. You win when you find the Web sites you're looking for. Here are some search pointers.

- **Keep your query short and to the point.** Long, rambling dissertations confuse the search tool and give poor results. "Garbage in, garbage out" definitely applies to Web searches. An example of an effective query is "Web search technique." On the other hand, the query "How can I search the World Wide Web effectively?" would not produce helpful results.

- **Check for spelling errors.** Typos ruin a great search query. Entering the keywords "Web search thechnigues" won't find any sites that hold information about Web search techniques.

- **Enclose phrases in double quotes.** Some search tools require quotes, and some don't. Because you don't know which tools need what, you should get into the habit of using double quotes to glue phrases together. For example, "web search technique" finds sites that show the exact phrase, rather than finding every site with the word *Web* or *search* or *technique*.

- **Use Boolean logic.** If you had a bad time in high school math, don't panic at the mention of Boolean logic! Here's a quick primer:

  - **AND:** The word AND between keywords limits your query. For example, Web AND search AND technique means that the sites found by the search tool must contain all three words. However, this doesn't mean that they need to be together in a phrase. AND is sometimes represented by the character &.

  - **OR:** OR is the assumed connection between words in a search query. OR produces the opposite result of using double quotes around words. In our example, the use of OR means that the search tool will find Web pages that contain the words *Web* or *search* or *technique*. OR is sometimes represented by the character.

  - **NOT:** Use NOT when you want to exclude a specific word. The query *"search techniques" NOT Web* tells the search tool to dismiss all Web sites that contain references to Web search technique but to show you the links to sites that contain references to any other search technique. NOT is sometimes represented by the – (minus sign) character.

6

Touring HotBot's Search Page

Originally an academic experiment, *HotBot* was developed at the University of California at Berkeley. HotBot is a search engine with first-rate speed and links to over 54 million sites on the Web. The HotBot search engine is located at www.hotbot.com.

Click to show results list with full descriptions, brief descriptions, or URLs only

Choose number of linked sites to be shown on results list

Click to search

Choose Web, Usenet News, or Web and Usenet search

Limit search to all words, any words, exact phrase, person, links to this URL, or Boolean expression

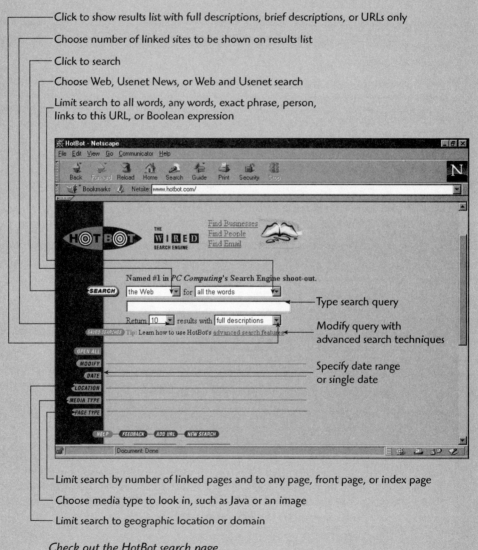

Type search query

Modify query with advanced search techniques

Specify date range or single date

Limit search by number of linked pages and to any page, front page, or index page

Choose media type to look in, such as Java or an image

Limit search to geographic location or domain

Check out the HotBot search page.

- **Start with a broad query and then narrow it down.** You don't want to miss anything, do you? Unless you're 100 percent positive of what you'll find, let the search tool do its job and find as many links as it can. After you've looked at the results, refine your query and search again.

- **Don't get discouraged.** So many Web pages exist that it may take a few tries before you find what you're looking for.

TIP

Many search tools contain links to helpful information about how the tools work. Look for a link to Advanced Techniques or Helpful Hints to get the most out of each tool.

TRYING OUT MORE SEARCHES

The following exercises enable you to experiment with various search tools and techniques.

Exercise 3: Searching with HotBot

In this exercise, you use HotBot to search for sites that refer to *lemon chicken.* Follow these steps:

1. Type **www.hotbot.com** in the Location/Netsite box and press Enter. The HotBot page appears.

2. Click in the text box and type **lemon chicken.**

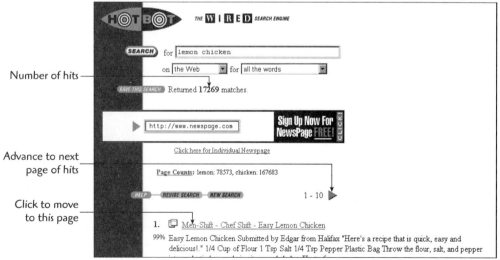

Number of hits

Advance to next page of hits

Click to move to this page

3. Click the Search button. While HotBot looks through its index of Web pages, fireworks flash in the Netscape icon.

4. Scroll through the links shown on the HotBot results page, which should look similar to the page shown in the following example. The links at the top of the results list most closely match the search query.

5. Jot down how many matches HotBot found for *lemon chicken*.

6. Click the Revise Search button. The HotBot search page reappears.

7. The current query reads "Search the Web for all the words." Click the drop-down arrow next to "all the words" and choose "the exact phrase" from the list, as shown here.

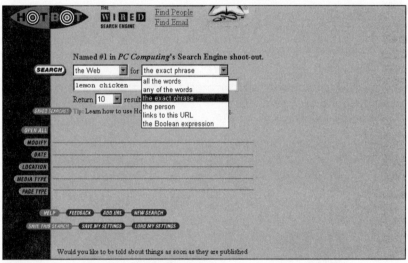

8. Click Search to run the search again. When the results appear, jot down the number of matches found with the revised query. The number of matches is considerably lower when you use "the exact phrase."

9. Click the Revise Search button once more.

10. When the search page appears on the screen, click the drop-down arrow next to "the Web" and choose "Usenet News" from the list.

NOTE

Usenet News is an Internet network of newsgroups where users exchange information and news. You learn more about Usenet News later in this book.

11. Click the Search button again. As HotBot looks through its index of Usenet News postings, fireworks flash in the Netscape icon.

12. Look at the results list. Instead of Web pages, you see links to articles posted by Internet subscribers.

13. Jot down the number of items on the results list. HotBot found fewer matches by looking through the indexed articles on Netscape News than by looking on the Web.

14. Click Revise Search to return to the original search page.

TIP

Don't be surprised if you run the same search in a couple of days and get a different number of hits. The Web is open 24 hours a day and changes constantly.

Exercise 4: Using advanced search techniques

In this exercise, you use HotBot's advanced query features to narrow the results list for the search you ran in the preceding exercise. Follow these steps:

1. "Usenet News" is still shown in the Search drop-down list, from Exercise 3. Click the drop-down arrow and select "the Web" from the list. Your query should read "Search the Web for the exact phrase," with **lemon chicken** typed in the text box.

2. Click the Date tab below the query. The date modification section opens, as shown in the following example.

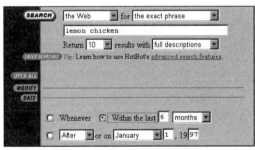

3. Click the option button next to "Within the last" to narrow the search for Web pages placed on the Web within the last six months.

4. Click Search. In a few moments, the results page appears. Note that fewer matches appear now than when the time frame was unlimited — as it was when you conducted the search in the last exercise.

5. Click Revise Search to return to the original search.

6. In the Date area, click in the box that displays a number on the "Within the last" option line and replace the number that's currently displayed with **1**. (You need to type it, as there are no spin controls.)

7. Click Search. In a few moments, the results page appears. Jot down the number of matches found, if any.

8. Click Revise Search once more to return to the original query.

9. Click the button in the date area next to "Whenever" to extend the date range.

10. Click the Location tab. Choose from Anywhere (the default option), CyberPlace for a specific domain name, or GeoPlace for a geographic location.

11. Click the option button next to GeoPlace and choose Europe from the drop-down list.

12. Run the search by clicking the Search button, and review the results list.

As you can see, changing the search query and related search criteria produces varied results.

Changes you make to any of HotBot's default settings, shown when you open the HotBot page, won't be loaded the next time you use HotBot. If you want to permanently change a setting (for example, changing the date range or looking for the exact phrase instead of all the words), make the changes you want and then click the Save My Settings button. The next time you use HotBot, the changes will be saved as your HotBot default.

Navigator has provided you with a bookmark to HotBot. To use it, click the Bookmark QuickFile icon, click the Search folder, and then click HotBot. If you need help with bookmarks, review Lesson 2.

Exercise 5: Harnessing the power of many search engines

The explosion in the number of search engines led Internet gurus to create "meta" search tools, often referred to as multithreaded search engines. Meta-engines search multiple search engines simultaneously. While meta-engines can't take advantage of all the controls that a single search engine such as HotBot offers, they enable you to look quickly through the indexed databases of a number of large search engines. In this exercise, you use the GO2SEARCH/MetaCrawler meta-engine. Follow these steps:

1. Type **www.go2search.com** in the Location box and press Enter. The GO2SEARCH/Metacrawler search page appears.

2. Click in the Search text box and type **"supreme physical fitness"** in double quotes.

3. Click the button next to "as a phrase" to have MetaCrawler look for the phrase *supreme physical fitness*, rather than the individual words.

4. Click Fast Search. MetaCrawler posts messages on the screen as it searches through the indexes of several search engines.

5. Scroll through the MetaCrawler search results. The results from the search engines that MetaCrawler looked through are collated onto one page. Note that your search query appears in the title of the page.

Change the organization of the results list by clicking the down arrow next to Relevance and then selecting Location. Instead of information about the linked pages, you'll find the location name of the linked sites.

6. Click the Fast Search button.

7. Click the Back button on the Navigation Toolbar to return to the MetaCrawler search page.

8. Delete the quotes around the phrase to change the query to **advanced physical fitness**.

9. Click the option button next to "Any" to search for any of the words.

10. Click the Complete button. The Netscape icon is active as MetaCrawler conducts the search. Scroll through the results list.

Exercise 6: Searching through Yahoo's site directory

Yahoo, a classic site directory, takes a different approach to finding Web pages than HotBot or MetaCrawler do. Yahoo's index of Web sites is arranged by categories. Under certain categories you find subcategories.

You can enter a few keywords and enable Yahoo to look for matches, or if you're not sure what you're looking for, select a category that interests you from Yahoo's main page. Using Yahoo's category organization, you could find Web sites without having to enter any keywords! Of course, to refine your search, you could select some categories and then enter a keyword.

In this exercise, you find sites that reference the film *Gone with the Wind*. The first part of this exercise takes you through many of Yahoo's subcategories. The final part shows how to jump directly to *Gone with the Wind* sites. Follow these steps:

1. Type **www.yahoo.com/** in the Location box and press Enter. The Yahoo main page appears.

2. Click the Entertainment link. An index of entertainment-related categories appears.

3. Scroll down the page and click the Movie and Films link. An index of categories about movies appears. The number of sites referenced to the link appears in parentheses beside the index title.

4. Click the Titles category link.

TIP

As you jump from category to category, you're bound to find a link that doesn't pertain to your original search but looks enticing. Feel free to follow another link and see where it leads you. Click Back on the toolbar when you're ready to return to this exercise.

5. Click the Classic Hollywood category link.

6. Click the *Gone with the Wind* category link.

7. Click any of the links to *Gone with the Wind* sites.

8. Click the Top link to return to the main Yahoo page.

9. Type **"Gone with the Wind"** (remember to use quotes) in the text box.

10. Click the Search button to tell Yahoo to look through a master index of all of its categories that contain references to *Gone with the Wind.*

OTHER INTERNET SEARCHES

Just a few years ago, searching the Web was a confusing, often frustrating proposition. Two search tools were used to help look through the maze of documents.

WAIS (Wide Area Index Searching) was developed by Apple Computer, Dow Jones, and Thinking Machines Corporation to provide an effective way to search the Internet. WAIS requires the use of special WAIS servers that look through the text of Web documents, instead of the page title or selected keywords. Go to `www.einet.net` to see an example of a WAIS server.

Gopher, developed at the University of Minnesota in 1991 and named for its mascot, provides another way to search through documents on the Internet. Mostly students and researchers use Gopher. The documents you find in Gopher are not Web pages; instead, they are textual and look primitive compared to Web pages.

Gopher uses two search tools to look through its sites. *Veronica,* the first tool, searches through all the Gopher sites in the world for matches to your query. *Jughead,* the second tool, looks through the Gopher site you're visiting currently. Gopher arranges its documents in directory folders, just like the files on your computer are arranged. Instead of the links and graphics you're used to, Gopher uses icons similar to those in Windows Explorer or My Computer. Go to `www.nova.edu/Inter-Links/` and follow the links to visit a Gopher site.

Although both WAIS and Gopher have a devoted following, they are rapidly becoming obsolete. As more documents appear on the Web and search tools index these documents more effectively, WAIS and Gopher are disappearing.

11. Yahoo organizes the links on the Yahoo search results page into Category Site Matches.

12. Click any link on the page to visit sites about *Gone with the Wind*.

By taking two different approaches to search for references to *Gone with the Wind*, you end up with very different results. For a broad-based search, type your search query and click Search if you're not sure what you're looking for. If you're looking for specific results, such as links to pages about *Gone with the Wind*, use the category method.

Understanding telnet

Telnet, a special utility, enables your computer to connect with and log in to other computers on the Internet. The Telnet links on Web pages look like normal links. When you telnet to another computer, you can access programs or databases stored there. A popular use of telnet is accessing job listings with the U.S. government. Many people use telnet to play interactive games. When you've finished using telnet, exiting or *logging out* of the host computer takes you back to Navigator. Think of telnet connections as one-way links. Even though your computer is connected to another computer when you're using telnet, the other computer does not have access to the files on your hard drive.

Exercise 7: Using telnet

In this exercise, you use telnet to establish an account with FedWorld and search through jobs available with the U.S. government. Follow these steps:

1. Type **www.shu.edu/academic/arts_sci/Graduate/communic/ joblinks.html** in the Location box and press Enter. A Web page appears (this page was set up at Seton Hall University and contains links to many different pages).

2. Select Edit → Find.

3. Type **FedWorld** in the text box and click Find Next. The FedWorld listing is highlighted.

4. Close the Find dialog box by clicking Cancel.

5. Click the telnet link that's on the same line as the FedWorld listing. The connection to the host computer is established and a Telnet window appears over the Navigator screen, as shown in the following figure.

6. Because this is your first time at the FedWorld telnet site, you need to type **NEW** at the prompt and then press Enter.

7. Type the correct responses to the subsequent questions, such as your name and address, pressing Enter after each one.

6

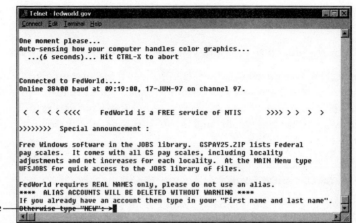

Type NEW here

8. You'll be asked to provide a password. Write down your password and your user name so you can refer to them later.

9. When your account has been set up, you'll receive an onscreen message. After you've read the information, press Enter (which is called the Return key when you're using telnet).

10. Continue typing responses to the questions, remembering to press Enter after each one.

11. When the screen shown in the following illustration appears, type the number of the option you want to view and press Enter.

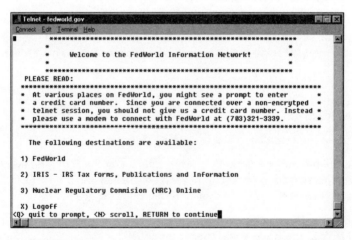

12. Scroll through the information on the screen, following the prompts at the bottom of the window.

13. When you've finished, follow the prompts to log off. When the connection with telnet is broken, the box shown in the following illustration appears. Click OK.

14. Click the Close button to the right of the Telnet title bar to return to Navigator.

Now that you've set up an account with FedWorld, you can telnet to the site for 180 minutes each day, as long as you enter your user ID and password.

The site at `http://www.spectracom.com/islist/inet2.html#HYTELNET` *contains links to hundreds of telnet servers.*

SKILLS CHALLENGE: SEARCHING FOR SPECIFIC DOCUMENTS

In this Skills Challenge, you use different search tools to find sites relating to Elvis Presley. Once you master searching techniques, you can use any search tool with ease.

1. Click Search on the Navigation Toolbar.

2. Choose the WebCrawler search tool from the Net Search window.

3. Type a query in the text box to look for Elvis Presley sites. Note the total number of documents found.

 Name two ways to set up a query so that you include all the words in the search.

4. Go back to the Netscape Net Search page. Refine your search by looking for references to Elvis Presley that do not contain the word *Graceland*.

2 *How should you structure a search query to find Web documents that contain Elvis Presley without the word Graceland?*

5. Search again. Note the total number of documents found now. Are there more or fewer than you found in Step 3?

6. Move to HotBot's search engine page at `www.hotbot.com/`.

7. Set up a query that looks for sites that reference Elvis Presley, the person.

8. Conduct the search and record the number of documents found.

9. Modify the query so that HotBot looks for documents about Elvis Presley dated in the last six months.

10. Run the search again. How many documents did HotBot find this time?

 How do search engines build their indexes of Web documents?

11. Move to Yahoo at www.yahoo.com/.

 What is the main difference between Yahoo and HotBot?

12. Search for links that contain both *Elvis Presley* and *Graceland*. How many sites were found?

13. Go back to the main Yahoo search page and move to the Entertainment category.

14. Type the same search query that you used in Step 12.

15. Click the option button to make sure Yahoo looks only through the Entertainment category.

16. Run the search. How many documents were found when you limited the search to one category?

17. Return to the Netscape home page.

TROUBLESHOOTING

You may hit the wall or get unexpected results as you use different search tools. The following table shows how to proceed when you encounter problems.

Problem	Solution
I set up a search and got pages of links on the results list. However, most of the links don't seem to go to working pages.	This problem hits everyone in the face now and again. Because Web spiders only go forward when finding new pages, pages that have been changed or removed don't get "un"-indexed. There isn't much you can do about it.
I'm using HotBot. How do I know I've found all of the Web pages I need?	You don't! Make sure that you search with a broad query first and then narrow it. Also, if you're really concerned, run the search through a couple of search tools.
How should I proceed if I only have a general idea of what I want to find?	Use a site directory such as Yahoo to start the search. A word of caution, though — it may take several tries to find sites that contain the information you're looking for.

WRAP UP

Once you complete this lesson, you have gained control of the Web. You now have the skills you need to find anything! In this lesson, you learned the following:

- The difference between search engines and site directories
- Basic rules for Web searching
- How to use HotBot, Yahoo, and MetaCrawler
- What telnet is

Practice, practice, practice! Redo the searches you ran in the exercises and visit the links shown on the result lists. String complicated search queries together using AND, OR, and NOT and see how the results change. Bookmark the search tools you're most comfortable with. When you have free time, move to some sites shown on the Netscape Net Search page and try some sample searches. In Lesson 7, you explore cool Web sites.

6

Having Fun on the Web

45 MINUTES

GOALS

This lesson takes you on a tour of fun sites. Some of your accomplishments in this lesson include the following:

- Using Switchboard to find someone
- Finding people with Netscape's help
- Seeing what's new and what's cool
- Letting Netscape guide you around the Web
- Visiting Talk City

7

GET READY

In this lesson, you get to have some fun on the Web. To complete this lesson, the drill's the same — you need to be connected to the Internet through your ISP or your company's direct connection. Navigator should be open on the screen.

When you finish this lesson, you will know how to search for people (as shown in the first figure following this paragraph), find the latest and greatest sites (as shown in the second figure), and participate in a chat site.

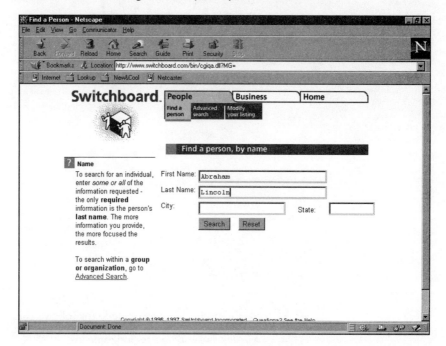

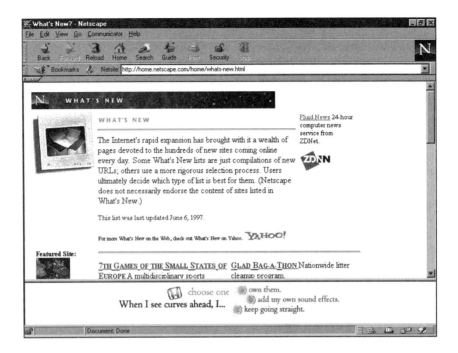

LOOKING FOR PEOPLE THROUGH THE WEB

Have you ever awakened from a sound sleep with thoughts of someone you haven't seen for years? Do you ever search fruitlessly for the phone book when you need to look up the phone number of someone across town? (The last time I went looking for the phone book, I finally found it under my son's bed!) Several sites on the Web make it easy to look for people — even friends you haven't contacted for years.

Many sites on the Web specialize in finding people. Some may furnish only the person's e-mail address. Others provide more detailed information, such as the street address, city, state, and phone numbers. The odds that you'll find a missing person increase with the amount of information you bring to the search.

Exercise 1: Using Switchboard to find someone

In this exercise, you use a search engine called *Switchboard* to look for people. Switchboard contains one of the most comprehensive directories on the Web. With 106 million residential listings and 11 million business listings, the Switchboard Internet directory is a great place to start when you're looking for someone. Follow these steps to begin your search:

1. Open Navigator (if it isn't already open and visible on the screen).

2. Type **www.switchboard.com/** in the Location box and press Enter.

7

3. When Switchboard appears, move your mouse to the Find People link (the mouse pointer takes the shape of a hand) and click the left mouse button. The Find a Person form appears.

4. Click in the First Name text box and type the first name of the person you're looking for. Press Tab to advance to the next field.

5. Type the remaining information in the other boxes, pressing Tab to advance to each box. If you're not sure about a box, leave it blank. The only box you absolutely must fill in is the person's last name. A completed form is shown in the following illustration.

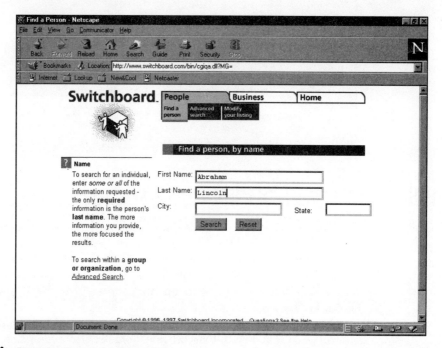

6. Click the Search button.

7. As the search is conducted, various messages may appear on the status bar. In a few moments, the Switchboard results window appears.

8. Look through the names and addresses to find the person you're looking for. If the person is not on the current page, click More Listings to move to the next page.

9. If necessary, click Modify Search to return to the form you completed and change the information. To use some of Switchboard's advanced options, click Advanced Search. To begin a new search, click New Search.

Exercise 2: Finding people with Netscape's help

Netscape has compiled a large list of search guides containing highly specialized search tools to help you find whatever you're looking for. The People Guide provides easy access to many directory services designed to help you find anyone. Most directories used by Netscape work like your phone company's white pages directory, but instead of a phone number, you'll probably get an e-mail address. In this exercise, you tap Netscape's list of available directories to locate the person you want to find. Follow these steps:

1. Click the Lookup folder on the Personal Toolbar.

2. Choose People from the submenu. The People page of the Netscape Guide appears, as shown.

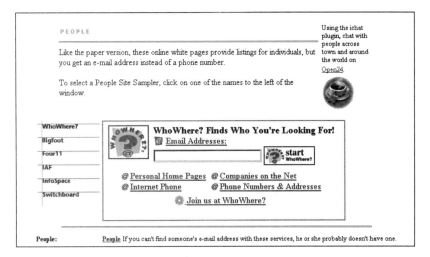

3. Scroll down the page and click the People link. You'll see a list of links to search engines and to services designed to find people. Table 7-1 describes some of the sites listed.

TABLE 7-1	NETSCAPE'S PEOPLE FINDERS	
Name	**URL**	**Description**
Bigfoot	www.bigfoot.com/	Offers a lifetime e-mail forwarding service called "Bigfoot for Life." An additional " FEETure" links you to personal home pages.
InfoSpace	www.infospace.com/	Offers online directories including yellow pages, government listings, and individuals.
WhoWhere?	www.whowhere.com/	Enables you to find URLs, Internet video phone numbers, and e-mail addresses in English, French, and Spanish.

(continued)

TABLE 7-1	NETSCAPE'S PEOPLE FINDERS (CONTINUED)	
Name	**URL**	**Description**
Switchboard	`www.switchboard.com`	Contains listings of millions of personal and business phone numbers and addresses.
Internet Address Finder	`www.iaf.net`	Enables you to search by individual names or e-mail addresses.
Four11	`www.four11.net`	Enables you to search for individuals by name, e-mail, or Internet phone number. Also contains celebrity and government listings.

4. Click one of the links on the People page. A blank form that contains fields such as Last Name and First Name appears. After you complete the search information and click the Search button, the corresponding people finder search engine is accessed.

5. If you'd like to go directly to the page for a specific search engine, instead of using a form on the Netscape Guide page, move to the site by typing one of the URLs shown in Table 7-1. Follow the instructions on the page to find the person you're looking for.

6. If you want to try another link, click the Back button to move back to the People page of the Netscape Guide.

Although you need to type carefully as you enter the next two URLs, each one offers a wide range of directory services. Access to listings for all directory servers in the world (at least, that's what they claim) and phone books from several continents can be found at `gopher://gopher.nd.edu/11/Non-Notre%20Dame%20Information%20Sources/Phone%20Books—Other%20Institutions`. *The page at* `http://ils.unc.edu/emailpro/public_html/p.html` *provides much information about searching for people, as well as links to several unusual directories. Although the sites are off the usual track, they're both worth a look.*

TOURING SOME HAND-PICKED SITES

Decisions, decisions. The volume of information on the Web can sometimes be intimidating. Often, people don't know exactly what they want to look for; they may prefer to let someone else choose where to visit.

If you fit into this category, the folks at Netscape have done a lot of advance work for you. They've come up with many sites that they think you'll enjoy. Letting Netscape direct your Internet trip is like going cross-country in a luxury van — all you have to do is enjoy the ride! Of course, you can jump off any time and take control of your search by using the skills you learned in the previous lesson. Even if you conduct many searches on your own, take a break and let Netscape show you around for a while.

Exercise 3: Seeing what's new and what's cool

This exercise shows you how to explore some interesting sites that Netscape has chosen. Follow these steps:

1. Click the Guide button on the Navigation Toolbar. The submenu appears.

2. Click What's New. The What's New page of the Netscape Guide appears, as shown in the following illustration.

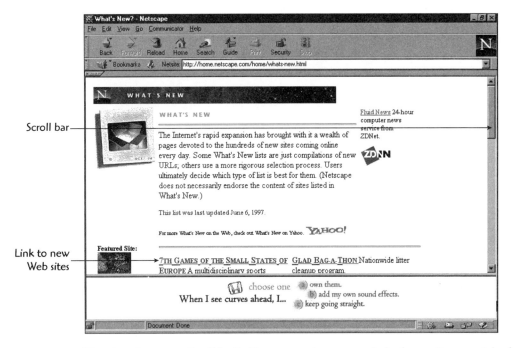

The sites shown on the What's New page change regularly. Some sites are picked for their content or design, while others are selected simply because they're new.

3. Scroll down the What's New page and find a link to a site with a description that interests you. (You know you're on a link when the mouse pointer takes the shape of a hand.)

4. Click the link to move to the new site.

5. If you find any interesting links at the new site, follow them. Or, click the Back button to return to the What's New page.

6. When you've explored all the sites you want to see on the What's New page, click the Guide button on the toolbar.

7. Click What's Cool from the submenu. The What's Cool page appears on the screen.

The What's New and What's Cool pages are both split into frames. One of the frames contains advertising, while the larger frame displays the destination page information. You can click a link on the advertising frame to visit the advertiser's site. Review Lesson 3 if you need help working with frames.

8. Explore the links that interest you, as you did on the What's New page.

For fast access to What's New and What's Cool, click the New & Cool folder on the Personal Toolbar. The folder holds bookmarks to both sites.

VISUAL BONUS

The Latest and Greatest — Yahoo Style

The following illustrations show the Yahoo screen and how to find links to some really great sites on the Web. On a daily basis, Yahoo assembles some of the most interesting pages for your enjoyment. Yahoo is located at `www.yahoo.com/`.

Yahoo buttons to explore.

What's New for Tuesday March 18, 1997

HARDCORE GAMERS WELCOME HOME.
YOUR PLACE TO CHAT, POST CHEATS, GET FREEBIES AND MORE!
CHECK OUT THIS WEEKS PRIZES.

New Additions to Yahoo!	Daily Picks
click a day for hierarchical, complete, or split listings of newly added sites	World Flight 1997 - follow Linda Finch's attempt to complete Amelia Earhart's famous flight. (in Travel:Virtual Field Trips)
Monday Mar. 17 - 1618	Mr. Blackwell - find out who made this year's list. (in Design Arts:Fashion)
- Sunday Mar. 16 - 441	
- Saturday Mar. 15 - 679	GameWorks - we've come a long way since Pac-Man and Donkey Kong. (in Games:Arcades)
Friday Mar. 14 - 1425	
- Thursday Mar. 13 - 1971	No Greater Love - Mother Teresa's life and words. (in Books:Christian)
- Wednesday Mar. 12 - 1418	
- Tuesday Mar. 11 - 2023	Laura Ashley Home - ideas and accessories to brighten your home

Previous days / Links to great sites

Click the New button for daily Web page picks.

VISUAL BONUS

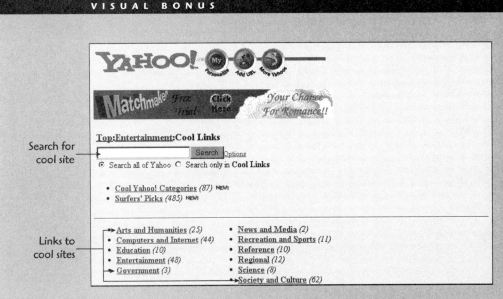

Search for cool site

Links to cool sites

Click the Cool button to search for cool sites.

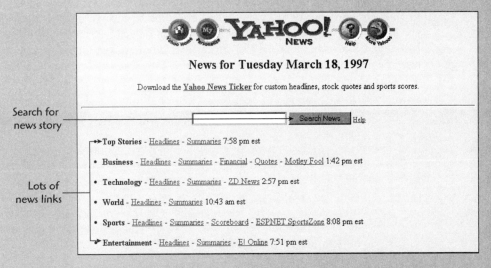

Search for news story

Lots of news links

Click the Today's News button for the latest headlines.

7

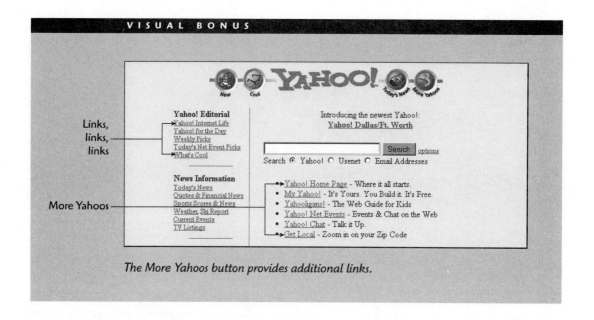

VISUAL BONUS

Links, links, links

More Yahoos

The More Yahoos button provides additional links.

Understanding the Netscape Guide

In previous exercises, you used the Netscape Guide to find Web pages. Netscape and Yahoo have teamed up to provide samples of several types of pages. The Netscape Guide takes some of the effort out of finding great Web sites, by providing links to a vast range of diverse topics. Table 7-2 shows how the Guide is organized.

WHAT'S COOL?

It seems that every page offers a cool sites link. Many of the supposed cool sites really are great, but many are not. In fact, many cool sites are nothing more than advertisements. Who determines what's cool on the Web? Because no criteria or rules exist for rating a site's coolness, the Web designer who set up the referring page adds the link to the page he or she chooses. Why do so many pages have cool sites links? Many Web designers believe that everyone who explores the Web wants to be told where to go and what to do.

In fact, most of us do! We continue to click the cool links in our quest for the ultimate site. We want to know what's the latest fad, and we want to feel like we're part of the " in" Web crowd. I've been disappointed hundreds of times by following a cool link to a site that isn't very good. (Not to mention that I've deserted the great page that contained the referring link!) I know I'll do it again. You will, too. Just don't expect too much from most cool links. And who knows — when you learn to create a Web page later in this book, maybe you can add some cool sites to a link on *your* page.

TABLE 7-2	NETSCAPE GUIDE SECTIONS
Section	*Description*
Home	Contains links to the seven other sections. Also has links to various Web resources, news, and important information about Netscape and its products.
Business	Provides links to business news, as well as employment and company listings. The section contains subsections for Careers and Jobs, Small Business Information, and Business on the Web.
Computers and Internet	Holds links to a wide array of computer-related sites. This section contains subsections for Software, Internet, Hardware, and Intranet.
Entertainment	A comprehensive set of links for all facets of entertainment. In addition to the main Entertainment page of links, subsections of Movies, Music, Books, Television, and Games can also be found.
Finance	Get hooked into the latest finance sites on the Web. Subsections for Quotes, Mutual Funds, Taxes, Banking, and Real Estate exist here.
Shopping	Links to some of the best Web merchants are here. Automotive, Music, Classified, Computers, and Electronics subpages are available.
Sports	A great way to find the greatest sport sites. In addition to the Sports main page, visit the following subsections: Baseball, Basketball, Football, Hockey, Soccer, Golf, and Tennis.
Travel	Plan your dream vacation using the links you find here. Subsections for Travel Agents, Guides, Lodging, and Air Travel are assembled.

Although the Netscape Guide pages provide most of the information and links you'll ever need, you can customize the Guide pages by following the simple instructions from Netscape. At the time this book was written, customizing the Guide pages was limited. However, in the near future, Netscape and Yahoo plan to enable greater customization.

Exercise 4: Letting Netscape guide you around the Web

In this exercise, you use the Guide to tour some of Netscape's hand-picked sites. Follow these steps:

7

1. Click the Guide button on the toolbar and then click The Internet from the submenu. The Netscape Guide home page appears, as shown in the following figure.

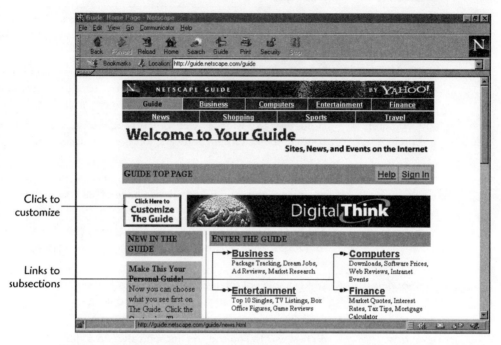

Click to customize

Links to subsections

2. Scroll down the page and click the Computer link. A page similar to the one shown in the following example appears.

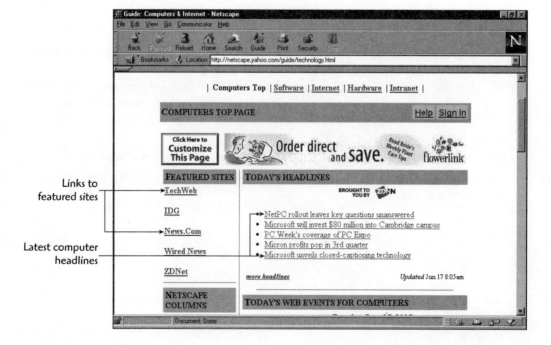

Links to featured sites

Latest computer headlines

3. Click a link to a featured site to view the new page. In a few seconds, the linked page appears.

4. If a link on the new page interests you, follow it (by clicking it).

5. Click the Back button on the Navigation Toolbar as many times as necessary to return to the Netscape Guide home page.

6. Instead of scrolling through the text links, you can click the tabs at the top of the Netscape Guide page to move to any of the Guide subsections. Click the tab to Shopping.

7. Explore the links to the various shopping sites on the Web.

8. When you've finished shopping, click the Netscape icon to return to the Netscape home page.

A FEW NEAT TRICKS

Here are a few "insider" Navigator tricks — some are useful, most are not!

- Press Control+Alt+F. You're whisked to the famous fish tank in Netscape's corporate office.

- Type **about:mozilla** in the Location box and press Enter. Make sure you don't use any spaces. You'll read some scripture supposedly taken from the Book of Mozilla. (In case you don't know, Mozilla Gorilla is the official Netscape mascot.)

- Type **about:jwz** in the Location/Netsite box and press Enter to move to the Web site of Netscape's Jamie Zawinski. Follow some of the links for a wild Web ride.

- Press Control+Alt+S to hide the status indicator. This is useful if you want to see a bit more of the Navigator screen. Press the same keys again to redisplay the status indicator.

- Type **about:global** in the Location/Netsite box and press Enter. You see a list of all the sites you've visited, taken from your Global History file. Bringing up the Global History is especially useful if you've forgotten the URL of a site to which you really want to return.

- Bet you thought that virtual reality meant going to a video arcade and putting on weird headgear! Navigator lets you enter the world of virtual reality from your computer with the help of the Live 3D plug-in. Type the following URL in the Location box: **home.netscape.com/comprod/products/communicator/multimedia/live3d/cool_worlds/maubie2.wrl**. Press Enter. A virtual reality demo of Maubie the Dog appears after the interval specified in the status bar.

7

UNDERSTANDING WEB SECURITY

The shopping sites you just visited in Exercise 4 were fun to look at, but did you buy anything? The biggest stumbling blocks to Web shopping are security issues. Aren't you a bit nervous about sending your credit card number through cyberspace? Many people are. Many people also worry that there's no way of knowing if the merchandise really exists. Are the merchants legitimate?

Netscape is aware of the security issues that concern you, and is working hard to protect you from unscrupulous merchants and Internet hackers. Any time you want to check the security of the site you're viewing, click the Security icon (the lock in the bottom left corner of the page) for information. As a system default, Netscape notifies you if you're about to submit information to a nonsecure source. Netscape is developing more security layers for the Internet. Even sites that don't use Netscape servers accept Netscape security as an Internet standard. The folks at Netscape have developed a protocol called *Secure Sockets Layer* (SSL) that encrypts the data that is transmitted over the Internet.

In addition to SSL encryption, some sites are developing their own security solutions to Web transactions. First Virtual (www.fv.com/) charges a nominal fee to maintain your name, credit card information, and other information in their records. You can purchase items at some Web sites with your First Virtual PIN (account) number, instead of your live credit card information. Another company called Cybercash has come up with a type of digital cash using another form of encryption. You can visit the Cybercash site at www.cybercash.com.

Anytime you want to learn more about security and Netscape, click Help → Security from the menu. You'll find several documents containing relevant information.

Always give yourself plenty of time when you look through the sites that Netscape's chosen for you. As you explore, you may find an interesting link that leads to another, and so on. Suddenly, you realize you've been busy at the computer for hours!

Java is the hottest thing to hit the Web! It's been called sexy, it's reported to be the future of the Internet, and, for sure, Java is the most talked-about Web feature right now. What is Java? It's a programming language that's used to create miniprograms, called *Java applets*, that can be placed directly into Web pages. One of the most exciting features of Java applets is that they work on any type of computer system, such as Mac, Windows, and even UNIX. Additionally, Java can be used to create full-fledged software applications.

Java applets can assume many forms — scrolling marquees, games, or even sales forms that calculate totals automatically. It's important to know that Java applets can't run by themselves — they require a Web browser such as Navigator.

Navigator 4.0 is set up to play Java applets. The Java source code or program is added directly to the HTML code of a Web page. When Navigator encounters a Java applet, the program appears on the Navigator screen, and a message that the Java applet is running appears on the status bar.

To see Java in action, type **home.netscape.com/comprod/products/ navigator/version_2.0/java_applets/** in the Location box and press Enter. The Netscape Java Applets Demo page appears. Scroll down the page to the section containing links to samples of Java applets. Click the Crossword link to see an example of a Java application.

CHATTING ON THE WEB

Although visiting the Web is an amazing adventure, it's also quite solitary. It's difficult to Web-surf with a crowd. Have you ever wished that you could talk to someone who's having the same experiences? Or maybe you wish you could talk to an anonymous group about a problem you're having. The Web is full of *chat sites* that are waiting for you to join.

Understanding chatting

Generally, the term *chat* on the Web means you talk to someone by typing your comments in your computer. Your comments are posted to a board that appears on the computer screens of all the other people in the conversation. Chat conversations, even though they're typed, move quickly. After a while, you get so used to participating in a typed conversation that you actually forget it's not verbal. Internet chats are generally conducted in *chat rooms*, hosted by specific chat sites.

7

Exercise 5: Visiting Talk City

Here, you visit Talk City and engage in a real-time, typed conversation with other people on the Web. Talk City is one of the most comprehensive chat sites on the Web. Follow these steps:

1. Type **www.talkcity.com/** in the Location box and press Enter. The Talk City home page appears, as shown in the following illustration.

Click if you're a first-time visitor

2. If you want to learn more about Talk City, click the link for new Talk City visitors. The About Talk City page appears. After you read through the page, click the Back button on the Navigation Toolbar.

3. Click the Chat Live link. The Chat Live page appears.

4. When you first open the Chat Live page, a gray box appears on the screen. The box soon displays a form you need to complete before entering a chat room. Depending on your computer, it may take a few minutes for the form to appear. Fill in the form. (You don't have to fill in real information if you don't want to.) Only the Nickname field is required; you don't need to fill in your name, e-mail address, or the URL of your home page.

5. Click the button of the chat room you'd like to visit and then click Start Chatting. A message appears, advising you that EZTalk2, the special program used by Talk City, is loading. If someone else is using the nickname you entered in Step 4, you'll be asked to enter another one and click the chat room button again.

The first time you visit a Talk City chat room, it may take a few minutes before you connect. In the future, your connections to chat rooms in Talk City will be much faster (as long as you use the same personal information you entered in Step 4).

6. When the connection is established, a separate window appears on top of Navigator, as shown in the following figure. A list of the participants appears in one frame, and the conversation appears in a second frame. The bottom frame contains a text box for you to type your comments. Take a moment and read the conversation on the screen.

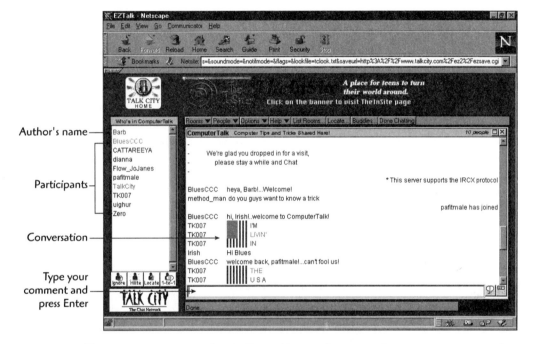

Author's name

Participants

Conversation

Type your comment and press Enter

7. Type a comment and press Enter. Your nickname and comment appear in the conversation in a highlighted color.

If you're shy or feel strange, identify yourself as a new visitor. Most people in the chat room will do their best to make you feel more comfortable.

8. Continue participating in the conversation for as long as you want.

9. (Optional) If you want to send a private message to someone in the room, double-click that person's nickname on the participants list. A separate window appears, with a box for you to type the message. Click the Close button to return to the regular conversation, when you've finished exchanging private messages.

10. When you're done chatting, click the Close button to dismiss the EZTalk window.

11. If you want to visit another chat room, choose that room from the list.

12. When you're done chatting, click the Back button on the toolbar to return to the Talk City home page.

13. Click one of the links on the home page to visit another of Talk City's features.

Talk City offers conferences and events to please everyone! Make sure you check out the Events Calendar link.

SKILLS CHALLENGE: LOOKING AT MORE COOL SITES

In this Skills Challenge, you find and follow links to interesting sites and use the skills you've gathered in some of the previous lessons. Remember, you can always look back through the lessons you've completed if you need a refresher. Follow these steps:

1. Move to the Netscape home page. The address is `home.netscape.com/`.

2. Go to the What's New page that Netscape has set up for you.

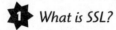 *What are two ways to access the What's New and What's Cool pages?*

3. Move to the fourth text link on the left side of the links and click it.

4. Follow a link on the new page to another page.

5. Use Global History to move to the Netscape home page.

6. Go to Switchboard. The address is `www.switchboard.com/`.

7. Search for your phone number. If you have an unlisted number, search for the phone number of a friend or relative.

8. When the results appear, look at the page in Print Preview.

9. Print the page that shows the phone number you were looking for.

10. Go back to the Netscape home page.

11. Move to the Netscape Guide and click the Shopping link.

12. Visit one of the shopping destinations.

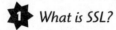 *What is SSL?*

13. Check the security of the shopping site.

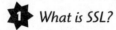 *How do you check the security of a site?*

14. Go to Talk City at `www.talkcity.com`.

15. Sign in and chat with another group that interests you.

16. Leave Talk City and close EZTalk2.

TROUBLESHOOTING

As you have fun on the Web, you may encounter a few unexpected surprises. The following table lists some common problems and concerns.

Problem	Solution
I was looking for some information about an old high school friend. Several of the search engines and services found him, but when I called the number, I found out that he'd moved.	Unfortunately, the information you get from any people-finding search servers may be a bit outdated. It takes a while for new information to supersede the information that's shown. (Don't forget, some services list in excess of 100 million records.)
I clicked a button marked Cool Links on somebody's Web page but got an error message on my screen instead of a list of sites. What happened?	Relax, you didn't do anything wrong. The page to which the link referred moved to a new URL or was removed completely. As you work with any kind of link, this problem often occurs.
I'm afraid that the people in the chat room can see the files on my computer.	They can't. The only thing they can see are the comments you type.
How do I know if the merchandise I'm ordering from the Web is high quality?	You don't. Just as mail-order shopping can be chancy, so can shopping on the Web. If you're nervous, look for a phone number or e-mail address and contact the merchant before you buy. If you're still not sure, don't do it.
An error message on my screen appeared when I was playing a Java applet. Did I do something wrong?	You didn't do anything to cause the error. The Java program may have been written in an older version of Java that's not used anymore, or it may have contained errors. If you find an e-mail address on the page that contained the program, you may want to send the Webmaster a note to let him know something was wrong.

7

WRAP UP

Good work! You're doing great! In this lesson, you learned the following:

- How to search for people on the Web
- How to view Netscape's What's New and What's Cool
- How to use the Netscape Guide
- How to chat on the Web

Practice these skills by visiting both Yahoo's and Netscape's What's New and What's Cool pages. Visit a new Netscape Guide every time you open Navigator. Search for anyone you've wondered about. Go on a shopping spree without ever leaving your computer. The next lesson explains how to download files and programs from the Web.

Downloading from the Web

8

45 MINUTES

GOALS

This lesson provides a smorgasbord of information about software programs and files that you obtain or use with Navigator. You work through the following lessons:

- Downloading a game
- Using SmartUpdate
- Locating plug-ins
- Downloading a file from an FTP site

GET READY

Before you begin this lesson, jot down the speed of your modem. (If you're not sure, you can find the name and maximum speed of your modem by clicking the Windows Start button and then selecting Control Panel → Modems.) Make sure you're connected to the Internet and that Navigator is open on the screen. If you're accessing Netscape through an intranet, check with your network administrator to make sure you can download plug-ins and other files from the Web.

When you finish this lesson, you will know how to download programs that you use outside of Navigator or that give Navigator additional capability, including those shown in the following figure.

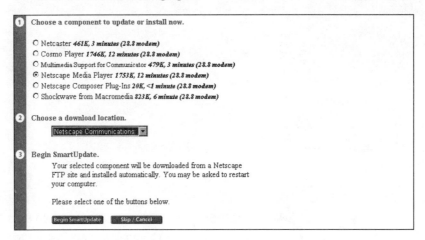

GETTING SOFTWARE FROM THE WEB

The software you download with Navigator's help falls into two categories:

- Programs you use on your computer outside of Navigator and that work independently from Navigator, such as games and virus-checking utilities.

- Programs you use within Navigator, such as *plug-ins*. Plug-ins extend Navigator's capabilities and include software such as movie players and special text readers.

Keep in mind that the terms *download* and *save* mean the same thing — a file from the Web is copied to your computer.

Hundreds of programs are available for downloading from the Web. You can find simple children's games or elaborate, role-playing games that contain exciting graphics and sounds. Games are the most popular Web download. Some programs are specialized, like a utility that converts graphic images to counted cross-stitch diagrams. Shop the Web for the programs you want. Obtaining software programs from the Web is a breeze with Navigator. Table 8-1 lists the types of software you can download from the Web.

TABLE 8-1	SOFTWARE TYPES
Type	*Description*
Freeware	Programs that you can use for free. Although some fairly sophisticated freeware programs exist, many are simple utilities. Freeware is distributed as is and doesn't come with a manual or any tech support.
Shareware	Shareware programs are obtained on an evaluation basis, or a kind of "try before you buy" plan. Some shareware is aggressive about having you register the program. Every time you open one of these programs, you'll see screens advising you how to register and how many days of the evaluation period remain. When the trial period expires, you can't use the program anymore if you didn't register. Other, less aggressive shareware programs let you go on using them, regardless of your registration status. When you register for a shareware program, usually for a low fee, you often get documentation and technical assistance. You should register and pay for shareware.
Commercial	Some of the big-name programs you can purchase from a computer store or catalog are now available on the Web. Commercial programs that you download may require an up-front payment before you can install them. Other commercial programs may be working demos of the actual program and will function in a limited manner.

Remember that each time you download and install a new program on your computer, you use up more hard drive space. Even if your computer has a gigantic hard drive, you don't want to litter it with programs you don't use. Choose the programs you download from the Web with care.

Exercise 1: Downloading a game

In this exercise, you find a game on the Web and download it to your computer. Even if games don't interest you, the steps for finding other types of programs are basically the same:

1. Open the Bookmark QuickFile on the Location Toolbar and choose Computers and Technology → Download.com, as shown. Or, type **www.download.com/** in the Location box and press Enter. Either way, in a few seconds the DOWNLOAD. COM page appears.

NOTE

Although many other sites offer a large selection of programs (most notably, Tucows at www.tucows.com/)*, the DOWNLOAD.COM site, maintained and updated daily by C/Net, is the most comprehensive.*

2. Scroll down the page to the Categories section and click the Games link.

3. Scroll down through the Subcategories section, which shows the types of games, and click the Cards and Casino link. In a moment, a list of the available games and their descriptions appears.

TIP

If you want to search for a program and you don't know its category, skip Steps 2 and 3. Instead, type some information about the program, such as **virus protection** *or* **calorie counter***, in the Quick Search box on the DOWNLOAD.COM home page; click Search. After a few seconds, a list of programs matching the information you typed appears.*

4. Click the link to a game you like. A page appears with information about the game.

5. Read the information carefully, as it may contain download or installation instructions. Print the installation instructions if they seem difficult or confusing. After you've read the information, click the appropriate link to download the game.

If you decide you don't want to download the game, click the Back button on the Navigation Toolbar.

6. As the download process begins, you may see one of several dialog boxes. The combination of different file types and different download sites triggers different responses from Navigator.

If Navigator doesn't recognize the filename and type, you'll see an Unknown File Type box. Click Save File to copy the file from the Web to your computer.

Or, you may see a dialog box, like the one in the following example, advising you that a possible security hazard exists. Don't be alarmed. Sites such as DOWNLOAD.COM and other commercial sites generally contain files that are virus-free and will not damage your computer. To proceed, make sure the option button next to Save it to disk is selected, and then click OK. On the other hand, if you're not sure about the reliability of the site from which you're obtaining a file, click Cancel to halt the download.

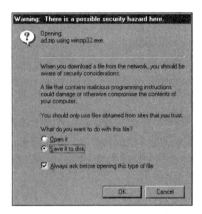

Or, you may simply see the Save As dialog box.

7. When the Save As dialog box appears, first select a folder in which to store the program (you can always use the WebSave folder you created in a previous lesson), and then click Save. A Saving Location dialog box, like the one shown in the following example, appears. The file is saved when the box disappears.

Minimize button ——

To monitor the progress of the download and still have access to your computer, click the Minimize button on the Saving Location dialog box. The box appears as a separate button on your Windows taskbar, with updates about the percentage of completion of the download as the file is copied to your computer.

8. When you're ready to install the game, use Windows Explorer to open the folder in which you saved the downloaded file. Follow the installation instructions. Double-click any text files (the file type says "Text Document") that appear in the folder, because they probably contain information you need to know. An example of this type of file is README.

You don't need to install games or other programs immediately after you download them. Wait until you have some free time. That way, you'll be sure to follow all instructions and not skip any steps because you're feeling rushed.

THE COMPUTER VIRUS THREAT

A *computer virus* is a program that attaches itself to another program or file. When you run the program or open the file that holds the virus, the infection enters your computer. Viruses are designed to replicate themselves when files are transferred from computer to computer. Some viruses are harmless (like the one that plays Yankee Doodle through your computer speakers every day at 5:00), but most are not. Many viruses reside silently inside your computer, quietly going about their business as you go about yours, until they destroy your files or drives. The following list shows some obvious virus symptoms:

- Programs suddenly take longer to load.
- Files on your hard drive have unrecognizable names or seem to double in size for no reason.
- Multiple general protection fault errors occur on your computer.
- A clicking or other annoying sound suddenly can be heard from your computer.

If any of these things are happening to your computer, you probably have a virus. Scared? You should be. Viruses are not accidental; someone, somewhere, had to work hard to develop the destructive programs. However, the good news about computer viruses is that unlike the common cold, most can be eradicated. Virus protection programs are available from the Web and from commercial sources. Download or buy a virus protection program today. Follow the manufacturer's instructions and scan your hard drive. Then, scan *every* file you download.

For some reason, many people who regularly download files and exchange files don't use virus protection. "Too expensive," or "Takes too much time," are the most common answers in response to the question, "Why not?" Neither answer makes sense. Let's face it — your computer represents a considerable investment of money and time. Protect that investment with virus protection.

8

Understanding plug-ins

A *plug-in* is a software component that gives Navigator some extra capabilities. You can use a plug-in to read files in a special format, listen to audio files, or even view movies. When you install Communicator, some basic plug-ins are included with the installation. Additionally, you can download over 150 plug-ins from various sites on the Web to extend Navigator's power. After you've downloaded a plug-in and installed it, Netscape seamlessly integrates the plug-in to work as an extension of Navigator.

Once you install a plug-in, you probably won't be aware that it's active. That's because Navigator activates the appropriate plug-in when you move to a page that needs it. For example, when you visit the Gap Get Dressed site, the Shockwave plug-in combines with Navigator to provide you with a great way to dress the Gap dolls. Sometimes, a plug-in opens in a smaller window, such as the Netscape Audio Player.

You don't need to do anything in advance to get the plug-ins you think you'll need. As you look through Web pages and click links, Navigator lets you know when you need a plug-in. Navigator finds the appropriate plug-in and, if possible, gives you a choice of similar types. You can also download a plug-in in advance if you know you're going to need it.

Not all plug-ins are free. As you read the licensing agreement, visible either during the download or the installation, be aware of the vendor's payment requirements. Table 8-2 lists a few of the most commonly used plug-ins.

TABLE 8-2	COMMONLY USED PLUG-INS
Name	**Description**
Acrobat Reader	Enables you to view files in Portable Document Format (.PDF) from within Navigator. Many government forms, such as those from the Internal Revenue Service and federal and state job listings, are placed on the Web in .PDF format.
Earthtime	Provides a clock interface that displays the local time and date for eight geographic locations in your choice of over 400 world capitals and commercial centers. An animated worldwide map indicates darkness and daylight.
Netscape Media Player	Brings high-quality streaming audio and synchronized multimedia to Navigator. Provides excellent sound quality over the Web for modems with speeds lower than 28.8Kbps.
Apple QuickTime Plug-In	Enables you to experience QuickTime animation, music, MIDI, audio, video, and objects in specially designed Web pages.
Live3D	Turns Navigator into a virtual reality player, enabling you to visit interactive sites.
Shockwave	Delivers exciting audio, video and graphics to Navigator.

Exercise 2: Using SmartUpdate

In this exercise, you use SmartUpdate, a feature of Communicator, to locate the Netscape Media Player plug-in and download to it your computer. The Netscape Media Player adds high-quality audio and multimedia to your computer. Once the Media Player is downloaded, you install and then configure it so that it works with Communicator. For the Media Player to work properly, you must have a sound card and speakers installed with your computer.

In early versions of Communicator, SmartUpdate provides easy access to some Netscape components or plug-ins that are not included in the initial Communicator download. In the future, registered Netscape users will be able to use SmartUpdate to get new versions of Communicator and its components. While SmartUpdate lists some common components and plug-ins that you can add to your copy of Navigator, it does not include all the plug-ins available.

Follow these steps to use SmartUpdate:

1. From anywhere in Communicator, click Help → Software Updates. The SmartUpdate page, similar to the one shown in the following example, appears. Because Netscape changes the SmartUpdate page regularly, the page you see may look different.

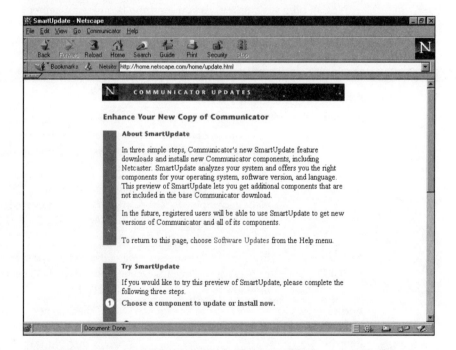

At some point, SmartUpdate will be available only to registered users of Communicator. If you haven't registered your copy of Communicator, consider doing so. For a small fee, you'll have access to all the latest and greatest Netscape software and upgrades. Registration information is available by clicking Help → Register Now.

2. Scroll down the page to the Choose a component section.

3. Click the option button next to the Netscape Media Player. Although you can download any of the components shown on the list, you must download them one at a time.

4. Move to the next section and choose a download location (if more than one is available) from the drop-down list.

5. Move to the third section and click Begin SmartUpdate.

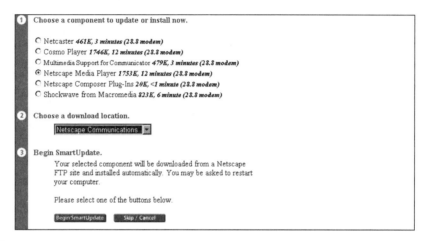

6. A box appears to inform you of the progress of the download. Press Continue when the download procedure is complete.

7. If you see a Java Security dialog box asking you to grant the privilege to install new software, click Grant to continue. A dialog box appears displaying the name of the Netscape component that you downloaded.

8. Click Install to begin the installation procedure.

9. Follow the onscreen prompts to complete the installation. When the installation is complete, a Netscape Media folder is added to your Windows Start menu. The open folder appears on the screen.

10. Double-click the Configure Media Player icon. The Netscape Media Player Properties dialog box appears, as shown in the following figure.

11. To accept the Media Player default settings, click OK. Change a setting only if you're an advanced user and very familiar with your computer.

12. The Media Player is now configured. The next time you start Navigator, all of Media Player's features will be available to you.

13. To install additional plug-ins, return to the SmartUpdate page, choose another plug-in, and repeat Steps 3 through 8 in this exercise. You can add the components shown on the SmartUpdate page any time you're using Communicator.

Exercise 3: Locating plug-ins

How do you know when you need a plug-in? As you move around the Web, Navigator lets you know when you need a plug-in to view a Web page. Although you can download plug-ins on an as-needed basis, you can also download any plug-ins you want, any time you want.

In this exercise, you learn different ways to locate plug-ins. You won't actually download any of the plug-ins to your computer. If you see a plug-in you want, however, bookmark the site and then download the plug-in later. Follow these steps:

1. Type **www.idgbooks.com/extras/shockwave/examples.html** in the Location box and press Enter. A page from the IDG Books Worldwide Web site appears.

2. Click the link to IDG Books Homepage — SHOCKED. A dialog box appears, instead of the page you expected to see, and informs you that a plug-in is needed.

3. You're not going to download the plug-in during this exercise, so click Cancel.

If you clicked Get the Plugin, Navigator would identify the type of plug-in needed to view the page and provide you with a list of available plug-ins to download. Read the information about each plug-in, choose the one you want to install, and click Download. (Make sure that the plug-in you choose matches your system requirements. For example, if you're using Windows 95, don't choose a plug-in designed for Macintosh computers.) Follow the instructions to download and install the software to your system.

As a rule, plug-in installation requires that you save the plug-in to your hard drive, and then double-click on the saved file to start the installation. After the installation is complete, you'll need to restart Navigator and reload the page you wanted to view.

4. To view all the available plug-ins, click Help → About Plug-ins. The About Plug-ins Netscape page appears.

5. On the line that reads "For more information about Netscape plug-ins," click the "click here" link. The Inline Plug-ins page appears, as shown in the following figure.

Plug-ins arranged by category

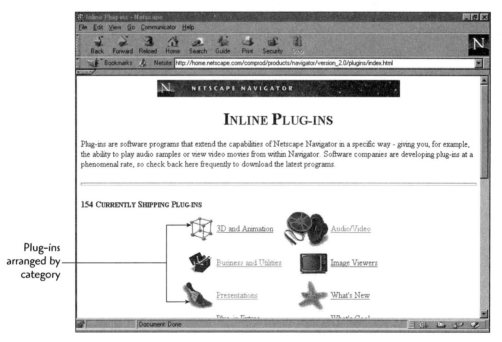

6. The Plug-ins are arranged in categories, such as 3D and Animation, Business and Utilities, and Presentations. Click the 3D and Animation link.

7. Scroll down to read the descriptions of all of the plug-ins available on the page. When you've finished, click the Back button.

8. Click the link to Business and Utilities. Scroll down the list and look at all the plug-ins available.

Although plug-ins extend Navigator's capabilities dynamically, don't download a plug-in if you're not sure you're going to need it. Unused plug-ins can fill up your hard drive.

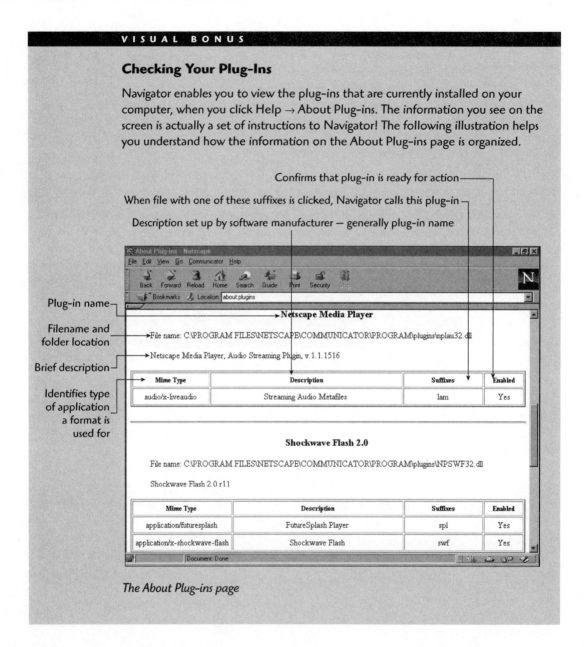

The About Plug-ins page

WHAT IS FTP?

FTP, or File Transfer Protocol, is the way you transfer files from the Internet to your computer. Following are two main types of files you can download or transfer:

- **Files that you save to your hard drive.** These files include program files, graphics files, or even files that contain Web pages.

- **Files that you view or play.** These files include music and sound clips or movie files.

FTP support is built directly into Navigator. Most of the time, the files you want to transfer to your computer look like ordinary links in Web pages; you simply click the link to begin the process of saving the file to your hard drive. At times, right-clicking a file begins the download process.

Navigator also enables you to transfer files from FTP sites. Looking at an FTP site is like looking at Windows Explorer — the files are arranged in directory folders. When you find the file you want, you select it for downloading by clicking it.

Because it's a bit more difficult than simply clicking a link, why bother using an FTP site? For one thing, some files are available only from FTP sites. Also, many Web page links are often busy, and using the FTP site ensures that you'll be able to download the files at your convenience — not at 3 a.m. because that's the only time the link to the file you want isn't busy.

Sometimes, the most difficult aspect of using FTP is finding the file you want to download!

FTP sites to visit

The following table lists some FTP sites you can visit:

URL	Site
`http://www.fedworld.gov/ftp.htm`	FedWorld (contains a searchable index of all files in the FTP libraries)
`ftp://ftp.netscape.com/`	Netscape
`ftp://ftp.microsoft.com/`	Microsoft
`ftp://ftp.aol.com/`	America Online

Exercise 4: Downloading a file from an FTP site

In this exercise, you download a file from the FedWorld FTP site. Follow these steps:

1. In the Location box, type the address of the FTP server you want to go to. For this exercise, type **ftp://ftp.fedworld.gov/pub/commerce/commerce.htm** and press Enter. The COMMERCE Library list of files appears, as shown in the following figure.

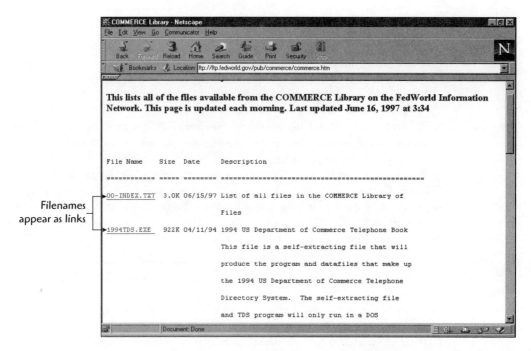

Filenames appear as links

2. Click the file you want to download, after you've scrolled through the file list.

3. Depending on the file you choose to download, you may see a warning advising you that the file is being downloaded from a network and may contain damaging contents. If you're sure that FedWorld is a reliable site, click the option button next to Save It to Disk and then click OK to continue.

4. If the file type you're downloading is not registered in your Windows settings, the Unknown File Type dialog box appears. Click Save File to bring up the Save As dialog box. If Windows recognizes the file type, the Save As dialog box appears.

5. From the Save As dialog box, select the folder on your hard drive where you want to save the file, and then click Save.

The file is saved to your computer. When the download process is complete, you return to the Navigator screen.

SKILLS CHALLENGE:
GETTING AND USING SOFTWARE PROGRAMS WITH NAVIGATOR

In this Skills Challenge, you recap some of the principles you learned in earlier lessons and tie up loose ends from this lesson. The challenge uses some of the work you did during the lesson exercises, so make sure that you've performed the steps for each exercise before you start here. If you need help with something you covered previously, review the material you need before you continue.

1. Move to the DOWNLOAD.COM site.

2. Type **virus** in the Quick Search box and press Enter.

3. Scroll through the programs listed on the search results and click the links to any of the programs that interest you.

4. If you don't already have virus protection installed on your computer, download one of the programs. Follow the installation instructions to install the program to your computer.

5. Move to the Barbara Kasser home page at `www.geocities.com/Paris/LeftBank/4487`.

6. After the page loads, click the picture of the café.

 How do you know when a plug-in is loaded?

7. Move to `www.gapinc.com/`, the Gap home page.

8. Click the Get Dressed interactive link.

2 *How do you know when you need a plug-in?*

9. (Optional) Follow the links to download the Shockwave plug-in and then install Shockwave to your computer.

3 *Why do you need to install plug-ins?*

10. Return to the Netscape home page.

TROUBLESHOOTING

The following table lists unexpected problems you could run into as you work with the software mentioned in this lesson.

Problem	Solution
I'm afraid of computer viruses. What should I do?	Be proactive, not reactive, when it comes to dealing with computer viruses. First, buy or download a virus-scanning program and make sure your computer is virus-free. Be very careful about sharing disks with anyone who isn't running virus protection. (If you don't know, ask before you share files or disks.) Follow the virus scanner's instructions and scan every file you download or that's given to you. Finally, make sure that your virus software provides regular updates, as new viruses appear daily.

Problem	Solution
I downloaded a plug-in, but when I went back to the Web page, Navigator didn't see it.	You probably forgot to install the plug-in after you downloaded the file. Getting and then installing a plug-in is a two-step process. Install the file and it will work just fine.

WRAP UP

You've finished this lesson. Take a brief walk to clear your head if you plan to complete the next lesson today. In this lesson, you mastered the following:

■ How to download software programs from the Web

■ How to use SmartUpdate

■ How to download and install plug-ins

Practice these skills by querying search tools for sites containing games and other programs you can download. When you encounter a page that requires a plug-in, don't be afraid to download and install it. Before you download any file, make sure you have enough space on your hard drive. Once you've downloaded a file, check it for viruses before you install it. In Lesson 9, you begin working with e-mail.

PART III

Communicating Electronically

This part shows you how to use e-mail, conference over the Internet, and join discussion groups. You work through the following lessons:

- Lesson 9: Sending Mail Messages
- Lesson 10: Reading Your Mail Messages
- Lesson 11: Working with the Address Book and Folders
- Lesson 12: Conferencing Across the Internet
- Lesson 13: Participating in Discussion Groups

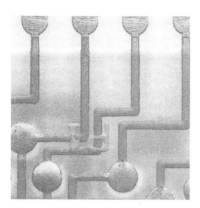

Sending Mail Messages

9

45 MINUTES

GOALS

This lesson helps you understand e-mail and shows you how to set up and send messages using Netscape Messenger. You work through the following exercises:

- Configuring your mail preferences

- Creating and sending a message

- Scheduling an e-mail message for delivery later

- Creating a draft message

- Attaching files to e-mail messages

- Attaching Web pages to e-mail messages

- Deleting a message before it's been sent

- Adding sending options to a message

- Creating a personal signature file

159

GET READY

To complete this lesson, you need to know the name of your incoming and outgoing mail server. If you're not sure, contact your ISP. Although you don't need to be connected to the Internet for some of this lesson, you can connect now if you like.

When you finish this lesson, you'll know how to send electronic mail messages with Messenger, as shown in the following figure.

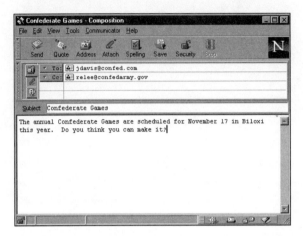

UNDERSTANDING AND CREATING E-MAIL WITH MESSENGER

Messenger is the component of Communicator that enables you to send and receive private electronic mail messages on your computer, via the Internet. Called *e-mail* for short, it is one of the most widely used features on the Internet. You've already sent e-mail through the mail links on Web pages and by filling out the resulting Messenger form. Messenger enables you to create messages from scratch.

E-mail works by transmitting messages over the phone lines instantly, from one computer to another computer anywhere in the world. Sending an e-mail message is just like leaving a message on an answering machine. The recipient doesn't need to be home or at work (or even connected to the Internet) when you send the message, because it's delivered directly to his or her mailbox.

E-mail provides a quick and easy way to communicate with your friends or business associates. Have you ever played "phone tag"? You know how it goes — you place an urgent call to someone who has the information you need to finish a job. Instead of talking to a person, you leave a message on the answering machine that picks up the call. Because the call is returned at the exact moment that you leave your desk for some coffee, you now have a message on your answering machine, instead of the information you need. Your return call is intercepted by the answering machine again. . . . and so on. If you had used e-mail instead of the phone, your question could have been received, answered, and sent back to you in a short period.

E-mail offers many advantages. For one thing, it's cheap. Aside from the cost of your call to your ISP (usually a local or free call), you don't have to pay long-distance or connection charges. Additionally, you can attach files such as sales reports or memos to e-mail messages. (The folks at IDG Books Worldwide and I used e-mail to send all files for this book back and forth.) You can send a message to a group instead of sending it to each individual. And best of all, you can maintain your e-mail contacts in Messenger's Address Book, so you don't need to look up the e-mail address each time you send a message.

Messenger is composed of various windows. The Message Center lists your mail server and the folders in which you store your messages. The Message List displays all messages contained in a folder — for example, all the messages stored in your Inbox. The Message window shows a specific message, and the Compose Message window appears when you're creating a new message.

Exercise 1: Configuring your mail preferences

In this exercise, you configure Messenger to send and receive messages. Unless you change Internet service providers or something else about your Internet account, you only have to perform these steps once:

1. Click Start at the bottom left corner of the screen.

2. Move your mouse up to Programs and slide across to Netscape Communicator. The Netscape Communicator submenu appears, as shown in the following figure.

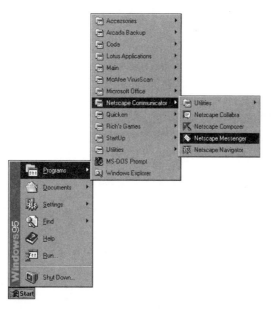

3. Slide the pointer over to Netscape Messenger and click once. Because this is the first time you've used Messenger, the Mail and Discussion Groups Setup Wizard dialog box appears. (If you've already set up Messenger or used a previous version of Netscape mail, your mail may be configured. If so, skip to Exercise 2.)

Wizards are step-by-step instructions that guide you through Windows tasks, such as setting up a particular feature or option. Many programs use wizards.

4. Read the information on the first screen and then click Next.

5. The next screen requires that you fill in your name, e-mail address, and the address of the outgoing mail server. Press Tab to advance to each field. If you're unsure about any of the information, contact your ISP. When you've entered all the information correctly, click Next. The following figure shows the dialog box with the information filled in.

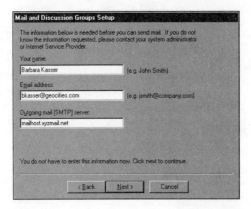

6. The next screen, as shown in the following example, deals with your incoming mail. Type your *user name* (which may be different from your real name) in the first field and the name of your incoming mail server in the second field. Click Next to proceed.

Select POP3 unless your ISP tells you otherwise

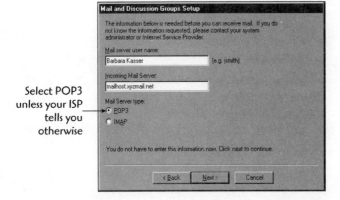

7. The last screen to appear deals with the News server. If you're unsure about the information requested, don't be concerned. You learn about discussion groups later in the book. Click Finish.

The setup is complete. You're ready for e-mail! Later on, if you need to change any information about your mail account, click Edit → Preferences → Mail and Groups and make the appropriate correction.

Understanding e-mail addresses

Before you can send an e-mail message, you need to understand how e-mail addresses work. Anyone who's connected to the Internet directly or through an online service, such as America Online or CompuServe, has an e-mail address. You or your coworkers may even have an Internet e-mail address at your company or business. (Check with your administrator to make sure.)

My e-mail address is an example of a fairly typical address: bkasser@ geocities.com

The first part of the address is the person's user name, which is already set up with the ISP. A user name can be composed of any combination of letters and numbers. My user name, bkasser, is somewhat unimaginative, but many people get creative with their user names. One of my good friends uses KidsMom, another friend uses Busnut, and my son uses Cairnman (we own a cairn terrier.)

The second part of the address is the @ sign; it is used as a separator between the name and third part of the address, which denotes the location. The third portion of the address, after the @ sign, shows the unique domain name of your mail host. Just like my postal mail address, my e-mail address tells the Internet how to direct the messages sent to me.

VISUAL BONUS

The Message Composition Window

The following Visual Bonus shows you the Message Composition window and explains all the options you can select as you compose e-mail messages.

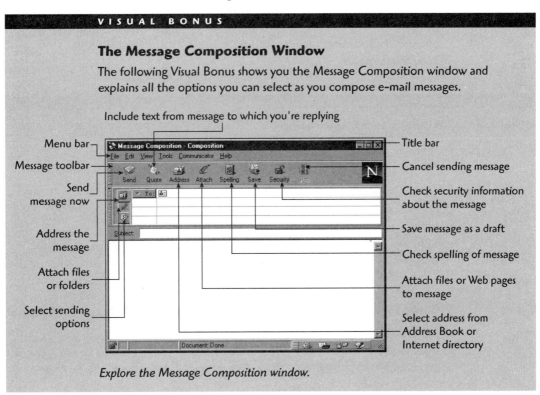

Menu bar
Message toolbar
Send message now
Address the message
Attach files or folders
Select sending options

Include text from message to which you're replying

Title bar
Cancel sending message
Check security information about the message
Save message as a draft
Check spelling of message
Attach files or Web pages to message
Select address from Address Book or Internet directory

Explore the Message Composition window.

Exercise 2: Creating and sending a message

In this exercise, you create and send an e-mail message. If you have a friend's or a family member's e-mail address, you can use it for this purpose. Otherwise, use the fictitious address in this exercise. You don't need to connect to the Internet to create messages. Follow these steps:

1. Open Messenger from the Start menu, if it isn't already open.

TIP

The Component Taskbar provides a quick way to jump to your Inbox in Messenger from any of Communicator's programs. The Component Taskbar may be docked (attached to a portion of the screen) or floating (you can drag it around the Netscape screen). Either way, click the Mailbox button — the one with the picture of the envelope — to quickly open your Messenger Inbox.

2. Click the New Msg button on the toolbar. The Message Composition window appears.

3. Click in the To box and type the recipient's e-mail address — for example, **jdavis@confed.com**. If you'd like to enter additional addresses, press Enter after you type each one. Each address appears in its own To box.

If you've set up an entry in your Address Book, you could use that instead. In Lesson 11, you learn how to use the Address Book .

4. (Optional) You can send mail to other types of recipients, as shown in Table 9-1. By default, Messenger shows only the To field. Click the down arrow to the left of To to view the other recipient types. Choose Cc and type **relee@ confedarmy.gov.**

TABLE 9-1	**OPTIONS IN THE CC FIELD**
Option	**Description**
Cc	A copy of the message is sent to this recipient
Bcc	The original recipient and any Cc recipients are not aware that a blind carbon copy of the message is sent to this recipient
Group	Send the message to a group of recipients you've set up previously in your Address Book
Reply To	Includes your e-mail address
Followup To	Enables you to specify a different address for replies to your message

5. When you've finished adding addresses, click in the Subject box and type **Confederate Games**. If you don't type in a subject, you'll be prompted to add one when the message is sent.

6. Click in the message area, or press Tab to advance to it, and type this message, as shown in the following illustration: **The annual Confederate Games are**

scheduled for November 17 in Biloxi this year. Do you think you can make it?

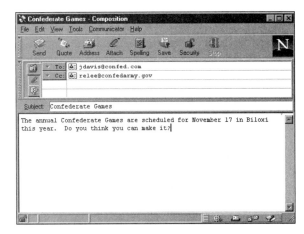

7. Click the Spelling button or choose Tools → Spelling to check your spelling. Unless you're an ace typist, this option is always a good idea.

8. To send the message now, connect to the Internet if you're not already connected. (If you're not sure, check for the Connected button on the Windows taskbar.)

9. Click the Send button on the toolbar.

The message is moved to the Outbox folder while your outgoing mail server is contacted to pick up the message and send it. Delivery can take anywhere from a few minutes to a few hours.

10. If you've typed a recipient's e-mail address incorrectly, you'll receive a message saying that your original message contained fatal errors and could not be delivered. You typed in fictitious addresses, so expect the message to bounce back to you.

Exercise 3: Scheduling an e-mail message for delivery later

Instead of creating messages while you're connected to the Internet, you can create them when you're offline, and then connect later and send them all at once. One of the main advantages of creating your messages offline is that you don't waste valuable connection time and dollars as you struggle for the exact word or phrase. Follow these steps:

1. Create a new message but don't click the Send button.

2. Click File → Send Later. The message is placed in the Outbox for delivery later.

3. Create any additional outgoing messages and place them in the Outbox by clicking File → Send Later after you've finished creating each one.

4. When you're ready to send your messages, connect to the Internet.

5. Click File → Send Unsent Messages. Your outgoing mail server picks up the mail and sends the message to the recipients you entered.

OTHER E-MAIL COMPOSITION OPTIONS

Messenger adds versatility to e-mail because it provides many options. For example, you can create a draft message, just as you'd create a draft of an important memo or letter. You can attach files and Web pages to e-mail messages and send them with your messages. You can add security options to the messages you send. You can even change the priority of your messages and request a return receipt when your message is delivered.

Exercise 4: Creating a draft message

If you need a little extra time to get the message just right before you send it, you can create a draft. For example, if you're waiting for the exact details on a project or plan, you can type the message now and add the final details before you send it. Follow these steps:

1. Create a message in the usual way. Click New Message to open the Composition window.

2. Type **alincoln@union.net** in the To line.

3. Click or tab to the Subject line and type **Honored Guest**.

4. Click or tab to the message area and type the following message: **We'd like for you to join us at the annual Confederate Games in Biloxi. Please let me know if you can attend.**

5. When the message is complete, click File → Save Draft. The message is inserted into the Drafts folder, one of Messenger's default folders for storing messages.

6. Remove the message from the screen by clicking File → Close or pressing Ctrl+W.

7. When you're ready to work with Messenger again, you can return to it by clicking the Mailbox folder on the Component Bar if you're working in Navigator. If you've closed Communicator completely, open Messenger from the Start menu.

8. When the Inbox appears on the screen, click the drop-down arrow next to Inbox to display your message folders, as shown in the following figure.

Choose the Drafts folder.

9. Click the Drafts folder to display the messages you've saved as drafts.

10. Double-click the message that contains the draft you're looking for.

11. With the message open, click the area in which you'd like to make changes. Click in the message area after the last sentence and type **We'll be able to send you airline tickets.**

12. If you're ready, click Send. If you need more time to work on the message, click the Draft button to put the message back into the Drafts folder.

E - M A I L   L I N G O

Who would have thought that e-mail would take the world by storm? Yet, like a whirlwind, e-mail has impacted much of our lives. I send and receive around 100 e-mail messages every day at work. My son is able to communicate with his cousins on the other side of the world by e-mail. My aunt and uncle have established a lively, family e-mail group. E-mail has made the world smaller and made its citizens more connected.

Along with this new form of communication come new rules and phrases. For example, you should never type e-mail messages entirely in uppercase letters. Using all caps is perceived as shouting, and in very poor taste. (I FOUND OUT THAT RULE THE HARD WAY.) The following list is a composite of some common acronyms used in e-mail, along with their translations.

Phrase	What it Means
BTW	By the Way
FYI	For Your Information
IMHO	In My Humble/Honest Opinion
TIA	Thanks in Advance (also sometimes written advTHANKSance)
RTFM	Read the Friendly Manual ("Manual" here refers to any documentation)
LOL	[I] Laughed Out Loud [at what you wrote]
ROTFL	[I am] Rolling on the Floor Laughing [at what you wrote]
RSN	Real Soon Now
:-)	Smiley Face

Use some of the terms in your e-mail messages. Amaze your friends. And above all, have fun!

Sending mail attachments

You can attach almost any type of file to an e-mail message you send. For example, you can send memos, graphic images, spreadsheets, or even saved Web pages. As I've mentioned before, I sent most of the lessons in this book to IDG Books Worldwide via e-mail.

Two problems may occur when you attach files to e-mail messages. First, unless the recipients have the exact program used to create the file (or a similar one), the attachment is useless. Think how frustrated you'd be if you received a file created in WordPerfect, but you didn't have WordPerfect on your computer.

The next problem is slightly more complex. When you send a file across the Internet — no matter what the format — it needs to be converted to text (ASCII code) at your end, sent over the Internet, and then converted back to its original format when it reaches the recipient. This process needs to take place for every file that's attached to a mail message. Fortunately, people smarter than you or me have figured out ways to make these mind-boggling file transfers work. Messenger automatically applies the translation process to any file you attach to an e-mail message. You don't need to do anything special.

TIP

Almost all current e-mail programs include an automatic process to decode sent files, so most of the time the attachments you send with Messenger will be readable when they reach their destination. It's a good idea, however, to make sure that the receiving program can handle what you've sent it. Test it in advance — especially if the e-mail attachment is an important file.

Exercise 5: Attaching files to e-mail messages

In this exercise, you attach a file that's saved on the hard drive of your computer to an e-mail message. Follow these steps:

1. From within Messenger, click the New Msg button to create a new e-mail message.

2. Complete the To line by typing in your own e-mail address.

3. Click or tab to the Subject line and type **File Attachment test.**

4. Click the Attach button on the toolbar. A list of the items you can attach to a message appears.

5. Choose File from the list. The Enter file to attach dialog box appears.

6. Find the file you want to attach, as shown in the following figure.

Filename is selected

Click to attach file

7. When you've located the file, click it once to select it (the filename appears highlighted) and then click Open.

8. The shortcut menu closes and you return to the Message Composition window. The filename you selected appears in the attachment box, as shown in the following figure.

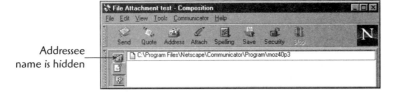

Addressee name is hidden

9. Repeat Steps 4 through 8 to attach additional files.

10. Send the e-mail now or place it in the Outbox, from which you'll send it later.

Exercise 6: Attaching Web pages to e-mail messages

Attaching a Web page to an e-mail message is simple. The steps are similar to those for attaching files:

1. Follow Steps 1 through 3 in the previous exercise to create a message, changing the subject line to **Test Web Page Attachment**.

2. Click the Attach button on the toolbar.

3. Choose Web Page. The Please Specify a Location to Attach dialog box appears.

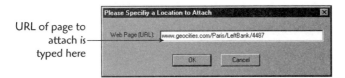

URL of page to attach is typed here

4. Type the URL for the page you want to attach to the message. You don't need to type the http:// portion; Messenger fills it in for you. For this exercise, type **www. geocities.com/Paris/LeftBank/4487**

5. When you've typed the URL, click OK to close the dialog box. The Web page is attached to the message.

In the next exercise, you learn how to delete messages while they're still onscreen.

Exercise 7: Deleting a message before sending it

The message you created in the previous exercise should still appear onscreen. Follow these steps to delete it:

1. Click File → Close.

2. A box appears, asking if you want to discard changes and advising you that the message is unsent, as shown in the following figure.

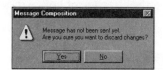

3. Click Yes. The message is deleted.

Deleting unsent messages is as easy as changing your mind!

Exercise 8: Adding sending options to a message

In this exercise, you add sending options to an e-mail message. Follow these steps:

1. Compose a message in the normal manner, but don't send it.

2. Click the Message Options button to view all of your sending options. Refer to Table 9-2 for a description of the options.

Message Options button

TABLE 9-2	MESSAGE OPTIONS
Option	**What it does**
Encrypted	Sends the message in a type of code that will be unencrypted when the message reaches its destination
Signed	Includes your personal signature file, if you've created one

Option	What it does
Uuencode instead of MIME for attachments	Deals with files you attach to messages. (Don't check this box unless you've checked with your network administrator or the person to which you're sending files.)
Return Receipt	Provides you with a delivery notice when the message is received (if the recipient's mail server supports this feature)
Priority	Choose from Normal, High, or Highest. (Normal is the default choice.)

TIP

Click the Security button on the toolbar for additional options designed to make your message more secure. Remember, however, that the Internet is not entirely secure. You can't predict what kind of security conditions exist when your message is received.

3. When you've selected your options, send the message.

Exercise 9: Creating a personal signature file

In this exercise, you create a personal signature file — a short text file that is attached to outgoing e-mail messages and reflects your personality or style. Think of your signature file as the front license plate on a car; if you have one at all, it makes a statement about you. Right now, you'll create a signature file with a general type message. Feel free to substitute another message than the one I've provided for this exercise. Follow these steps:

1. With Messenger still open, click the Start button, and then click Programs → Accessories → Notepad. The Notepad applet opens on your screen with the cursor flashing in the left corner.

2. Type **I love e-mail!** (or another sentence or two). Check the file carefully for spelling or grammatical errors.

3. Click File → Save. The Save As dialog box appears.

4. Move to the folder in which you want to save the file.

5. In the File name box, type **mysig,** as shown.

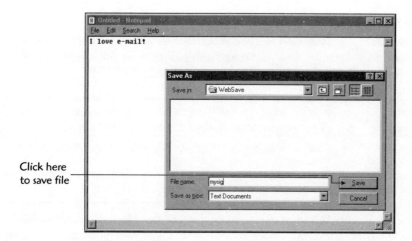

Click here to save file

6. Click Save. The file is saved and you return to Notepad.

7. Close Notepad by clicking the Close button or by clicking File → Exit.

8. Return to Messenger. If Messenger doesn't appear on the screen when you close Notepad, make it the active window by clicking the Inbox button on the Windows taskbar.

9. Now that you've created the file, you need to tell Messenger to include the text of the file in your outgoing e-mail messages. Within Messenger, click Edit → Preferences and click the Mail and Groups category on the left.

10. (Optional). If a + sign appears next to Mail and Groups, expand the subcategories by clicking the + sign. A - sign appears in place of the + sign and the subcategories are visible.

11. Click the Identity subcategory. In the Signature file text box, type the path and filename of the mysig.txt file you created. Or, instead of typing the filename and path, you can click Choose and move to the folder and filename. The following figure shows an example of a completed Identity sheet .

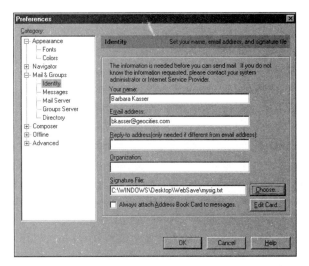

12. Click OK to close the Preferences dialog box. Now, each time you send an e-mail message, your signature file will be included as part of the message.

If you want to change the text, open mysig.txt in Notepad and edit the file. If you don't want to include the signature file, open the Preferences dialog box and delete the file from the Identity sheet of the Mail & Groups category.

SKILLS CHALLENGE: PREPARING E-MAIL MESSAGES

In this Skills Challenge, you practice what you've learned about sending e-mail.

1. Open Messenger to the Inbox folder.

1 *What are three ways to open the Inbox?*

2. Open the Message Composition window to create a new message.

3. Address the message to yourself.

2 *Can you explain the parts of an e-mail address?*

4. Include the word *Test* in the subject and include the sentence "This is a test." in the body of the message.

5. After the message is complete, place it in the Drafts folder rather than sending it.

6. Open the Drafts folder.

7. Reopen the message you placed there.

8. Attach a file called NOTEPAD.EXE from the Windows folder on your computer.

9. Change the sending option to High Priority.

10. Instead of sending the message now, save it for delivery later.

 Where does a message go when you schedule it to be sent later?

11. Send the message now.

TROUBLESHOOTING

Messenger offers a whole new realm of possibilities. You may encounter some unexpected problems, however, as you create and send messages. The following table discusses a few of these problems and offers simple solutions.

Problem	Solution
I'm sure that I typed the correct e-mail address, but I got an error message saying that the address was incorrect.	The most likely cause of this type of error is that the address you typed was in the wrong case. E-mail addresses are *extremely* case-sensitive and must be typed exactly as they appear on the recipient's mail server. Another alternative is that the address is no longer valid.
I couldn't find the Drafts folder or the Sent folder. The box at the top of my screen says Inbox.	Click the drop-down arrow next to Inbox to open the list of folders. Choose the folder you want from the list.
I sent a message in error and now I've changed my mind. Is there any way to get it back?	If the message you want to cancel is in the Outbox, delete it by opening the Outbox folder, clicking the message to select it, and pressing Delete. But if the message is in the Sent folder, it's gone! Like letters you drop in the mailbox, a message can't be retrieved once you've sent it through the Internet.

WRAP UP

You should feel great about how far you've come. In this lesson, you learned the following:

- How to configure Messenger
- How to create and send e-mail messages
- How to attach files and Web pages to e-mail messages
- How to add sending options to a message

Practice these skills by sending messages to friends and family. If you really want to give Messenger a workout, create and send messages to yourself.

In Lesson 10, you work with e-mail messages you've received.

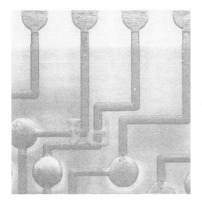

Reading Your Mail Messages

10

40 MINUTES

GOALS

This lesson helps you master the skills necessary to retrieve and manage the messages you receive. You learn about the following:

- Getting and reading new mail messages
- Checking for mail messages automatically
- Replying to an e-mail message
- Forwarding a message
- Viewing a file attached to an e-mail message
- Marking and flagging messages
- Sorting the messages in your Inbox
- Using mail filters to arrange your mail
- Finding a misplaced message

GET READY

To complete this lesson, you need to be connected to the Internet with Messenger open. When you finish the lesson, you will know how to reply to and manage the messages you receive in your Inbox, as shown in the following example.

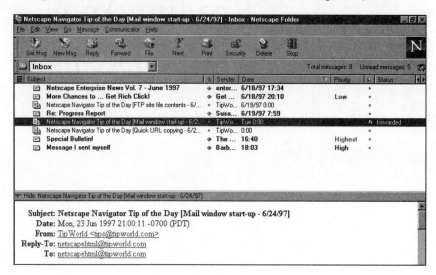

RETRIEVING AND WORKING WITH YOUR MAIL

Everyone loves to get mail! No matter how busy you are, sitting down to check your mail always provides a few moments of excitement. Whenever someone sends you a message, it's held in your personal mailbox on the mail server of your ISP or corporate network. When you ask Messenger to get your mail, it goes out to your personal mailbox, gathers the new messages, and then deposits them on your computer.

You determine when Messenger should check for new messages. You can set up Messenger to check for mail when you first open your Inbox, or to notify you as soon as a message is deposited in your personal mailbox on the mail server; you also can check for messages manually. Messenger understands that everyone likes to work differently, and enables you to configure your Inbox in several ways.

You work with mail messages the same way that you work with regular mail. You can send a response to a message, either to the sender or to everyone who received the message. Messages can be forwarded, printed, and filed in folders. You can delete the messages you don't need anymore.

Exercise 1: Getting and reading new mail messages

In this exercise, you retrieve your new messages from the mail server. Follow these steps:

1. If Navigator is open, click the mailbox icon on the Component Bar to open your Inbox. If you don't have any of Communicator's programs open, click Start and choose Programs → Netscape Communicator → Netscape Messenger to move to your Inbox.

2. Click the Get Msg button on the toolbar. When the Password Entry dialog box appears, as shown in the following illustration, type your e-mail password in the text box and click OK.

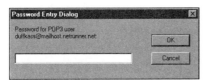

3. As Messenger checks for new messages, the Getting New dialog box appears on the screen, as shown in the following figure.

If you have new messages, Messenger places them in your Inbox. If you don't have any messages, a dialog box appears informing you that you have no new messages on the server. Either way, you return to your Inbox after Messenger checks for messages.

4. New, unread messages appear in your Inbox in bold text, with a closed envelope icon at the left. Unless you change the sort order, messages are placed in your Inbox in the order in which they're received.

5. To read a message, click its subject header. The text of the message appears. If it's a long message, you may need to use the scroll bars to move through the body of the message.

If you don't have any new messages to read, send yourself a few messages. Attach a file or two to one of the messages. If you need help with sending messages, review the exercises in Lesson 9.

Exercise 2: Checking for mail messages automatically

With a few mouse clicks, you can tell Messenger to check for your mail automatically at regular intervals. Messenger places an icon in the system tray to let you know you have mail waiting. When it's convenient, you can retrieve the messages. Follow these steps:

1. If you haven't opened Messenger yet, open it by clicking the mailbox icon on the Component Bar. (You can also use the Windows Start menu if you want.) The Inbox appears.

2. Click Edit → Preferences. The Preferences dialog box appears, with a list of categories on the left side.

3. (Optional) If a + sign appears next to Mail and Groups, expand the subcategories by clicking the + sign. A - sign appears in place of the + sign and the subcategories are visible.

When all the subcategories under the Mail and Groups category are visible, click the Mail Server subcategory.

4. A sheet showing information about your mail server appears. Click the button labeled More Options. The More Mail Server Preferences box appears on top of the Mail Server sheet.

5. Click the check box next to Check for Mail Every __ Minutes, as shown in the following illustration. If an X appears in the box, the feature is already enabled.

Feature is enabled
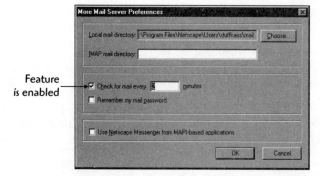

6. Type **2** in the text box so that Messenger checks for new mail every two minutes.

While you're in More Mail Server Preferences, check the box next to Remember my mail password, if you don't want to reenter your password each time you check for mail.

7. Click OK to save the changes and close the box. The Mail Server dialog box appears on the screen.

8. Click OK to close the Mail Server sheet of the Preferences dialog box and return to the Inbox.

Looking at the Inbox Folder

In this Visual Bonus, you look at the Inbox folder in detail.

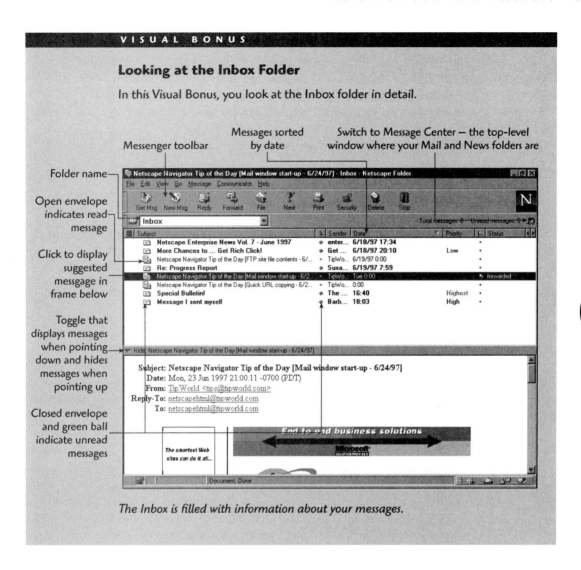

The Inbox is filled with information about your messages.

Messenger is now configured to check the mail server for incoming messages at the specified interval. When messages are found, an icon like the one shown in the following example appears in the system tray at the bottom right corner.

Screen tip says mail is waiting

Exercise 3: Replying to an e-mail message

In this exercise, you answer a mail message. Unlike snail mail (regular postal service mail), e-mail provides a fast and easy way to participate in a continuing dialogue. Follow these steps:

1. Launch Messenger by clicking the mailbox icon on the Component Bar, or by clicking the Start menu and choosing Programs → Netscape Communicator → Netscape Messenger. The Inbox appears.

2. Click the message you want to answer. The selected message appears highlighted, as shown in the following illustration.

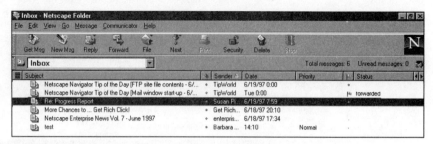

3. Click the Reply button on the toolbar. A submenu opens, as shown.

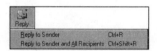

4. Choose Reply to Sender if you want to send the reply only to the person who sent you the message. Choose Reply to All if you want the reply to go to each person who received the original message. If the mail message was sent to a list that included your name, replying to all ensures that everyone on the list gets a copy of your reply.

The Message Composition window appears, with the fields in the header completed. Notice that if you chose Reply to All, the name of the sender appears in the To box, whereas the names of the other people who received the message appear in the Cc box. The Subject line contains the subject of the original message, preceded by *Re*. Although you can't see the text of the orig-inal message, the person who receives your reply will be able to see it.

5. Type your reply in the message area.

6. Click the Spelling button on the toolbar to spell check your message. It's better to take a second now to find embarrassing spelling mistakes, rather than discovering them after you've sent the message.

7. Send the reply by clicking the Send button. The Message Composition window disappears, and you return to your Inbox.

Exercise 4: Forwarding a message

In this exercise, you forward a message you received to someone else. Follow these steps:

1. The Inbox should be visible because you've just completed Exercise 3. If it's not visible, follow the directions shown in Step 1 of Exercise 3.

2. Click the message you want to forward. The message appears highlighted. Depending on the way you've set your Inbox, the text of the message may appear below the list of messages in the Inbox.

3. Click the Forward button on the toolbar. The Message Composition window opens on top of the Inbox.

The subject of the original message is preceded by Fwd, so that the recipient knows the message has been forwarded, as shown in the following example. Although you can't see the original message, the Attach button in the message header area appears pressed in, to indicate the original message is attached.

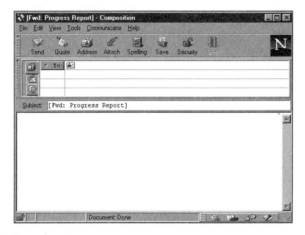

4. (Optional) If you want to include the original message as a quote, click Message → Forward Quoted, instead of using the Forward button on the toolbar.

5. Add the recipients' names, either by typing them or using the Address Book.

6. Type your message.

7. Click the Send button to send the message.

When the message is received at its destination, both your message and the forwarded message will be displayed.

Dealing with files attached to messages

The capability to send and receive files has elevated e-mail to a higher status, as an important element of daily communication. Being able to receive files, work with them, and if necessary, send the changed files back means that long-distance tasks now take a few hours instead of a few days. Receiving an attached file means that you can work collaboratively with someone either in the next cubicle or halfway around the world.

Different companies have different rules about receiving files attached to e-mail messages. Some companies allow any type of file, others allow only predefined file formats to be received, and other companies prohibit all e-mail attachments. If you have any questions about the policy at your company, check with your network administrator or the group that handles electronic mail.

The capability to transmit files has changed the personal e-mail picture, too. You may receive a file that contains an electronic greeting card. Or you may receive files that contain scanned family photos or children's artwork. My son exchanges files with his cousins several times a week.

You can change the way Messenger deals with file attachments. If, for the most part, you're going to view only attached files, tell Messenger to display them *inline*. Then, when Messenger detects an attached file, it shows you the contents of the attachment below the text of the message. (If it can't open the file, Messenger scans all the programs on your computer and attempts to match up the file you received with the program that created it.)

If you're going to use the files or make changes to them, tell Messenger to display them *as links*. When Messenger finds an attached file, it shows you the filename and other important file information. To view the file, you open the application in which the file was created. If you change the file, you must save it to a folder on your computer to make the changes permanent.

Exercise 5: Viewing a file attached to an e-mail message

In this exercise, you learn different ways to view a file attached to an e-mail. The exercise is divided into two parts; in the first part, you send yourself a message with a file attached, and in the second part you view that file. (The file you send is located in the Windows directory and tracks various Windows settings. Alternatively, you can choose any other file on your computer.)

1. Open the Inbox by using the Start menu or by clicking the mailbox icon on the Component Bar. If the Inbox is already open, switch to it.

2. Click the New Msg button and compose a mail message to yourself.

3. Type your e-mail address in the To portion.

4. Click the Attach button and choose File. The Enter file to attach dialog box appears.

5. Type the following in the file name text box: **c:\bootlog.txt**

6. Verify that you typed the filename and path correctly, as shown in the example, and click Open.

The Enter file to attach dialog box closes and the CONTROL.INI file is attached to the e-mail message.

7. Type **File attachment test** in the subject line.

8. Click Send to send the message.

9. Click the Get Msg button on the Messenger toolbar. The message containing the file you sent is received in the Inbox.

Messages, even those you send to yourself, may take a few minutes to go out to the Internet through your ISP or corporate connection, and then back to your mailbox. If the message doesn't appear when you click the Get Mail button, try again in a few minutes. Continue checking until the mail message is received.

10. Double-click the message to open it. The message opens in a new window.

11. Click View → Attachments.

12. Choose Inline. After the message, the text of the file is displayed, as shown in the following figure.

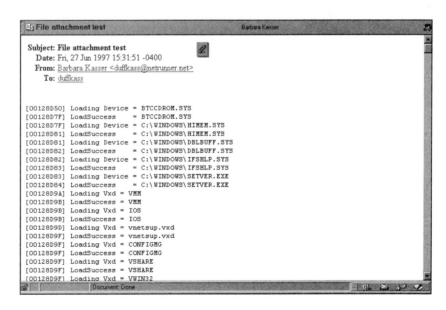

13. Click View → Attachments.

14. This time, choose As Links. Instead of seeing the text of the file, you see the file attached to the message as a link, as shown in the following figure.

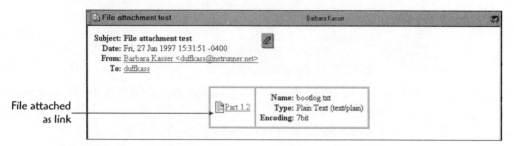

File attached as link

15. Click the file attachment link with the left mouse button. (The mouse pointer takes the shape of a hand.) The file opens in the Navigator window.

Text, graphic, and HTML files are the easiest file formats for Messenger to display. Files created with programs such as Word, WordPerfect, Excel, Lotus, PowerPoint, or other applications may require a few extra steps.

16. If Messenger has to open a program first on your computer to display the file, a Warning box, similar to the one shown in the following figure, appears. Read the warning and decide whether to proceed with opening the file.

TIP

Always be on guard when you open a file attached to an e-mail message. If you aren't sure who sent you the file, think twice before opening it. You can always save the file and then run it through your virus protection program. If you receive an unsolicited file from someone you don't know, however, delete the message. You can't be too careful when it comes to your computer.

17. To open the file, click the option button next to Open it and then click OK. In a moment, the program in which the file was created opens in a separate window, with the attached file displayed. If the program that created the file isn't installed on your computer, you'll receive an error message. At that point, your best bet is to contact the person who sent you the file.

MANAGING YOUR MESSAGES

Just like the correspondence you receive at home or at the office, your e-mail messages can pile up quickly. Messenger provides several ways for you to arrange your mail so you can always find the message you're looking for.

Exercise 6: Marking and flagging messages

Have you ever received paper mail that you want to set aside and take care of later? Messenger lets you *mark* selected messages so that you can deal with them later. You can mark a message to show that you've read it (even if you haven't) or to pretend that you haven't read it yet. Follow these steps:

1. If Messenger's not active, click the mailbox icon on the Component Bar or open Messenger from the Windows Start menu. Your Inbox appears.

2. Click a message you want to mark.

3. Click Message → Mark. A submenu appears.

4. Choose from As Read, As Unread, Thread Read, Category Read, All Read, By Date, or For Later. The message icon changes on the message list. If you've marked a message as unread, for example, its envelope icon appears closed and the entire message information is highlighted.

If you receive lots of e-mail, you may want to thread your messages. When you thread your messages, the replies to a message are displayed below the original message. Although threading messages makes it easier to keep track of a specific conversation, you won't be able to tell when the threads (replies) were received. To thread a message and its subsequent replies, click the message and then click Message → Watch Thread.

5. To place a flag icon next to a message, click the message you want to flag.

6. Click Message → Flag. A flag icon now appears next to the message.

You can flag messages for any number of reasons. You may wish to flag a message so you remember to reply to it later, or you can flag it to remind yourself that you need to follow some instructions shown in the message. The Flag feature works like a toggle switch. If you want to unflag a message, repeat Steps 5 and 6.

10

Exercise 7: Sorting the messages in your Inbox

Everyone likes to arrange correspondence differently. In this exercise, you arrange the messages in your Inbox the way you like them to be sorted. Follow these steps:

1. If it's not already open, launch Messenger by clicking the mailbox icon on the Component Bar or by clicking Start → Programs → Netscape Communicator → Netscape Messenger. The Inbox appears.

2. Click View → Sort. You see the following submenu.

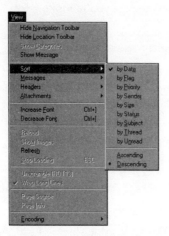

3. Choose one of the options listed in Table 10-1.

TABLE 10-1	MESSAGE SORTING OPTIONS
Option	**What It Does**
by Date	Sorts your messages by the date on which they were created.
by Flag	Sorts your messages by the flags you've set up, if any.
by Priority	Sorts your messages by the priority in which they were sent, such as High, Normal, and so on. Keep in mind that this option may not be available to many senders.
by Sender	Sorts your messages by the alphabetical order of the names of the senders.
by Size	Sorts your messages by the size of the message file.
by Status	Sorts your messages by their status, such as Forwarded.
by Subject	Sorts your messages by the information on the subject line.
by Thread	Sorts your messages by the threads, if any, that you've already set up.
by Unread	Sorts your messages according to whether or not you've read them, and places the unread messages together.

4. Click Ascending if you want to change the secondary order from descending to ascending. For example, if you chose to sort your messages by Date and then you chose Ascending order, your newest messages appear at the top of your message list.

You can also sort your messages by clicking the corresponding buttons at the top of the messages in the Inbox. For example, if you want to sort your messages by date, click the Date button at the top of the list of messages. The following illustration demonstrates how to sort messages by date, using the Date button.

These buttons change sort order

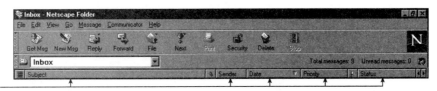

Exercise 8: Using mail filters to arrange your mail

In this exercise, you create a mail filter to automatically move the messages you send yourself for practice to the Trash folder, instead of the Inbox. Mail filters constitute several fields, called *conditions*, which you change to match the action you want to occur. Follow these steps:

1. Open the Inbox by clicking the mailbox icon on the Component Bar or by using the Windows Start menu. (The Inbox should already be open, however.)

2. Click Edit → Mail Filter. The Mail Filters dialog box appears.

3. Click New. The Filter Rules dialog box appears.

4. In the Filter name text box, replace the word *untitled* with **Mail from Myself**. Press Tab to advance to the next field.

5. If necessary, click the drop-down arrow next to the word *The* and select the word *sender* on the list. (If *sender* is already selected, proceed to Step 6.) Press Tab to advance to the next field.

6. The next word after *sender* should be *contains*. If another word appears, click the drop-down arrow and choose *contains* from the list. Press Tab to advance to the next field.

7. Type your user name or the first portion of your e-mail address in the text box. The first line should read: "The sender of the messages contains *yourname*." Press Tab to move to the next field.

8. The first field on the second line should be Move to folder. If it's not, click the drop-down arrow and choose Move to folder from the list. Press Tab to advance to the next field.

9. Click the drop-down arrow and choose the Trash folder.

10. In the Description text box, type **Move practice messages to myself to the Trash folder**.

11. Make sure that the option button next to Filter is selected.

The following illustration shows my completed filter rule. (Yours should look the same, except that your user or e-mail name should appear instead of mine.)

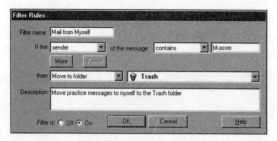

12. Click OK to close the Filter Rules dialog box. The rule you just created appears on the list of existing Mail Filters.

13. Click OK to close the Mail Filters dialog box and activate the rule.

The next time you send practice mail to yourself, the incoming mail message will automatically be moved into the Trash folder. Messages that you sent before you set up the mail filter will not move automatically.

The first rule you set up is simple. Messenger enables you to create both simple and complex rules to handle incoming mail. Additionally, you can change the order in which your filter rules are executed. If you're using e-mail for business, filter rules are a great way to manage large volumes of e-mail and keep your Inbox from becoming cluttered.

Exercise 9: Finding a misplaced message

No matter how organized you are, it's easy to lose track of important messages. You may remember the subject of a particular message or a few words of text, but aren't sure where the message itself is located. In this exercise, you search through the header information of your messages to find a particular message. Because you've been working through the exercises in this lesson, the Inbox should already be open and visible. If it's not, refer to the first step of the previous exercise to open Messenger. Follow these steps:

1. From within the Inbox, click Edit → Search Messages. The Search Messages dialog box appears. Notice that the Search Messages dialog box looks like the Mail Filters dialog box with which you worked in the last exercise.

2. If you want to search for items in all the folders, click the drop-down arrow and, if necessary, use the scroll bar to select the top folder called Local Mail. Otherwise, Messenger looks through the Inbox or whichever folder is selected. Press Tab to move to the next field when you've selected a folder.

3. Click the drop-down arrow next to the word *the* to open the list of available header fields in which Messenger will look. Click the field *subject* from the list and then press Tab to advance to the next field.

4. The next field enables you to choose an operator. Choose the operator *contains* from the drop-down list. Press Tab to move to the next field.

Most of the time, you should use contains as an operator when you're searching for message headers or message text.

5. Type **attachment** in this last box, making sure you type carefully. Always type as few characters as possible. For example, simply by typing *attachment*, you'll find all messages with the word *attachment* in the subject header. The following figure shows a completed Search Messages dialog box.

6. Click Search. Messenger looks through all the messages and finds those you're looking for, as shown in the following figure.

Double-click a message to open it

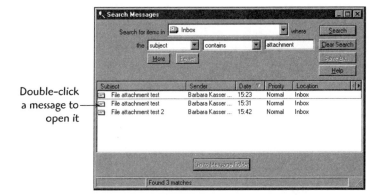

7. Double-click any message on the list to open it.

8. If you didn't find the message you were looking for, refine your search by changing some of the information (perhaps by shortening the text or looking in a different header field). Click Search to run the new search.

SKILLS CHALLENGE: STRETCH YOUR INBOX TRAINING

Great work! You're a Messenger expert. The best way to maintain your Messenger skill level is to use electronic mail often. In this challenge, you practice the mail skills you've learned. To complete this challenge, connect to the Internet and open the Inbox.

1. Sort your messages by Date.

 What are two ways you can sort your messages?

2. Select a message you sent to yourself.

 How can you tell if a message is selected?

3. Reply to the message and then send your response.

4. Change your settings so that the system checks for new mail every five minutes.

5. Mark a message that you've looked at, as unread.

 How can you tell if a message has been read?

6. Flag a message in your Inbox.

7. Open one of the messages you sent to yourself.

8. Close Navigator.

TROUBLESHOOTING

Receiving messages is much more exciting than sending them. But as hard as you try to avoid them, some unforeseen surprises can occur as you work with the messages you've received. The following table discusses a few unwelcome surprises you may encounter, and how to deal with them.

Problem	Solution
I added a mail filter to move messages from my family into a special folder. It's working on the new messages, but the old messages that I received before I set up the rule are still in my Inbox.	You're right. Mail filters work only on messages that you receive after you've set up the filter. If you want to move a message into a different folder, select the message and then click the File button on the toolbar. Choose from the list the folder to which you want to move the message.
Someone sent me a file but I can't open it.	The file was probably created with a program that you don't have on your computer. Both the sending computer and the receiving computer need to have the same software or, at least, compatible programs. Your best bet is to contact the person who sent you the file.

Problem	Solution
Why didn't Messenger find a message that I moved to the Trash folder, when I searched for it? I know I typed al the information in the Search box correctly.	Most likely, you emptied the Trash folder after you moved the message into it. Emptying the Trash folder is like taking out the trash and home — it's gone!

WRAP UP

Great work! In this lesson, you learned many skills, including the following:

- How to retrieve new messages
- How to sort and flag messages
- How to create mail filter rules
- How to find misplaced messages

Practicing these skills is more like fun and less like work. Check your mailbox often for new mail. In Lesson 11, you learn how to put the Address Book to work.

10

Working with the Address Book and Folders

11

25 MINUTES

GOALS

This lesson helps you organize your mail messages. You work through the following exercises:

- Adding a quick entry
- Creating a manual entry
- Editing an Address Book entry
- Deleting an Address Book entry
- Creating mailing lists
- Using the Address Book
- Creating a mail folder
- Understanding the Trash folder

GET READY

To complete this lesson, you should have set up your mail preferences in Lesson 9. After you work through this lesson, you will know how to use Messenger's Address Book feature, shown in the following example. You will also know how to organize the folders that hold your mail messages.

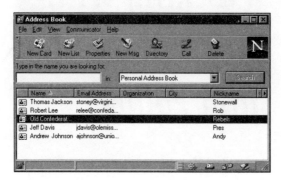

WORKING WITH THE ADDRESS BOOK

Netscape's Address Book functions both as an e-mail directory and a typical address book. Each entry is treated as a separate card, as in a Rolodex file. The Address Book enables you to enter both basic information, such as phone and fax numbers, and Internet information, including e-mail addresses. Many programs in Communicator share the Address Book.

Managing e-mail information with the Address Book makes good sense. After all, many e-mail addresses are complex combinations of user and domain names, such as SEVERNUSA!HQLEGAL01!rdole@pschy.mail.com. If you type one wrong character, your e-mail message never reaches its destination. After you've entered the address once in the Address Book, you don't need to worry about it again.

Exercise 1: Adding a quick entry

You can add a quick entry to the Address Book from any message you've received. Quick entries, because they're based on the return address of a message, contain little else besides a name and an e-mail address. You can always edit a quick entry later, however, if you want to add information. Follow these steps to add a quick entry:

1. Click your Inbox.

2. Click the Get Msg button on the toolbar to receive your new messages.

3. Double-click any message you've received to open it.

NOTE

If you have no messages in your Inbox, the world hasn't found you yet! As you become more familiar with Messenger, you'll receive lots of messages.

4. From within the message, click Message → Add to Address Book.

5. Choose Sender, as shown, if you want to add an entry for the person who sent you the message, or choose All to add all the addressees if the message was sent to multiple names.

That's it! The names and e-mail addresses are added to your Address Book. Add entries to your Address Book by performing these simple steps with any message you receive.

Exercise 2: Creating a manual entry

In this exercise, you add a manual entry to your Address Book.

1. Click Communicator → Address Book within any open Communicator program. The Address Book opens in its own window.

2. Click the Add Name button. The Add User dialog box appears.

3. The Add User dialog box is divided into three tabs. The first tab, Name, is already open. Enter the information in the Name tab, pressing Tab to advance from field to field. Use the entries from the following example of a completed Name tab.

Tabs—

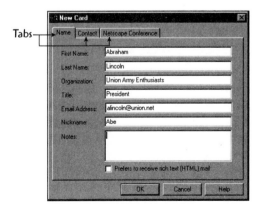

4. Click the Contact tab.

5. Complete the fields, as shown in the following figure. If you don't know the information for a field, leave it blank.

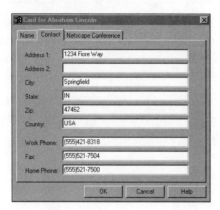

6. Click OK to add the entry to the Address Book. Don't worry about completing the Conference tab. You learn about Netscape Conference in Lesson 12.

7. Create dummy Address Book entries for the following users by following Steps 1 through 6:

Name	Nickname	E-mail address
Andrew Johnson	Andy	ajohnson@union.net
Thomas Jackson	Stonewall	stoney@virginia.net
Robert Lee	Rob	relee@confedarmy.gov
Jeff Davis	Pres	jdavis@olemiss.com

Exercise 3: Editing an Address Book entry

People move around all the time. You can edit any entry in the Address Book to change information, or fill in the blanks after you've added the name using the quick entry method. Follow these steps:

1. Open the Address Book.

2. Click the entry for Abraham Lincoln. The entry appears highlighted.

3. Click Edit → Card Properties.

4. The entry appears in a dialog box that shows the information you entered when you created the card.

5. Click in the Nickname field under the Name tab.

6. Change the nickname from Abe to Honest Abe.

7. Click OK when you're finished. The dialog box closes.

Exercise 4: Deleting an Address Book entry

In this exercise you delete an entry in the Address Book that you don't need anymore. Follow these steps:

1. If it's not already open, open the Address Book by choosing Communicator → Address Book from any program in the Communicator Suite.

2. Click the entry for Abraham Lincoln to select it.

3. Click the Delete button on the toolbar. The entry is removed from the Address Book.

Exercise 5: Creating mailing lists

In this exercise, you learn how to organize the names in your Address Book into lists. You can add the entries in your Address Book to as many lists as you like. If you change the information for a person in one of the lists, the person's other entries are automatically updated.

Lists make sending e-mail to everyone in a group as simple as sending one message. For example, you could send one message about the Confederate Games to hundreds of people at once, instead of addressing individual messages to each member of the Old Confederate Soldiers Club. Follow these steps to create an entry list:

1. If it's not already open, open the Address Book by choosing Communicator → Address Book from any program in the Communicator Suite.

2. To create a list within your Address Book, click the New List button on the toolbar. The Mailing List dialog box appears, as shown in the following figure.

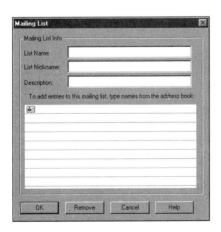

3. In the List Name text box, type **Old Confederate Soldiers.**

4. Tab to the List Nickname field and type **Rebels**.

5. Move to the Description box and type a brief description of the list: **Former members of the Confederacy**.

6. Tab to the member names area and type **Thomas Jackson**. Notice that as you type, Messenger completes the entry for you, based on the information you entered in the Address Book.

You must type the names of the list members exactly as they appear in the Address Book, pressing Enter after each one.

7. Type **Rob** on the second line of the list box and press Enter.

Instead of typing the complete names, you can type the Nickname you used in the original entry. When you press Enter, the complete name is substituted for the nickname.

The following illustration shows a list in the process of being created.

8. When you've added all the names to the list, click OK. The Address Book appears. Along with the individual entries, an entry for the list is shown, as you see in the following figure.

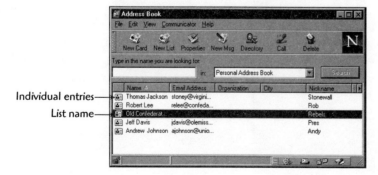

Individual entries

List name

9. To change the way entries in the Address Book are sorted, click the View menu.

The View submenu appears, as shown in the following figure.

10. Choose how you want the list to be sorted: By Type, By Name, and so on. A check mark next to an item indicates that it's currently selected.

11. If you want, change to Ascending or Descending order.

Don't remember who belongs to the mailing list? Double-click the list name in the Address Book. You'll see a listing of the members, plus all other information you entered for the list.

Exercise 6: Using the Address Book

You've done all the advance work to set up your Address Book. In this exercise, you use the Address Book in various ways to address an e-mail message. Follow these steps:

1. If Messenger is not open, open it now. You can click the Mailbox icon on the Component Bar or open Messenger from the Start menu. If Navigator is open, go to your Inbox by clicking Communicator → Messenger Mailbox.

2. Click the New Msg button on the toolbar. A Message Composition Window appears.

3. Click in the To box.

4. Instead of typing the e-mail address of the recipient, type **Stonewall**, one of the nicknames you added when you set up the Address Book entry. As you type, notice that Messenger completes the entry for you, as shown in the following figure.

Messenger tries to complete the entry for you based on the alphabetical order of the names in your Address Book. If you have two or more similar entries, such as Stonewall and Stonewill, keep typing if Messenger fills in the wrong name. Your letters override the filled-in letters.

Letters you typed
appear dark

Letters filled in
for you appear
light

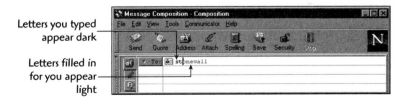

5. Press Enter to move to the next To line.

6. Instead of using a nickname to address the message, you can use the recipient's full name. Type **Andrew Johnson**, the full name you entered in the Address Book. Notice that again Messenger identifies the recipient and fills in the letters for you.

7. Press Enter to move to the next To line.

8. To send the message to all members of a list, type **Rebels**, the nickname of the Old Confederate Soldiers list you set up earlier. The message will be sent to each individual on the list.

9. If you didn't enter a nickname or you can't remember it, click the Address button. The Select Addresses dialog box appears, as shown in the following figure.

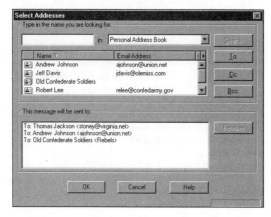

10. Select a name from the list and click the To button. The name you selected appears in the bottom portion of the window.

11. If you want to send the message to additional names, select each one from the list in the same manner. Use the scroll bar to move through the list if necessary.

12. Click OK when all the names have been selected.

13. (Optional) Repeat the procedure for other recipient types, such as Cc or Bcc.

14. Finish the message and send it as usual.

VISUAL BONUS

Searching for Names on the Internet

If you want to send a message to someone on the Internet, but you don't know that person's e-mail address, Messenger's Address feature may help you find it. This Visual Bonus takes you through the search process and explores its various options.

From the Messenger Inbox, click New Msg. Then, click the Address button on the toolbar in the Message Composition window. The Select Addresses dialog box appears. Follow the steps shown in the following two figures.

Type name
you're
looking for

Choose Internet
directory to
search through

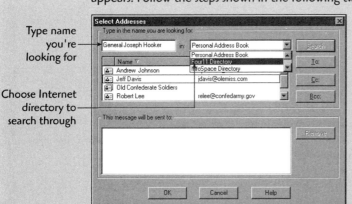

The Select Addresses dialog box helps you find an e-mail address.

Click to begin
search

You're ready to start your search.

When the search is complete, scroll through the list of matching names, click the name to whom you want to send the message, and then click the To, Cc, or Bcc button. The name and e-mail address are added to the This message will be sent to: box. If your search didn't find the match you were looking for, change some of the search criteria and try the search again.

After you've entered in the box all the names to whom you want to send the message, click OK. The Select Addresses dialog box closes, and your message is addressed. Type the message subject and text, and the message is ready to be sent.

WHY USE FOLDERS?

It takes a long time to find something on a messy desk, right? Just like a desk, your Inbox folder can become messy and cluttered before too long. Before your Inbox folder becomes overwhelming, set up some folders to store and organize your mail.

Messenger provides Inbox, Outbox, Sent, and Drafts folders for your use. You can create other folders that make sense to you. For example, I have a folder called Book for all the correspondence I get regarding this book. You may want to name your folders something like Business and Personal. If you're super-organized, you can even create subfolders.

TIP

Your e-mail folders are also used by Collabra to store discussions and newsgroup postings. You learn more about Collabra later in this book.

Exercise 7: Creating a mail folder

In this exercise, you create a folder to store your mail. Follow these steps:

1. Messenger should be open and on the screen. If it's not open, you can click the Mailbox icon on the Component Bar or open Messenger from the Start menu. If Navigator is open, go to your Inbox by clicking Communicator → Messenger Mailbox.

2. Click the Message Center icon. Or, click the drop-down arrow next to the folder titled Inbox and choose the Local Mail folder, as shown in the following figure.

Click and choose Local Mail

Message Center icon

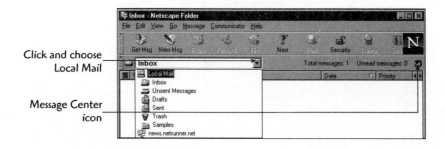

3. No matter which option you selected in Step 2, the Message Center appears, as shown in the following figure.

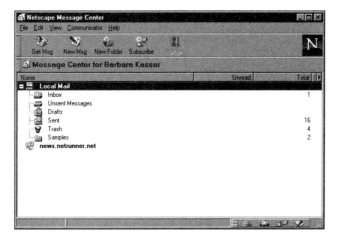

4. Click Local Mail to select it as the top-level folder.

Be sure to note which folder is selected when you begin creating a new folder. If you want the new one to be a top-level folder, click Local Mail before you begin. Otherwise, any new folder you create will appear as a subfolder of the one that was selected (highlighted) when you began the process.

5. Click File → New Folder. The New Folder dialog box appears.

6. Type **Tips** in the name box and click OK.

7. The dialog box closes and your new folder appears on the list.

Exercise 8: Understanding the Trash folder

The Trash folder is one of the folders that Messenger creates for you. When you delete a message, it's moved to the Trash folder. Because messages in the Trash folder are no different than messages in your Inbox, you can open and reread them at any time. You need to empty the Trash folder every so often, however, to keep deleted messages from taking over your hard drive.

1. Click the Inbox folder.

2. Click the drop-down arrow next to Inbox and select Trash from the list of folders in the Message Center.

3. When the Message Center appears in its own window, click File → Empty Trash Folder.

The trash folder is emptied; the messages in it are gone. You should make it a habit to empty the trash at regular intervals.

SKILLS CHALLENGE:
TESTING YOUR ADDRESS BOOK AND FOLDER KNOWLEDGE

You're an e-mail specialist! In this challenge, you have the opportunity to measure your Messenger knowledge.

1. If you're not already connected, establish a connection with your ISP.

2. Open Messenger.

3. Find a message that you sent to yourself.

4. Open the message.

5. Create a quick entry to the Address Book from the message.

1 *How do you create a quick entry to the Address Book?*

6. Create a manual Address Book entry for the following individual:

Name: **Ulysses Grant**

E-mail address: **ugrant@union.net**

7. Open the Message Composition window to create a new message.

8. Create a dummy message using the nickname General.

2 *How do nicknames work in the Address Book?*

9. Send the message for delivery later.

10. After you send the message, switch to the Outbox folder.

11. Delete the message from the Outbox folder.

3 *Where do messages go after they've been deleted?*

12. Compose and send a message to yourself.

13. Move to the Message Center and create a folder called Test Messages.

14. Click Get Msg to retrieve the message you sent.

15. Move the messages you've sent to yourself from the Inbox to the Test Messages folder.

16. Delete the messages from the Test Messages folder and empty the Trash folder.

TROUBLESHOOTING

Some problems may occur as you work with the Address Book and e-mail folders. The following table discusses a few common problems you may encounter, and offers simple solutions.

Problem	Solution
I was changing the sort order of the entries in my Address Book, and the toolbar disappeared. Where did it go?	You accidentally chose to Hide the toolbar. Redisplay it by clicking View → Hide Toolbar from the Address Book menu.
I deleted the Outbox folder, but it came back. Why?	The Outbox folder is a Messenger default folder. The Inbox, Drafts, Outbox, and Sent folders will be re-created by the program when Messenger needs them.
I emptied my Trash folder, and now I want to look at one of the messages that was in it.	Bad news. When you empty the Trash folder, the messages are gone forever. Maybe you can ask the person who sent you the message to resend it.

11

WRAP UP

You've earned a break! In this lesson, you learned the following:

- How to create different types of entries in the Address Book
- How to use the Address Book
- How to look for e-mail addresses on the Internet
- How to work with mail folders

Practice these skills by making as many entries as you can in the Address Book. (Ask around at work or school for your friends' e-mail addresses.) Think about how you want to organize your folders and then set up folders of your own. In Lesson 12, you work with Netscape Conference.

Conferencing Across the Internet

45 MINUTES

GOALS

This lesson shows you how to use Netscape Conference to talk with people through the Internet. Because Conference uses telephony, you actually make voice contact with another Conference user. You work through the following exercises:

- Setting up Conference

- Initiating a conference using the Netscape Conference Directory

- Using Speed Dial

- Answering a Conference call

- Talking over the Internet

- Sharing images on the Whiteboard

- Using Text Chat

- Exchanging files during a conference

- Using the Collaborative Browsing tool

GET READY

Before you begin this lesson, connect to the Internet. For audio conferencing, you need a sound card and speakers. Make sure that your microphone is plugged in and operational. When you complete this lesson, you will be able to talk with another Conference user across the Internet.

WHAT IS NETSCAPE CONFERENCE?

Netscape Conference is an exciting new component of Communicator. With Conference, you attach your computer to another computer that's running Conference. It doesn't matter if the computers are side by side or thousands of miles apart. Once you're connected, you're ready to begin your conference.

With Conference, you bypass telephone charges by speaking to a colleague or friend over the Internet. Instead of talking into a telephone receiver, you speak into a microphone that's attached to the sound card in your computer. Conference sends your voice across the Internet to the computer that's connected to yours. You hear your friend's replies over your computer's speakers.

Also included with Conference are a *Whiteboard* (similar to a chalkboard) and a *chat tool*, which enable you to text-chat with other Conference participants. Additionally, during a Conference session, one participant can lead the other around on a Web tour of different sites. You can record the addresses of the people you talk to the most and set them up on your Conference speed dialer. You can also place a Conference call to someone for whom you have an entry in your Address Book. Finally, you can select a person's name from the Web Phonebook, which displays a list of all the people who are currently using Conference.

USING CONFERENCE

Everyone is excited about Conference. Being able to sit at your computer and talk to someone on the other side of the world is amazing. When you use Conference, your computer can be connected to only one other computer. As you use Communicator, keep in mind that the audio may not seem as clear as a voice you'd hear on the phone. Also, keep in mind that using Conference requires a considerable amount of your computer's resources, so you may find that your computer seems slow.

The Conference Attendant is an excellent helper that launches whenever you open Conference. A telephone icon appears in your system tray to let you know Conference is open and available for calls — even if you've switched to another program:

    Conference is open and waiting to make or receive calls

    Conference is active and connected to another computer

For more details about Conference's status, position the mouse pointer in the Conference Attendant and read the connection details in the pop-up message.

Exercise 1: Setting up Conference

Conference is a separate component of Communicator. Before you use Conference, you have to set it up on your computer. Connect to the Internet and follow these steps, guided by the Setup Wizard:

1. Click Start and choose Programs → Netscape Communicator → Netscape Conference. If you're already using Navigator or another Communicator program, click Communicator → Conference. The Welcome to Netscape Conference setup dialog box appears.

If you installed the standard version of Communicator, you may not have the Conference software. Switch to Navigator and click Help → Software Updates to bring up the Netscape SmartUpdate page. Follow the onscreen prompts to download and install Communicator before you proceed with the exercises in this lesson.

2. Read the information and click Next to continue. The next box, as shown in the following figure, informs you that you need to know your name and e-mail address and how to connect to the Internet (such as by modem or direct connection) to set up Conference. If you know the information you need to proceed, click Next.

If you're not sure of your e-mail address or your Internet connection method, click Cancel to exit the setup procedure. When you've assembled the necessary information, you can start the setup procedure again.

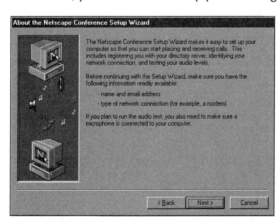

12

3. When the Setting Up Your Business Card dialog box appears, as shown in the following figure, type in your name (or an alias) and your correct e-mail address. The other information on the box is helpful in identifying you to the other conference participants, but it's not required.

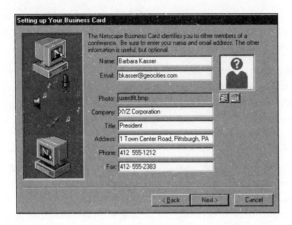

The name you type is the name that will appear to the other Conference users. If you're shy or unsure about using your own name, it's okay to type in an alias. For example, my son uses Cairnman. You can change the name anytime.

4. (Optional) If you have a scanned photo or a graphics image you'd like to place on your business card, type the folder path and filename in the Photo text box. The picture appears on the card.

5. When you've filled in all the information you wish to include, click Next.

6. In the Setting Your Directory Preferences dialog box, you choose how and where to list your name as a Conference participant. Unless you have the URL of another directory, such as your company's directory if you're using Conference from an intranet, don't make any changes to the default settings.

If you don't want your name shown on the list of users when you're using Conference, uncheck the box next to List my name in phonebook. (If you've made arrangements for a Conference call with a friend or coworker at a specific time, you may want to leave your name out of the Conference users list so you're not bothered by an unsolicited call.)

Unlike your personal Address Book, the Web Phonebook listing is dynamic, which means that your name appears on the list of active participants only when you're connected to the Internet and Conference. When you break your Internet connection, your name disappears from the list after a brief delay.

7. In the Specify Your Network Type dialog box, click the option button next to the entry that most closely matches your connection and modem information. Click Next to continue.

8. The next box, Detecting Your Sound Card, displays information that the Setup Wizard detected about your sound card. Click Next to continue.

9. The first of the two Testing Your Audio Levels dialog boxes gives you some tips about adjusting the audio levels on your computer. Read the tips and click Next to move to the second Audio Levels box, and adjust the sound levels on your computer. If you don't want to test the audio levels at this time, click Skip to conclude the Setup Wizard.

10. If you decided to test your computer's sound, the next box, Testing Your Audio Levels (2 of 2) contains three steps for testing audio levels. Perform the steps and, if necessary, make the adjustments indicated. When you've completed the third step shown in the dialog box, click Next.

11. Read the information in the final box, which is titled Setup Complete, and click Finish. Netscape Conference is launched!

VISUAL BONUS

Looking at the Conference Screen

The Conference screen contains buttons and icons that don't look familiar. This Visual Bonus breaks down the Conference screen.

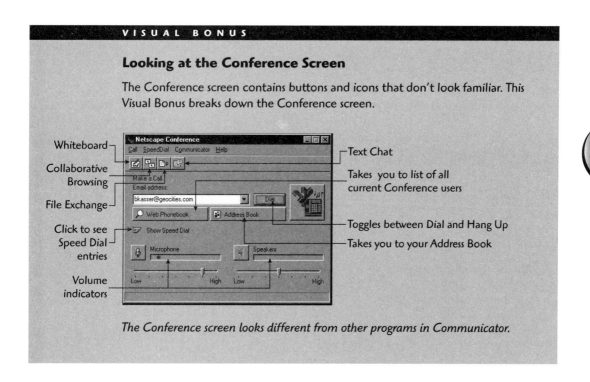

The Conference screen looks different from other programs in Communicator.

Exercise 2: Initiating a conference using the Netscape Conference Directory

In this exercise, you initiate a conference by choosing a name from the Netscape Conference Directory. Conference is open and on your screen from the last exercise, so you can continue with this exercise now. For this and the remaining exercises in this lesson, you may want to connect to a friend or colleague. If another one of your friends is using Communicator, see if you can set up a time for both of you to explore Conference together. Follow these steps:

1. Click the Web Phonebook button. The Netscape Conference Directory page appears in Navigator, as shown in the following illustration.

2. Click a letter to see the names of all the people who are using Conference right now, that begin with that letter. Or, click the View All Entries link to see the names of all users currently using Conference. In a moment, the Netscape Conference Directory Who's Online list appears.

3. The list includes the Conference user's name, e-mail address, and any other information the user included during setup, such as location. Find a name on the list and click the link to Call with Netscape Conference. Click a name from the list. As the call is dialed, the following dialog box appears on the screen. Additionally, you may hear a ringing sound coming from your computer.

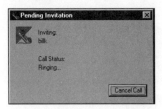

4. When your call has been accepted, the ringing stops, the Pending Invitation dialog box closes, and the Conference screen reappears. The e-mail address of the person to whom you're connected appears in the E-mail address text box. Additionally, you can position your mouse arrow in the Conference Attendant to see a screen tip showing the name of the party to whom you're connected.

Skip to Exercise 5 in this lesson to begin your audio conference.

5. If the person you're calling is unavailable or refuses to take the call, Conference gives you the opportunity to record a voice mail message that will be attached to an e-mail message and delivered to the person's Inbox.

When the Voice Mail dialog box appears, click Yes to record a message. Another dialog box appears, as displayed in the following illustration, that shows the e-mail address of the person you were calling.

Start recording

Stop recording

6. Click the Record Message button, the red dot, to start recording your voice mail message. Speak slowly and carefully. When you've finished recording, click the Stop Recording message button, which looks like a white square. Click Send to send the voice mail message.

In addition to using the Web Phonebook, you can initiate a conference call in two other ways. First, click the Personal Phonebook button and choose a name that you've entered previously in your Address Book. Or, type an e-mail address in the E-mail address text box and click Dial. If the party you're trying to reach is using Conference and is not connected to another Conference user, your call will go through.

Exercise 3: Using Speed Dial

If you call a particular person often, add the entry to Speed Dial. As with a regular phone, Speed Dial entries enable you to place a call with minimum effort. Follow these steps:

1. From the Conference menu bar, click SpeedDial.

2. Choose Speed Dial 1 through 6 and then Edit. The Speed Dial Edit dialog box appears.

3. Type the person's name in the Name text box.

4. Type the person's e-mail address in the Email text box.

5. (Optional) Even though you can select a Conference partner by using his or her name or e-mail address, Conference actually calls the IP (Internet Protocol) number of the computer. If you know the person's permanent IP address, type it in the Direct Address text box.

12

6. When you've filled in the lines, click OK to close the Speed Dial Edit dialog box. A completed Speed Dial entry is shown in the following figure.

You can leave
this line blank

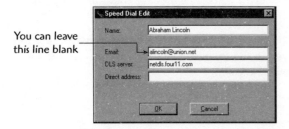

7. Repeat these steps for each entry you create. You can set up to six Speed Dial entries.

8. When you're ready to use Speed Dial, click the triangle that's pointing to the right, next to the words Show Speed Dial. The Speed Dial entries appear.

9. Click the entry you want, to initiate the call.

Exercise 4: Answering a Conference call

Although you can't initiate a call to yourself, enter Conference and wait a few minutes. Conference generates so much enthusiasm that someone will see your name on the list of Conference users and call you shortly after you open the program. Follow these steps to answer a conference call:

1. Open Conference, if you closed it after the previous exercise, by clicking Start and choosing Programs → Netscape Communicator → Netscape Conference.

2. If you want to use another program while you're waiting for a call, switch to any other application on your computer, including Navigator, by clicking the program's button on the Windows taskbar if the program is already open. If it's not open, use the Windows Start menu to open the program you want.

3. When a call is placed to your computer, you hear a ringing sound (if you have speakers), and a dialog box, similar to the one shown in the following illustration, appears.

4. Click Accept Call. Skip down to the next exercise, now that you're ready to talk!

5. If you don't wish to answer the call, click Reject Call.

Exercise 5: Talking over the Internet

In this exercise, you participate in a telephone conference. You need to have an active connection to complete the steps. Beware: Talking over the Internet can be habit-forming. Follow these steps:

1. Turn on the microphone by clicking the microphone icon on the Conference screen. The microphone icon appears pressed in.

2. Talk slowly and clearly into the microphone.

3. When you've finished talking, click the microphone icon again to turn off the microphone. While this step is not required, turning the microphone off when you're not speaking ensures that the background noises in your home or office (such as ringing phones, barking dogs, and people talking in another room) are filtered out.

4. Listen to the reply. Depending on how your system is set up, you may have to click the speaker icon to hear the response.

5. Click the microphone icon again when it's your turn to speak, and speak into the microphone.

6. Continue the conversation for as long as you want.

7. When you're ready to end the conversation, click Hang Up.

8. Close Conference, if you've finished conferencing, by clicking Call → Exit.

USING OTHER CONFERENCE TOOLS

Along with providing the capability to speak with someone over the Internet, Conference offers other options. While you're participating in a Conference call, you can use Conference's other tools. The Whiteboard tool enables you to share images. The Collaborative Browsing tool enables one party engaged in a Conference call to lead a tour of the Web. The File Exchange tool makes it easy to transfer a file from your hard drive to the connected computer. Use the Text Chat tool to communicate by writing words instead of speaking.

12

Exercise 6: Sharing images on the Whiteboard

The Whiteboard, one of Conference's tools, is a great way to share images during the conference. After the image is placed on the board by a participant, each person in the conference can draw pointers to parts of the screen or even collaborate on a drawing. Follow these steps to share images:

1. While a conference is active, click the Whiteboard button on the Conference toolbar to open the Whiteboard. The Whiteboard appears on the computer to which you're connected.

The Whiteboard contains a palette of drawing tools on the left side, as well as a regular toolbar and menu bar.

2. If you want to draw a freehand picture, click the Freehand Drawing tool. Move the mouse pointer onto the Whiteboard area. The mouse pointer takes the shape of a pencil. Hold the left mouse button down and drag the mouse pointer on the screen, as if you were using a pencil. Draw any shape you like.

3. If you want to bring up an image, click File → Open to display the Open dialog box. If necessary, change the file type in the Files of type box to one of the listed file types, and then navigate to the folder in which the image file is stored. When you locate the file, click it once to select it and then click Open. The image appears on the Whiteboard.

4. Although you can't open a nongraphics file, such as a word processing document or a spreadsheet, you can *capture* the image of a file that is already open on your computer and move it to the Whiteboard.

Within the Whiteboard, click Capture → Window. Your mouse arrow changes to a cross. Switch to the program window that contains the file you want to capture, such as a Lotus spreadsheet or a Word memo, by clicking the program's button on the taskbar. When the program appears, click its title bar, located at the top of the window. (The title bar shows both the name of the program — for example, Lotus 1-2-3 — and the name of the open file.) Switch back to the Whiteboard and click in the top right corner of the white area. The image of the file that you *captured*, or copied, from the other window appears, as shown in the following illustration.

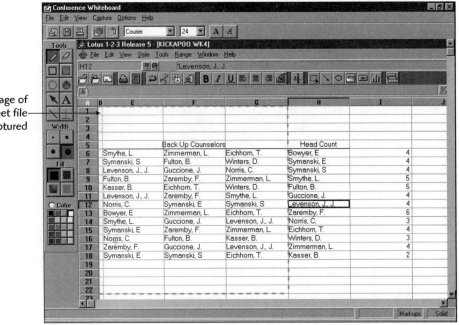

Image of spreadsheet file was captured

To capture the image of your computer desktop in the Whiteboard, click Capture → Desktop. When you click in the top right corner of the Whiteboard, the image of the desktop appears.

To capture a portion of the screen, click Capture → Region. After you've switched back to the program whose screen you want to capture, drag the cross-shaped mouse pointer over the portion of the screen you want to display on the Whiteboard. When you switch back to the Whiteboard and click in the top right corner of the white area, the area you selected appears.

5. Select a tool, such as the Pointer or Freehand Line tool, and then choose a corresponding Width, Fill, and Color from the other sections on the tool palette.

6. When you've selected a tool, move the mouse pointer onto the Whiteboard and mark the image. Because the image on the Whiteboard appears on the computer screen of the other Conference participant, you each see the other's markups and notations.

7. Print the image on the Whiteboard by clicking the Print button on the Whiteboard toolbar.

8. Click File → Close to close the Whiteboard. Because the Whiteboard opens in its own window, closing it does not close Conference.

Exercise 7: Using Text Chat

In addition to the audio conferencing, Conference provides a great Text Chat tool. When the audio is difficult to follow or one of the participants doesn't have a PC microphone, Text Chat is a great help. Like the Whiteboard, Chat opens in a separate window, complete with its own menu and toolbar. Follow these steps:

1. When your computer is connected to another computer in Conference, open Text Chat by clicking the Text Chat button on the Conference toolbar. The Text Chat program opens in its own window.

2. Type your comments in the lower Personal Note Pad located in the bottom half of the screen. After you've read them over, click the Send button or press Ctrl+Enter on the keyboard.

NOTE

Remember, you must send the text after you type it. Unless you click the Send button or press Ctrl+Enter each time you want to submit a comment, the person on the other end won't see what you typed.

3. The comments you send are identified as Local User on the Log File portion of the screen. The typed comments of the other participant are identified as Remote User. Type as many comments as you want.

4. On the Text Chat's menu bar, click Options and make sure that a check mark appears next to Pop Up on Receive, to ensure that you'll see all typed communication during a Conference session. Pop Up on Receive acts as a toggle, so if you don't see a check mark next to the menu selection, click it to turn on the feature.

5. Close Netscape's Text Chat by clicking File → Close.

NOTE

Text Chat enables you to write messages back and forth with one person. Lesson 7 shows you how to use a chat site, such as Talk City, to talk textually with a group of people.

Exercise 8: Exchanging files during a conference

File Exchange enables you to exchange files with another party during a Conference session. If you're sending files, make sure you know their folder location beforehand so you don't waste valuable connection time hunting for them. Follow these steps:

1. When your computer is connected to another computer in Conference, click the File Exchange button on the Conference toolbar. File Exchange appears.

The top portion of the window is the Send window, where you list the files to be sent. The bottom portion of the window is the Receive window, where the files you've received are displayed.

2. If the file you're sending is a text file, click Options → Ascii. For application and data files, click Options → Binary.

3. Click File → Add to List and move to your WebSave folder.

4. Click a file from the WebSave folder to select it, and then click Open. The filename and folder location appear in the File(s) to send box, as shown in the following figure.

Click to send——→

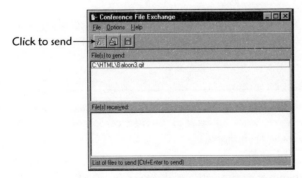

5. If you want to send additional files, repeat Steps 2, 3, and 4 for each file. If the files are not in the WebSave folder, move to the correct folder location and choose the files you want to send.

6. When you're ready to send the files, click the Send button or press Ctrl+Enter. In a moment, the files are transferred to the other computer.

7. If the other party has sent you files, each filename will appear in the File(s) received box. Click a filename to select it (the file will appear highlighted) and then click File → Save. When the Save As dialog box appears, move to the location in which you want to store the files, and click Save. After you've saved the files to your computer, the filenames disappear from the File(s) received box.

8. When you've finished sending the files, click File → Close to close the File Exchange tool and return to Conference. If you don't want to send the file from your WebSave folder, click File → Close now.

Be extremely careful about exchanging files. Computer viruses are often transmitted unsuspectingly during file exchanges. If you don't know the origin of a file you've received or if the file was unsolicited, don't save the file.

Exercise 9: Using the Collaborative Browsing tool

The Collaborative Browsing tool enables you to display a specific Web page in Navigator on both connected computers, during a Conference session. As you tour the Web during your conference, the person to whom you're connected is whisked to the same site. Once you begin a browsing session, you are the session leader and can control the browser display. Unfortunately, the Collaborative Browsing tool does not fully support pages that contain frames. Try not to access any framed Web pages. Follow these steps:

1. When your computer is connected to another computer in Conference, click the Collaborative Browsing button on the Conference toolbar. If you're not connected, follow the steps in Exercise 2 to link your computer to another.

2. When the Collaborative Browsing dialog box appears, click Start Browsing. If it's not already running, Conference opens Navigator and sends an invitation to the connected computer. If the invitation is accepted, the participant's copy of Navigator is launched; if the invitation is refused, Conference notifies you with a dialog box.

3. Check the Control the Browsers box and then click Sync Browsers to synchronize both copies of Navigator, so that they both display the same URL.

4. Click the Navigator button on the Windows taskbar to make Navigator the active window.

5. Move to a Web page by typing a URL in the Location box or by clicking one of your bookmarks. The same page that appears on your screen appears on the other computer, as well.

6. (Optional) Move to other sites on the Web.

12

7. When you've finished touring the Web, switch back to the Collaborative Browsing tool by clicking Stop Browsing.

SKILLS CHALLENGE: CONDUCTING A CONFERENCE

This Skills Challenge helps you to review what you learned about Conference. You'll initiate a Conference — so, if possible, you should set up a conference with a friend or coworker. Alternatively, choose a name from the list of available participants.

1. Open Conference from the Communicator menu in Navigator.

2. Establish a connection with another Conference user.

 *How does Conference identify the computer you're calling?*

3. Open the Whiteboard.

4. Draw a picture of a cat or dog with the Freehand tool and invite your conference partner to help you with the drawing.

5. Close the Whiteboard.

6. Click the Collaborative Browsing button. When the Collaborative Browsing dialog box appears, click the Start Browsing button. Type **home.netscape.com/** and lead your conference partner to the Netscape home page.

7. Open the Text Chat tool.

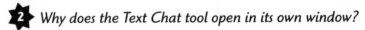 *Why does the Text Chat tool open in its own window?*

8. Type a comment and send it.

9. Send a follow-up reply to the comment you receive.

10. Close Text Chat.

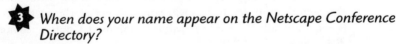 *When does your name appear on the Netscape Conference Directory?*

11. Continue chatting. When you're ready, politely break the connection.

TROUBLESHOOTING

The questions in the following table are commonly asked by new Conference users.

Problem	Solution
I've never used my microphone before, so how can I tell if it's working?	You can test your microphone in the Sound Recorder applet in the Accessories program group. If you need help finding the applet, click the Windows Start button, choose Help, and type **microphone** in the Help text box. Follow the prompts to check if your mike is working.
Can I erase the image that's currently showing in the Whiteboard?	To erase the image, click Edit → Clear Whiteboard. The current image disappears, along with any markups you've made to it.
How will I know if someone is using the Text Chat tool?	By default, Text Chat is designed to become the active window as soon as you enter text into it. So, if the other member of the conference uses the Chat Tool, the chat program will open in an active window on your computer.

WRAP UP

Great work. In this lesson, you learned the following:

- How to configure Conference
- How to set up a conference
- How to use the Speed Dial feature
- How to use the Whiteboard and Chat Tool to enhance Conference's capabilities

Practice these skills by using Conference to contact as many people as you can. Have a great time! In Lesson 13, you learn how to use Collabra to participate in Internet discussion groups.

Participating in Discussion Groups

30 MINUTES

GOALS

This lesson introduces you to Netscape Collabra, a utility for posting and reading messages on discussion groups, including Usenet News. You work through the following exercises:

- Setting up Collabra

- Obtaining a list of available discussion groups

- Subscribing to discussion groups

- Reading discussion group postings

- Replying to a posting

- Getting and reading new messages

13

GET READY

To complete the exercises in this lesson, you must be connected to the Internet. If you're using your company's intranet, find out from the people who administer the system whether you have access to Internet discussion groups. (Some companies may let their employees view only work-related discussion groups.) As you work through this lesson, complete each exercise before you move on.

When you complete this lesson, you will have set up Collabra and joined discussion groups of Internet users that share a common interest, as shown here.

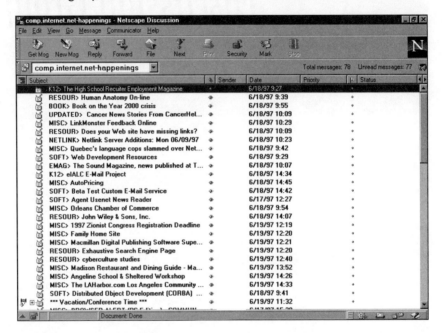

WHAT IS COLLABRA?

Collabra is the component of Communicator that enables you to read and post messages to Internet bulletin boards. These electronic message centers work much like the corkboard and pushpin bulletin boards you see at school or at the local supermarket. Someone posts a message and then somebody else replies, either to the group or to the individual who posted the original message.

Internet bulletin boards are called discussion groups. Each discussion group centers on a particular topic or interest. With over 15,000 discussion groups, you can probably find one that holds court on something you'd like to pursue. Additionally, discussion groups exist on the intranets of many companies. These company discussion groups provide employees with a virtual forum to collaborate on projects and exchange ideas.

Many of the discussion groups you see in Collabra are actually part of the Internet's Usenet News. Although most groups originate in Usenet, groups can be formed in a company, an ISP, or a source such as CompuServe.

Collabra shares many of Messenger's features. The discussion group postings appear in the form of messages stored in folders. Because Collabra uses the Message Center as its base, you can read and file discussion group messages in the same way you handle your mail. In fact, you can store postings from discussion groups in the same folders as your mail, which means that you only need to look in one place for stored messages.

PREPARING TO JOIN DISCUSSION GROUPS

Before you can find a group that shares your interests, you need to set up Collabra. Once it's configured, you can get started with finding the groups that interest you. Unlike some "live" discussion groups, these discussion groups don't charge a subscription fee. Best of all, you can subscribe and unsubscribe whenever you like.

Exercise 1: Setting up Collabra

Before you can use Collabra, you have to provide some basic information about yourself and your ISP. If you're not sure about the exact name of your ISP's *news server*, the tool your ISP uses to give you access to the groups, call them before you proceed. Follow these steps:

1. Click Start and choose Programs → Netscape Communicator → Netscape Collabra. If Navigator is open, click the Discussion Groups icon on the Component Bar. The Netscape Message Center appears.

2. Click Edit → Preferences. The Preferences dialog box appears, with a list of categories on the left side.

3. (Optional) If a + sign appears next to Mail and Groups, expand the subcategories by clicking the + sign. The - sign appears in place of the + sign, and the subcategories are visible.

When all subcategories under the Mail & Groups category are visible, click the Groups Server subcategory.

13

4. A sheet showing information about your news server appears. In the Discussion Group (news) server text box, replace news with the exact name of your ISP's news server. I have typed my news server's name in the following example.

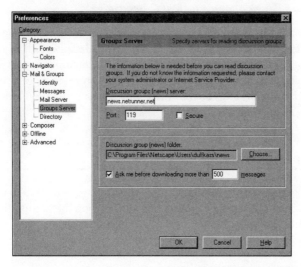

5. (Optional) In the Discussions Directory text box, change the folder in which your discussion group messages are stored, if you wish. (Change the default location only if you have a good reason!)

6. Click OK to enter the settings and return to the Message Center.

Now, you're ready to dig in!

Exercise 2: Obtaining a list of available discussion groups

In this exercise, you look at the discussion groups that you can join. Keep in mind that although more than 15,000 discussion groups exist on the Internet, your ISP may subscribe to only a fraction of them. Additionally, your ISP may offer subscriber-only discussion groups that the general population can't access. Your company may have some work-specific discussion groups, as well. Follow these steps:

1. From within the Message Center, click File → Subscribe to Discussion Groups. The Subscribe to Discussion Groups dialog box appears.

2. Click the All Groups tab at the top of the box. Most likely, no group names (or very few) are displayed on this tab.

3. Click the Get Groups button on the right side of the box. Collabra instructs the news server to download the list of available groups to your computer. As the group names are listed in the box, a status indicator tracks the current percentage of the total groups, as shown in the following figure.

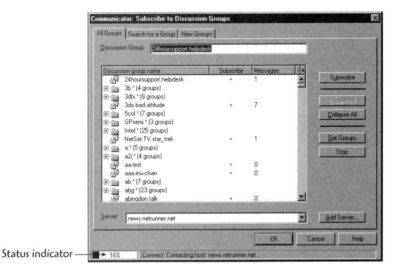

Status indicator

The first time you display all discussion groups, it takes a while for the news server to provide the complete list. Future visits to view the available discussion groups won't take as long to load.

4. When `Document:Done` appears in the bottom left corner of the dialog box, all of the groups are downloaded. Scroll through the list to find a group that interests you.

The master list of group names is arranged in a hierarchical structure, with the group categories in alphabetical order. Many categories contain subgroups. For example, the group "alt.acting" tells you that the group is an alternate group about acting. The + sign next to a category name indicates that it's *collapsed* so that the subgroups are hidden. Subgroups may have subgroups underneath them. Discussion groups at the top layer of the list tend to be somewhat general. The lower the layer of a subgroup, the more specialized it becomes.

13

5. Click the + sign next to the alt category to expand it. The alt group becomes *expanded* and the names of the subgroups appear. Additionally, the + sign switches to the - sign, as shown in the following figure.

Collapsed —

Expanded —

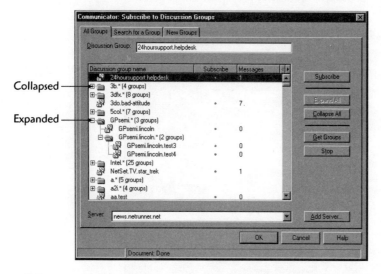

If you want to find a special discussion group or conduct a comprehensive search on all discussion groups, visit `http://sunsite.unc.edu:80/usenet-i/groups-html/` *on the Web. You'll find each group listed, along with a brief description.*

Understanding discussion group names

Discussion group names can seem like secret codes, as you see when you scroll through the list. Collabra allows user-friendly discussion group names (for example, the name Windows 95 Network Installation Issues makes more sense than comp.win95.net.inst.iss) The group names that come from Usenet News on the Internet, however, are difficult to break down. Sometimes, the names are so severely abbreviated that it's almost impossible for a *newbie* (a person who's new to discussions) to decode them. Unless you're looking at your company's discussion group list or groups set up by Netscape, most of the names you see will need to be translated.

Regional names are the easiest to decipher. For example, the discussion group called alabama.schools deals with the schools in Alabama. Even the regional names that are abbreviated can be figured out. Table 13-1 explains some of the most common group name abbreviations from Usenet News.

TABLE 13-1	MOST COMMON DISCUSSION GROUP CATEGORIES	
Abbreviation	*Description*
alt	Alternative topics that may be controversial or offensive (but aren't always)
comp	Topics relating to computers, including hardware and software
misc	Miscellaneous topics
news	Topics having to do with Usenet News and related issues
rec	Recreation of all sorts, including hobbies, sports, and TV
sci	Science-related topics
soc	Issues of social nature
talk	Hot topics that lead to debate and heated discussions

When people talk about Usenet discussion groups, they often don't count the alt group as a part of Usenet's main listings. The groups that use the alt designation are diverse and can be offensive or just plain confusing to most people, as with the group named "alt.buddha.short.fat.guy." Alt groups, because they're alternative, are not subject to the rules and guidelines followed by most other discussion groups.

PARTICIPATING IN DISCUSSION GROUPS

Because so many discussion groups exist, you're sure to find a few that interest you. For example, I belonged to a group of technical writers, a group of people interested in counted cross-stitch, and a group that loved a popular Tuesday night cop show, all at the same time. When I got too busy to keep up with the postings of all three groups, I unsubscribed to the group that wasn't quite as enjoyable as the other two.

Exercise 3: Subscribing to discussion groups

Follow these steps to subscribe to a discussion group:

1. If the Subscribe to Discussion Groups dialog box is closed, open it by following Step 1 in the previous exercise.

2. Click the Search for a Group tab.

3. Type **newbie** in the Search for text box.

13

4. Click the Search Now button. In a moment, the results of the search appear, as shown in the following example. Your news server may find the same groups or different ones.

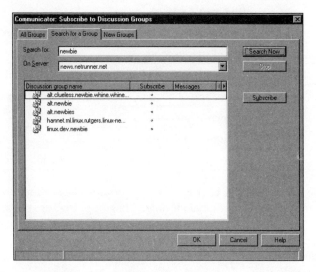

5. Review the names of the groups. On my list, the last two groups don't appear to have anything to do with people who are new to discussion groups.

6. Click the group alt.newbies to select it.

7. Click Subscribe. A check mark appears in the Subscribe column next to the group name.

8. Click the All Groups tab. Now you can scroll the list to find a group that seems interesting.

9. Move down to the Comp group and click the + sign to expand the list.

10. Find the group comp.internet. If more than one subgroup appears under comp.internet, choose one. I clicked comp.internet.net-happenings.

Click a group to select it (it appears highlighted).

11. Click Subscribe. A check mark appears in the Subscribe column next to the group name. The total numbers of postings are also displayed.

12. Click OK to close the Subscribe to Discussion Groups dialog box. You can find discussion groups by searching for them by name, or you can scroll the list and find groups that might be interesting.

Exercise 4: Reading discussion group postings

Now that you've joined some discussion groups, it's time to read the postings. Follow these steps:

1. If you're following the exercises in order, the Netscape Message Center window should be open on the screen. If it's not, click Start and choose Programs → Netscape Communicator → Netscape Collabra.

2. In the area next to your news server name, notice that a + sign is showing, indicating that the group is collapsed. Click the + sign.

NOTE

Think of the + sign as Collabra's way of shouting, "There's more!" Whenever you see a plus sign, you know instantly that you're not looking at the whole picture.

3. The two groups to which you subscribed appear below your news server's name, as shown in the following illustration.

4. Double-click a group name to open it. As the group opens, various messages flash on the status bar.

When the group is opened, it looks similar to any mail folder — with a few subtle differences, as illustrated in the following figure.

13

Group name —

Indicates a thread

Tab indicates that postings are hidden

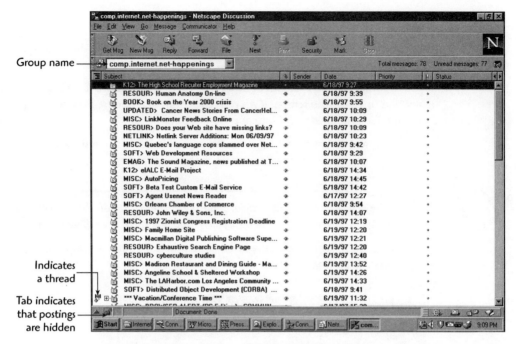

5. Double-click the first message on the list to read it. The message opens in its own window.

The message shown in the following example contains a link to a URL. Because Collabra is tightly integrated with Navigator, you can click a link in a discussion newsgroup (or mail) message to view the Web site.

Link to URL on Web —

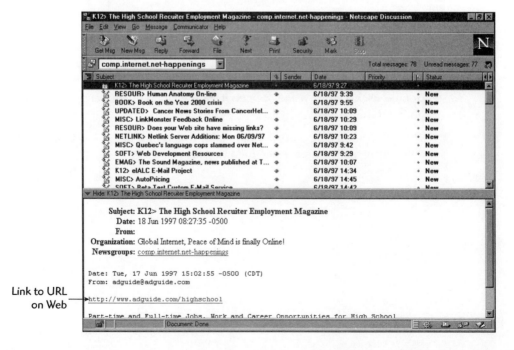

VISUAL BONUS

Setting Disk Space Rules

It's easy to see how discussion group postings can take over your computer. A small discussion group can generate 10 to 20 postings a day. Some larger discussion groups generate 1,000 postings every day.

If you belong to several discussion groups, the space inside your computer can easily be eaten away. Therefore, you should set a few rules for your system to follow. From the Message Center, click Edit → Discussion Group Properties and click the Disk Space tab. Setting these defaults creates a good starting point for Collabra messages. After you work with Collabra for a while, you can always change the defaults again. When you've finished making your selections, click OK to close the Discussion Group Properties and return to Collabra.

The following Visual Bonus shows you the options available to keep messages from taking over your computer!

Select this option ⟶

Option checked
by default

Change to 14. If you haven't looked at messages in two weeks, you're probably not going to.

Click for additional options

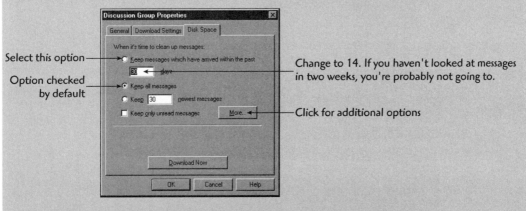

The Disk Space tab of the Discussion Group Properties dialog box

Check this box ⟶

Change to 180. Six months gives you a lot of time.

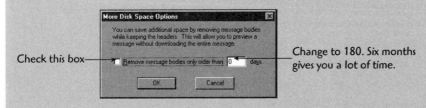

More Disk Space options to save space on your computer

13

6. If you don't want to read the posting in a window other than the list of postings window, click the triangle that's pointing upward, at the bottom of the Netscape Discussion window.

When you click a posting on the list, the message opens below the list of messages.

7. Scroll down the list of postings, reading those that interest you. As you can see, you have several messages to look through.

8. If you want to search for a particular posting, click Edit → Search Messages. Complete the Search Messages dialog box and click Search.

You learn how to get the new postings to a discussion group in Exercise 6. The number of daily postings can vary from just a few to thousands, depending on the group.

Exercise 5: Replying to a posting

Replying to a discussion group posting is a lot like sending an e-mail message. Follow these steps:

1. Click the message to which you'd like to post a reply.

2. Click the Reply button on the Messenger toolbar, as shown in the following figure. From the submenu that appears, click Reply to Sender if you want only the person who posted the message to receive your reply; click Reply to Sender and All Recipients if you want all members of the discussion group to receive a reply; click Reply to Group to publicly post your reply; or click Reply to Sender and Group if you want to send your reply to both.

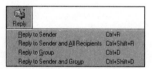

3. The original message appears in the Composition window with > characters in front of the subject line and the recipient box filled in. Type your reply, as shown in the following illustration.

Spelling button —

Recipients —

Subject line is filled in

Type your reply here

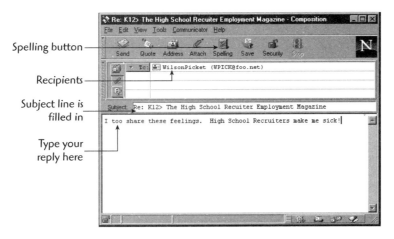

4. Click the Spelling button to spell check your reply before you send it.

5. Click the Send button on the Messenger toolbar to post the reply. The message is transmitted to the recipients.

TEN DISCUSSION GROUP DON'TS

Discussion group conversations often get heated. Follow the rules listed here to practice some good *netiquette* (Internet etiquette) and avoid getting *flamed* (receiving violent, nasty e-mails and comments).

1. Don't forget that the other members of the discussion group are people, just like you. Be courteous and polite.

2. Don't rely on your readers to figure out when you're serious and when you're trying to be funny or sarcastic. Writing serious stuff is difficult. Writing sarcastic wit is even more difficult.

3. Don't make statements that could be construed as official company policy. You can get yourself (and your company) in a lot of trouble by writing something like "My company, The XYZ Corporation, hires only people from Omaha."

4. Don't retype the entire posting you're replying to in your reply. People don't have time to wade through lines of stuff they've already read.

5. Don't post an answer like "Me too" or "I don't know." Paraphrase a line or two of the original thread or posting so everyone knows what you're talking about.

6. Don't give in to the temptation to post a comment like "Rodney is a moron" or some other insult. Other people may like what Rodney has to say — even if he is a moron. An insulting posting just creates a flame war.

(continued)

13

TEN DISCUSSION GROUP DON'TS (CONTINUED)

7. Don't jump into someone else's flame war, unless you want to get hurt. After all, you wouldn't stand between two people who were whacking each other with sticks, would you?

8. Don't come across like a know-it-all. Who likes to talk with someone who claims to be an expert in everything?

9. Don't send a message in all uppercase letters. IT'S VERY BAD FORM AND PEOPLE WILL THINK YOU'RE SHOUTING.

10. Don't forget that posting to a discussion group is voluntary. No one is forcing you to post replies. If you don't like the people in the group, or the conversation becomes too banal, unsubscribe to the group and find a new one.

Stick to these ten simple rules. Learning some netiquette and corresponding language may take a while, so be prepared to *lurk* (hang back for a while) before you start posting. **IMHO, FWIW,** you'll find that Collabra's discussion groups are fun and informative. **BTW, YMMV.** (Translation: **In my humble opinion, for what it's worth**, Collabra's Discussion Groups are fun and informative. **By the way, your mileage may vary.**)

Exercise 6: Getting and reading new messages

In this exercise, you complete a few simple steps to get the new messages that have been posted to the group since the last time you checked.

1. Open Collabra Discussions. The Message Center appears.

2. Click the discussion group folder for which you want to get the new messages. (The line appears highlighted.)

3. Click the Get Msg button on the Messenger toolbar. The new postings for that group are added to the respective discussion group folders.

4. Open the alt.newbies discussion group folder. Look through the folder for the new postings.

5. Reply to, forward, or file the postings you want to answer.

Collabra is tightly integrated with Messenger, so the rules for both programs are very similar. The menu system for both programs is the same, so you can reply to, forward, or file discussion group messages in the same way you handle mail messages.

Unsubscribing from a discussion group

It's a snap to unsubscribe from a discussion group. Within the Message Center, click the group from which you want to unsubscribe. When the group is highlighted, click Edit → Delete Discussion Group. The group disappears from your list. You can subscribe to that group, or any other group, at any time.

SKILLS CHALLENGE: GETTING THE MESSAGE WITH COLLABRA

In this Skills Challenge, you revisit the list of newsgroups and search for new groups. Along the way, plan to pick up additional Collabra tips, as you combine some new tricks with those you already know.

1. Open Collabra, if it is not open already. Collabra deals with Internet bulletin boards.

 What is another term for Internet bulletin board?

2. Click File → Subscribe to Discussion Groups.

3. Click Get Groups.

4. When the list of groups appears, expand all groups by clicking the Expand All button.

5. Look through the alt groups for discussion groups that contain the word *paranormal*.

 What is different about the alt discussion groups?

6. Join one of the paranormal groups.

7. Open the new paranormal group you just joined.

8. Read the first message.

9. Send a reply to the discussion group.

 To whom can you post a reply to a discussion group message?

10. Mark all the messages you've read by clicking Message → Mark → All Read. (This trick comes in handy if you don't have time to read any of the messages, or none of them seems interesting.)

11. Close the message folder that holds the paranormal group by clicking the Close button.

12. In the Message Center window, click the paranormal group you joined to select it.

13. When the group is highlighted, click the right mouse button and choose Remove Discussion Group. The group is removed from the list of groups to which you subscribe.

13

TROUBLESHOOTING

Now that you've been introduced to Collabra, think about how you can put it to work for you. Find groups that hold discussions on topics that interest you, or that might help you with a problem or give you some needed support. Remember that you don't have to join a discussion group for life — you can quietly unsubscribe at any time. The following table shows some of the common questions newbies ask about Collabra.

Problem	Solution
I'm overwhelmed by the number of groups. How do I find the ones I want?	Use the Search for a Discussion Group tab to look for groups' names that contain the keywords you want. You can always cruise to the Web and go to `http://sunsite.unc.edu:80/usenet-i/groups-html/` for a list of the groups and their descriptions. As a third alternative, take a few minutes and just scroll through the list of group names for some that interest you.
I'm too shy to post a message, but I don't want the group members to think I'm rude.	Don't worry, they don't even know you're a member of the group. It's a good idea to hang back for a bit after you've joined a new group, and follow the message threads for a while before you speak up (it's called *lurking*). When you're ready to post, let everyone know you're a newbie. Or, if you decide you're really not interested in what the group is posting about, unsubscribe from the group.
What's the difference between intranet groups and Internet groups?	Internet discussion groups are out there for everyone. Intranet groups can be seen and joined only by people who work for the same employer or who have obtained permission from the site's administrator. Also, although Internet group membership and participation is voluntary, sometimes you're required to post to your company's group.

WRAP UP

Collabra fitness is a snap! In this lesson, you covered the following topics:

- How to set up Collabra
- How to locate and join discussion groups
- Understanding discussion group names

Practice these skills by looking for groups that share your interests or desires and then reading and posting messages. In Lesson 14, you shift gears and learn how to create some basic Web pages.

13

PART IV

Composing Web Pages

In this part, you create your own Web pages using Netscape's tools and Composer. You work through the following lessons:

- Lesson 14: Creating a Basic Page with the Page Wizard and Templates
- Lesson 15: Designing Your Web Page from Scratch

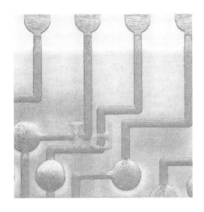

Creating a Basic Page with the Page Wizard and Templates

GOALS

This lesson shows you how to build your own Web pages without having to learn HTML. Some of the topics you learn include:

- Creating a basic page with the Page Wizard
- Changing the look of your page with the Page Wizard
- Saving your new page with the Page Wizard
- Exploring a page template
- Personalizing the text and formatting of a template page
- Adding a few finishing touches

14

GET READY

To complete this lesson, you need to be connected to the Internet with Navigator open. When you've finished this lesson, you will know how to compose basic Web pages (such as the one shown here) with the help of Netscape's Page Wizard and templates.

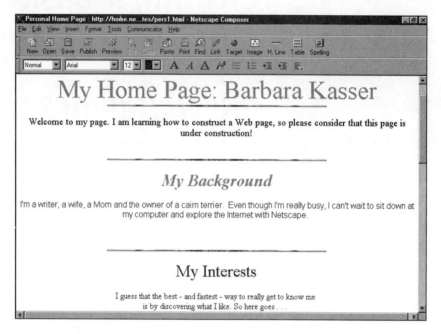

CREATING SIMPLE WEB PAGES

Now that you've spent all this time learning about people, places, and things on the Web, you may want to tell the world about yourself by creating your own Web page. Rather than jump in over your head and build your first page from scratch, use Netscape's Page Wizard and templates to make the process easier.

Web pages are written in a language called *HTML*, which stands for HyperText Markup Language. HTML documents contain the text of the Web page, along with instructions about how to format that text. Additionally, the HTML for a Web page includes information about the images on the page, the page background, and other presentation details. When you view a Web page in Navigator, the HTML code is converted into the page you see onscreen.

Fortunately, the tools provided with Communicator make it easy to build Web pages without learning HTML. One of these tools is the Page Wizard, which guides you through the process of building a page using preformatted elements provided by Netscape. Templates can also help you set up pages that look great with minimum work. After you select a template, you use Composer to personalize it with finishing touches.

USING THE PAGE WIZARD

Netscape understands that you want to create Web pages as quickly as possible. To keep you from poring over thick technical journals about HTML, the Netscape design team has put together a sampler of elements from which you can choose. The Page Wizard enables you to create great-looking Web pages with minimum effort.

Exercise 1: Creating a basic page with the Page Wizard

In this exercise, you meet your friend the Page Wizard and create a basic page with some text and links. The Page Wizard is run through Netscape's Web site, so make sure you're connected to the Internet before you begin this exercise. Follow these steps:

1. Open Netscape Navigator.

2. Click File → New → Page from Wizard.

3. Scroll down the Preview frame and click the Start button. Instructions for building your new page appear in the left frame, and a preview of the page replaces the text in the frame on the right.

4. Click the "give your page a title" link in the Instructions frame. A text box containing the sentence "Type your title here" appears in the Choices frame at the bottom of the screen.

5. Highlight the sentence in the text box by dragging your mouse over it while holding down the left mouse button.

6. While the original text is highlighted, type your name. The original text is replaced by your name.

7. Click Apply. Your name appears as the title in the preview page.

8. Click the "type an introduction" link in the Instructions frame. A box appears in the Choices frame for typing your introduction text.

9. Highlight the text in the box by dragging your mouse over it while holding down the left mouse button. Type **Welcome to my home page. I'm telling the world all about me!**

14

10. Click Apply. Your text is visible in the preview page, as shown in the following figure.

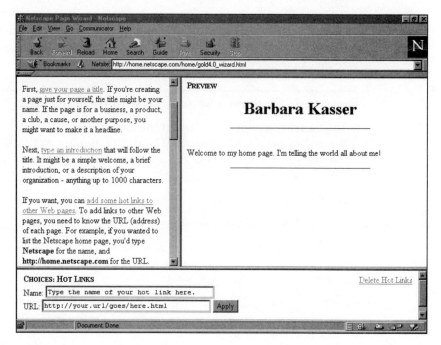

11. Scroll down in the Instructions frame and click the "add some hot links to other Web pages" link. A box for the name of the link and a box for the link address appear in the Choices frame.

12. Highlight the text in the name box and type **Barbara Kasser's Geocities Page.**

13. Highlight the text in the URL box and type **http://www.geocities.com/Paris/ LeftBank/4487**.

14. Click Apply. The link appears in the Preview frame.

Your page would be a bit lacking if the only link you had was to my page (although I would be flattered). If you want to add links to your other favorite sites, repeat Steps 11–14 for each link you want to add.

15. Scroll down the Instructions frame and click the link to "type a paragraph of text to serve as a conclusion." A conclusion box appears in the Choices frame.

16. Highlight the text in the conclusion box and type **Thanks for coming. Please visit again.**

17. Click Apply. The text appears in the Preview frame.

18. Scroll down the Instructions frame and click "add an e-mail link."

VISUAL BONUS

The Page Wizard

This Visual Bonus shows you the Page Wizard and explains the purpose of its three frames:

Instructions frame ——

Preview frame ——

Choices frame ——

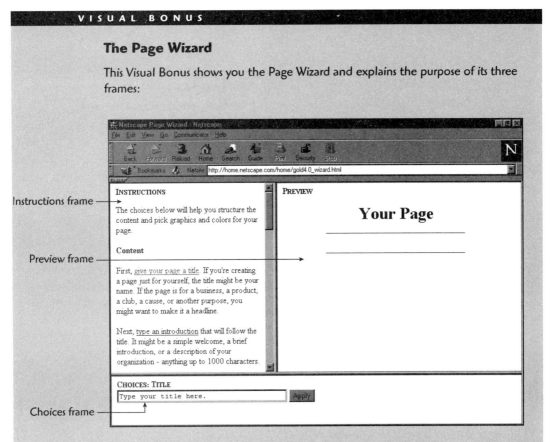

The Page Wizard screen is divided into three parts.

Preview frame: As you make changes to your Web page, the changes appear in this window. Most of the elements that appear in your first Web page are visible here.

Instructions frame: This is the frame you use to decide on the content and look of your Web page. You click each hyperlink in this frame to create a section of your page. The elements you can change include:

- **Title.** The name of your page. This should be your name, your company name, or some other type of headline.

- **Introduction.** Text that follows the title. Use it as a brief welcome area for your page. You can type up to 1,000 characters here.

- **Hot links.** This is where you insert links to other pages on the Internet. You add each link individually.

- **Conclusion.** Use this section to end your page. Once again, you can type up to 1,000 characters in this section.

14

- **E-mail link.** Add a hyperlink that links to an e-mail message box, so someone can send you a message.
- **Preset color combination.** Choose a color scheme for your page.
- **Background color, background pattern, text color, link color, visited link color.** Change the color or pattern for each of these items.
- **Bullet style.** Choose a bullet type for your lists.
- **Horizontal rule style.** Choose a style of separator line.

Choices frame: In this frame, you input the details of what you want to appear on the page. When you choose any option in the instruction frame, you'll see a box that you can use to enter the text you want to appear.

19. Highlight the text in the e-mail link box and type your e-mail address. An e-mail link appears on the preview page. People who visit your page use this link to send e-mail to you. Notice that Netscape was nice enough to put some text before the link for you. At this point, your page should look like the one in the following figure.

 It's easy to correct misspellings or change your text. Simply click the link in the Instructions frame for the section you want to change. When the text box containing the text you typed appears, make the correction. The Preview frame is updated when you click Apply.

Great job! But don't stop now. Jump into the next exercise so you can make the page look even better. If you don't have time to move on to the next exercise now, make sure you complete Exercise 3. By saving your page, you ensure that it will be available later.

Exercise 2: Changing the look of your page with the Page Wizard

In this exercise, you spiff up your new Web page by changing the colors of the text, background, and links, and by adding some graphics. You should have just completed Exercise 1 and should still be connected to the Internet when you begin this exercise. If not, redo the first exercise before going on to this one. Follow these steps:

1. With your new Web page in the Preview frame, scroll down the Instructions frame to the Looks section.

2. Click the link to "a preset color combination." A list of different color schemes appears in the Choices frame. Each scheme contains a background color, a text color, a link color, and a visited link color. The illustration here shows the schemes from which you can choose.

Pick a preset color scheme

3. Click one of the color schemes. The preview page changes to reflect the new color scheme.

4. Scroll down in the Instructions frame and click the "choose a bullet style" link. A list of different bullet types appears in the Choices frame. The list contains stars and animated bullets, as well as the standard bullets you're used to seeing.

If you want to design a custom color scheme, use the links below the preset color combination link. Each link enables you to change one aspect of the page appearance. For example, you add a background image to your page by clicking the "background pattern" link and selecting a pattern from the choices that appear in the Details frame.

5. Click one of the sample bullets. The bullet style you chose appears in the Preview frame before the hot link you added.

6. Scroll down in the Instructions frame to the "choose a horizontal rule style" link.

7. Click the link. A list of sample separator bars appears in the Choices frame.

8. Click one of the horizontal rules (separator bars). The bar you chose now appears as the separator between sections in the Preview frame.

You've just finished creating and spiffing up your first Web page. Now, what do you do with it? Later on, you may want to make changes to this page, and you may also want to put it on the Web, eventually. Before you can do either, you must save it to your computer. Beware! When you shut down Navigator, the page is erased, so if you haven't saved your page, you lose all your hard work. Proceed to Exercise 3.

14

Exercise 3: Saving your new page with the Page Wizard

In this exercise, you save the Web page that appears in the Preview frame. Complete this exercise immediately after Exercise 2, while your page appears in the Preview frame. Follow these steps:

1. Scroll to the bottom of the Instructions frame.

2. Click the Build button. In a moment, the page you created appears in its own Navigator window, complete with a Netscape logo.

TIP

If you don't have a WebSave folder, or forgot how to navigate to it, take a peek back at Exercise 3 of Lesson 4. You'll be saving your new Web page to that same folder.

3. Click File → Save As. The Save As dialog box appears.

4. Navigate to the WebSave folder you created earlier.

5. Click in the File name box and highlight yourpage.html, the default name of the page file.

6. Type **mypage**, as shown in the following figure. The highlighted text is replaced by the text you typed. You don't need to type the .html file extension, as it is added automatically.

When you've completed this exercise, go back to your desktop and open your WebSave folder. You'll see a number of new files in there besides the page you saved. What are these? These files are the images (the Netscape button, the bullets, and the horizontal rules) that appear on your page. They were stored in the WebSave folder when you saved the page.

Give yourself a big pat on the back, because not only have you created your first Web page, you've saved a copy as proof.

USING PAGE TEMPLATES

As an alternative to the Page Wizard, you can use Netscape's page templates to design your page. Templates consist of a set of pre-made pages that you change to meet your needs. You'll find templates for different types of pages, including personal, business, special interest, and just plain fun. You can use these templates as a starting point for creating your own pages.

Exercise 4: Exploring a page template

In this exercise, you explore one of the templates Netscape has provided for your use. Follow these steps:

1. If it's not open already, open Navigator by clicking Start → Programs → Netscape Communicator → Netscape Navigator.

2. Click File → New → Page from Template. The New Page from Template dialog box appears, as shown in the following figure.

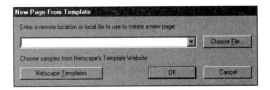

3. Click the Netscape Templates button. A page on the Netscape Web site appears that contains links to a variety of templates, along with some general instructions about how to use them.

4. Scroll down the page until you see the list of templates, shown in the following figure.

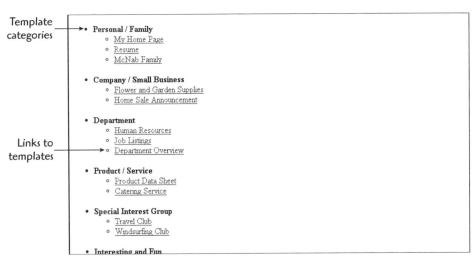

5. Click the link to My Home Page. A sample home page appears. You'll use this sample as a base for your own page.

6. Click File → Edit Page to download the template to your hard drive so you can edit it. In a moment, the downloaded page appears in Netscape Composer.

Although the page looks similar in Navigator and Composer, the title bar shows Netscape Composer.

7. Click File → Save As. The Save As dialog box appears.

8. If the Save in box does not show the WebSave folder, navigate to the WebSave folder now. (The WebSave folder should appear in the box, as it was the last folder in which you saved a file.) Notice that mypage.htm, the first page you built with the Page Wizard, appears in the WebSave folder.

9. Highlight pers1.html in the File name box and then type **homepage,** the new name of the file, in the File name box.

10. Click Save. (If the Confirm Save File dialog box appears, click Yes to resave the image now8.gif, the Netscape button, which appeared on the page you saved previously.) The page is saved to the WebSave folder of your computer. Notice that the filename, homepage, appears in the title bar.

TIP

Take some time to look at the sample pages in the page templates. You'll find many designs and ideas that you can easily adapt for your own use. Remember, you don't need to "reinvent the wheel" every time you set up a Web page!

11. Even though you've saved the page, you can't make any changes to it when you're still viewing it in Navigator. If you want to edit the page from Navigator, click File → Edit Page to open the page in Composer. Now you're ready to personalize the template.

Exercise 5: Personalizing the text and formatting of a template page

While I'm sure that J. B. Cabell, the gentleman on the sample page, wouldn't mind having his name and interests all over the Web, you may want to make some changes to this page. (That is, of course, unless your name is also J. B. Cabell, and Xena: Princess Warrior is one of your favorite sites!)

In this exercise, you change some of the content and formatting of the template page. Follow these steps:

1. The top portion of the page contains a set of instructions about how to use the template. After reading these instructions, highlight them and press Delete to delete the instructions from the page. (After all, you don't want the rest of the world to know your secrets, do you?)

2. Highlight J. B. Cabell at the top of the page.

3. Type your name. Your name appears in place of the highlighted text.

4. Highlight the entire first line now (including your name).

5. Click the arrow in the Font Color button to open a drop-down list of available colors. Click the color you want for the title. The box closes and the first line is displayed in the color you chose.

6. Highlight the introduction text. Type in some text of your own, welcoming people to your new Web page. You may want to use this sentence:

Welcome to my page. I am learning how to construct a Web page, so please consider that this page is under construction!

7. Highlight the text you just typed. Click the Font Size button on the Formatting toolbar and choose 14 from the list of font sizes, as shown in the following figure. The highlighted text increases in size.

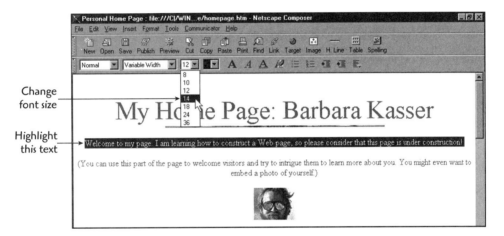

Change font size →

Highlight this text →

8. Unless you want people to think you look like J. B. Cabell, click both the text about including a photo of yourself and Mr. Cabell's picture, and then press Delete on your keyboard. The photo and text are removed from the page.

9. Highlight My Background and click the Italics button on the Formatting toolbar. My Background appears in italics.

10. The highlight bar still covers the text My Background. Click the Bold button on the Formatting toolbar. The text is now bold, as well as italicized. Notice also that the Bold and Italics buttons look pushed in on the toolbar.

NOTE

Although an option exists for underlined text in HTML (and a button for it exists on the Format toolbar), avoid using this option. Why? Underlined text is typically one of the indicators of a link. If you underline text that is not a link, it may be confusing to the people who view your page, especially if you change the text color.

14

11. (Optional) Change the color of the highlighted text, if you like.

12. Highlight the existing text in the My Background section. Type your own text. Rather than tell your life's story, just add a few brief sentences, for now.

13. Click the arrow in the Font button on the Formatting toolbar, and choose Arial from the list of available fonts. The text in the background section now appears in the Arial font.

14. Click outside the highlighted text to remove the highlight bar. When you've finished, your page in Composer should look like the one in the following illustration.

Sections you changed

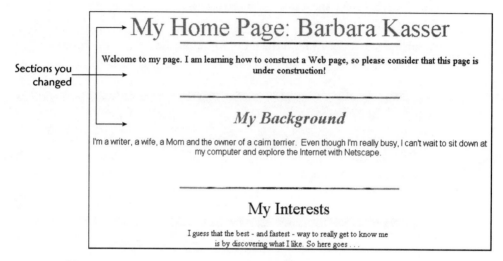

15. Before you make any more changes, you need to save the page. Click File → Save. After the changes you made are saved to your hard drive, you're ready to keep going.

Later on, you can reopen the page in Composer by clicking File → Open Page. Navigate to the WebSave folder (or wherever you saved the page), select the page file, and click Open. Watch out, though! If you open the page in Navigator, you won't be able to make editing changes.

Exercise 6: Adding a few finishing touches

The My Home Page template has provided a great start for your emerging masterpiece. You have the beginnings of a nicely designed Web page on your system now, and eventually you may want to put it up on the Web for the world to see. Now, it's time to add some underlying information so that people can find your page and know what it's about. To accomplish this, you need to insert a title and add some information to help Web spiders classify your page.

When you're ready to publish your page, make sure that you contact your ISP or network administrator for instructions on the best way to proceed.

1. Click Format → Page Colors and Properties. The Page Properties dialog box appears. Think of the box as a form you use to tell the world about your page.

2. Choose the General tab if it's not already chosen.

3. Click in the Title box and type a title for your page. The title will appear in the title bar of Navigator when someone views your page. It will also be used as the text for the link to your page in most search engines.

4. Click in the Author box and type your name if it isn't already displayed.

5. Click in the Description box and type a brief (about 25 words) description of your page. Don't worry if the text scrolls to the right and you can't read all the words in the box.

6. Click in the Keywords box and type some keywords that best describe your page.

7. (Optional) Click in the Classification box and type a classification for your page.

The completed General tab of the Page Properties dialog box is shown in the following illustration.

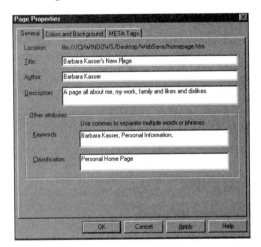

8. Click OK. The new page title appears in the Composer title bar, along with the name of the file.

You may have noticed that besides the title, none of the other text you typed in the Page Properties box appears on the screen. HTML contains some special commands, called META tags, that list the information for search engines, but don't display it on the page. It is possible, however, to see this information, as well as the rest of the HTML source code for your page.

9. Click View → HTML Source. The underlying source code for your page appears as a new window. The following illustration shows some of the source code for the sample page in this lesson.

14

```
Netscape                                                                    _ □ ×
<HTML>
<HEAD>
   <META HTTP-EQUIV="Content-Type" CONTENT="text/html; charset=iso-8859-1">
   <META NAME="GENERATOR" CONTENT="Mozilla/4.01 [en] (Win95; I) [Netscape]">
   <META NAME="Author" CONTENT="Barbara Kasser">
   <META NAME="Classification" CONTENT="Personal Home Page">
   <META NAME="Description" CONTENT="A page all about me, my work, family and likes and dislikes.
   <META NAME="KeyWords" CONTENT="Barbara Kasser, Personal Information,">
   <TITLE>Barbara Kasser's New Page</TITLE>
<!--<meta http-equiv="Content-Type" content="text/html;charset=iso-8859-1">-->
</HEAD>
<BODY TEXT="#000000" BGCOLOR="#FFFFFF" LINK="#0000EE" VLINK="#551A8B" ALINK="#FF0000">

<HR width="100%">
<HR width="100%">
<CENTER></CENTER>
```

Look at all that code you generated! Isn't it nice to know that you don't need to learn the technical details of HTML? You can build your own page by pointing and clicking.

10. Close the dialog box by clicking the Close button.

SKILLS CHALLENGE: CREATING A NEW PAGE

You put your page-building skills to the test in this challenge. Now, you're going to recap all the knowledge you gained in this lesson, so make sure you're comfortable and alert before you begin. If you get stuck or are unsure about how to complete one of the steps, flip back to the section in this lesson that contains the information. Ready? Here you go!

1. Open the Netscape Page Wizard.

2. Create a new page including title, introduction, links, conclusion, and an e-mail link.

3. Change the color scheme of the page.

4. Save the page as secondpage.html.

> **1** *Why do you need to save the page?*

5. Open the homepage.htm file you created earlier.

6. Change the appearance of the heading in the My Interests section.

> **2** *Why shouldn't you underline text on a Web page?*

7. Replace the existing text in the My Interests section with a few lines about your own interests.

8. Save the page as testpage.htm in the WebSave folder.

9. Add a title, author name, and keywords.

Why don't the keywords appear on the page?

10. Save the page again and close Composer.

TROUBLESHOOTING

You've made the leap from Web surfer to amateur Webmaster — great job! With the help of Netscape's Page Wizard and templates, you've created your first Web page, and you're well on the way to even greater creations. Before you move on, here are a few things that you might encounter or wonder about.

Problem	Solution
I'm afraid to mess with my page. What if I make a change and then decide I want it the old way?	No problem. First, keep in mind that until you save the changes, they exist in temporary memory only. So, if you decide to play around and then don't save the changes, nothing changes in your page. If you make changes that you think you may want, use the Save As command and save the changed page with a different name. Now, you have two versions of the page to work with. Of course, once you decide which page you want to use, delete the other one.
I tried to reopen the page I saved with Composer and I couldn't find it. What happened?	If you're certain that you saved the page to your hard drive, then maybe you didn't save it to the WebSave folder. Did you remember to navigate to that folder when you saved it? If not, the easiest way to find it would be to use the Windows 95 Find feature. You can get there by clicking Start → Find → Files or Folders. Make sure the Name & Location tab is selected, and type the filename (**mypage.htm** or **homepage.htm**) in the Named box. If you did save it, it will show up on the list in the lower half of the Find box. Just double-click on the name to open it.

14

Problem	Solution
How do I know when my page is finished?	When it looks the way you want it to! You'll find that you may tinker with a page quite a bit to get it to look just right. If you make some changes you're not sure you like, save the page with a different name and compare the changes to the original page later.

WRAP UP

Good work! You're on a roll! In this lesson, you learned the following:

- How to create a basic Web page with the Page Wizard and templates
- How to save your Web pages
- How to change the style of text
- How to add underlying information about your page that identifies it to search engines.

Any time you want to practice these skills, open the pages you've created and continue to make changes. Feel free to create new pages based on the templates. Experiment a bit! In the next lesson, you design a Web page from scratch with Composer.

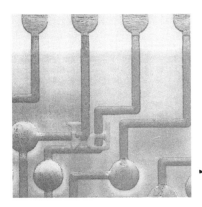

Designing Your Web Page from Scratch

15

50 MINUTES

GOALS

This lesson shows you how to create a Web page from scratch. Among other skills, you learn the following:

- Getting started with Composer
- Configuring preferences
- Changing the look of text
- Adding some pizzazz to your page
- Grabbing a graphics image
- Adding an image to your page
- Including a list on your page
- Editing your page
- Adding a link on your page

GET READY

Before you begin this lesson, contact your ISP or network administrator to find out the steps you need to take to share your completed Web pages with the world. Connect to the Internet before you start the exercises.

When you've finished this lesson, you will know how to create and enhance a Web page with Composer, shown in action in the following illustration.

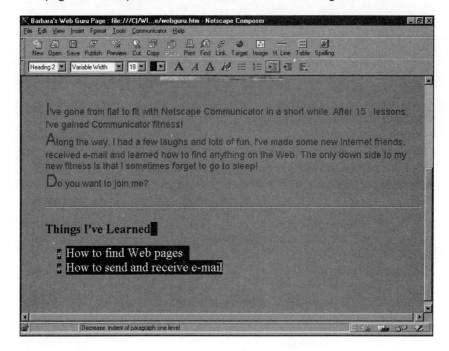

WHY USE COMPOSER?

As you learned earlier, HTML is the language that defines all Web pages. HTML documents contain text and graphics that you see onscreen, and instructions, called tags, that control the placement of the text and graphics. When Navigator or any other browser launches a Web page, the HTML tags determine how the page is laid out.

Even though HTML is a relatively recent language, new tags and specifications are added all the time. To simplify a complex process, Netscape has included Composer as a main component of Communicator. Composer's tools do most of the work in building a Web page. You concentrate on the content of your page instead of studying the proper syntax and placement of HTML tags.

As explained in the previous lesson, Composer takes over when you want to set up Web pages. Along with adding the tags and codes needed by Navigator and other browsers to display Web pages, Composer has a feature that enables you to upload your page to the Internet. This Publish feature works with only certain

ISPs, however, so check with your ISP first.

Exercise 1: Getting started with Composer

In this exercise, you open Composer and begin creating a Web page. Although you can use Composer for any type of page, in this exercise you create a page announcing your Communicator confidence.

1. If Navigator is already open, click the Composer button on the Component toolbar. Otherwise, click the Start button and choose Programs → Netscape Communicator → Netscape Composer.

2. Type the following text, pressing Enter after each paragraph:

I'm a Web guru!

I've gone from flat to fit with Netscape Communicator in a short while. After 15 lessons, I've gained Communicator fitness!

Along the way, I had a few laughs and lots of fun. I've made some new Internet friends, received e-mail and learned how to find anything on the Web. The only down side to my new fitness is that I sometimes forget to go to sleep!

Do you want to join me?

If you make a typing error, use the arrow keys to move through the text. Erase the error with the Backspace and Delete keys and type in the correction.

3. Save your page by clicking File → Save As. When the Save As dialog box appears, type **webguru** in the File name box, navigate to the WebSave folder, and click the Save button. (You don't need to type the file extension; it is automatically filled in for you.)

4. The Page Title dialog box appears. Substitute **(Your Name)'s Web Guru Page** for the text that's already there, as shown in the following figure. Click OK to close the Page Title dialog box.

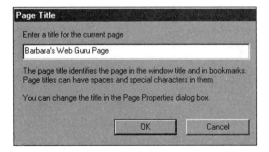

The page is saved to the hard drive of your computer and the filename appears in the Composer title bar. Your bare-bones page is now ready for some magic.

Exercise 2: Configuring preferences

Before you proceed, it's time to configure Composer. Taking a few minutes now will save a lot of time later, so it's worth the effort to set up a few basic Composer preferences. You need to set preferences that include the author's name and indicate how often the Web pages you're working on are automatically saved. Setting *AutoSave*, the feature that saves your work after a set interval, is the most important Composer preference. It's easy to become so wrapped up in the page creation process that you forget to save your work. Follow these steps to configure Composer:

1. In Composer, click Edit → Preferences. The Preferences dialog box appears, as shown in the following figure.

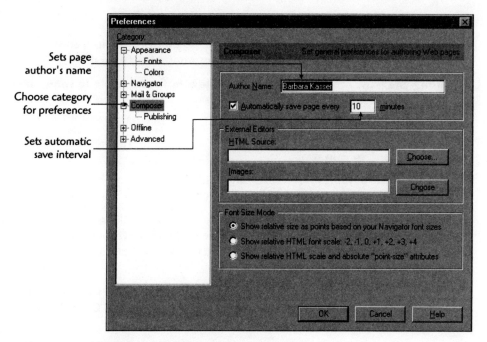

Sets page author's name

Choose category for preferences

Sets automatic save interval

2. Click Composer in the Category box.

3. Click the Author name box and type your name. Your name is now the default author for all new pages.

4. Make sure that the box next to Automatically save page every *x* minutes is checked. This turns on the AutoSave function that helps keep your work from disappearing if the power goes off or you exit without saving.

5. Click in the minutes box and type **10**, if it's not already listed. Now, your page is automatically saved to your hard drive every ten minutes.

6. Click OK to save your changes.

ENHANCING YOUR COMPOSER WEB PAGE

As you can see on your Web Guru Page, plain text can make a page look dull. Even the most interesting or outrageous page won't get a second look if it's not visually appealing! Fortunately, Composer provides many options to add some excitement to your page.

Exercise 3: Changing the look of text

The page you created in Exercise 1 is flat and unappealing. If you were looking for interesting pages on the Web, would you stop and read the Web Guru Page? Don't worry, with a few quick changes you can transform the page. Follow these steps:

1. If the Web Guru Page you created in Exercise 1 is not open in Composer, open it now by clicking Start and choosing Programs → Netscape Communicator → Netscape Composer. When Composer appears on the screen, click File → Open Page. Type **c:\windows\desktop\websave\webguru.htm**, as shown in the following figure.

NOTE

Recite the phrase "Select and Effect" as you work with text you've already typed. Highlight the text first. Then, when you've selected the text, choose an effect, such as bold, italics, or color from the toolbars or menu commands.

Type filename and location →

Or click to move to folder where file is stored

If you're comfortable navigating through folders, click Choose File, move to the WebSave folder, and click **webguru.htm**. Click OK to open the file.

2. Highlight the first line of text, "I'm a Web guru."

3. Click Format → Character Properties. The Character Properties dialog box appears. Make the following changes:

- Click the drop-down arrow next to the font in the Font Face box and select Arial from the list.

- Click the drop-down arrow next to the point size in the Font Size box and select 24.

- Check the Bold style box.

- Check the Italic style box.

- Check the Blinking style box.

- When you've made the changes, the dialog box on your screen should look like the one in the following illustration. Click Apply and then Close to close the dialog box.

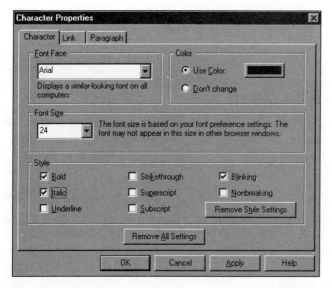

4. With the first sentence still selected, click Format → Align → Center. The text moves to the center of the page. Press the right arrow key to deselect the sentence.

5. Hold the left mouse button down and select the other three paragraphs so that they appear highlighted.

6. Click Format → Color. The Default color from browser preferences dialog box appears, as shown in the following illustration.

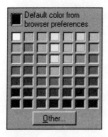

7. Click one of the darker colors and then click OK. The text is still selected.

8. Instead of using the menu command, you can change the font with the Font button on the Format toolbar. Click the drop-down arrow next to the Font button and choose Arial from the list of available fonts.

9. Change the font size of the three selected paragraphs by clicking the drop-down arrow next to the Font Size button on the Format toolbar. Choose 14 from the list of available point sizes.

10. With the text still selected, click Format → Increase Indent. The text moves to the right by one tab stop.

11. Deselect the text by pressing the right arrow key. All changes are visible now.

12. Click in front of the letter *I* in the phrase "I've gone from ...," and select the letter *I*. Use the Font Size button on the Format toolbar (as you did in Step 9) to change the size from 14 to 24. When you deselect the text, the first letter is larger.

13. Repeat Step 12 on the first letter of the first word in each remaining paragraph. When you've finished, the first letter of each paragraph is emphasized.

The page is starting to look interesting. Don't stop now.

Exercise 4: Adding some pizazz to your page

In this exercise, you add a background color and some elements to the page. Follow these steps:

1. Click Format → Page Colors and Background. The Page Properties dialog box opens.

2. Click the Colors and Background tab to bring it to the front.

3. Click the Background button. The Color dialog box appears.

4. Pick a color from the box and click OK. The color you chose is reflected in the sample box, as shown in the following figure.

Sample box —

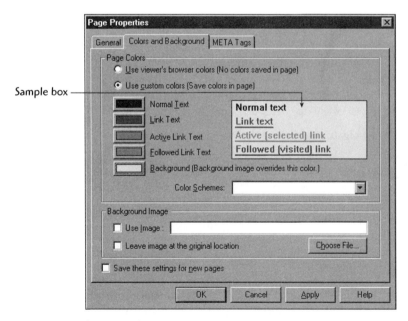

5. (Optional) If you love the background color you chose so much that you want to use it for future pages, check the box next to Save these settings for new pages.

6. Position the cursor after "guru!" on the first line.

7. Click Insert → Horizontal Line. A line separates the first line from the rest of the text.

8. You've been working in the editor to create your page. The way it looks in Composer, however, is not the way it will look in Navigator. Now, it's time to view the page as others will see it. Click File → Browse Page. When you're asked if you want to save the file, click Yes. In a moment, your page appears in a Navigator window.

Notice that some of the page elements look different in Navigator. For one thing, your first line is blinking. Also, the spacing and line breaks look a bit different.

9. Switch back to Composer when you've finished looking at your handiwork in Navigator, by clicking the Composer button on the Component toolbar.

 NOTE

Remember that the way the page looks in Navigator is the way the page will look to everyone who views it in Navigator. Even though Composer is a WYSIWYG (What you see is what you get) editor, your browser has the final authority. Toggle back and forth as you're creating your page, so you don't get an unpleasant surprise at the end. Do you really want the world to see the annoying blink on the first line of the Web Guru Page, for example? (You'll eliminate that blink later in this lesson.)

Exercise 5: Grabbing a graphics image

In this exercise, you spice up your page with a graphics image. If you don't have any great images gathering dust, search for clip art using Yahoo. You'll find a number of collections that have images in the public domain (free) or that you can obtain for a nominal fee. If you see an image on the Web that you want to use, make sure you get written permission from the page owner before you take it. (You wouldn't want the gendarmes knocking on your door!)

I own the image of the cairn terrier that's used on my page (it's actually a scanned photo of my dog, McDuff), so you can use it for your page.

1. Switch to Navigator by clicking the Navigator button on the Component toolbar.

2. Type the URL to Barbara Kasser's Geocities Page at **www.geocities.com/Paris/ LeftBank/4487** in the Location box and press Enter.

3. When the page loads, move to the bottom of the page and click the "and friend" text link in the copyright line. In a moment, the picture of my cairn terrier appears.

4. Position your mouse pointer over the dog and click the right mouse button once. When the pop-up menu appears, click the left mouse button on the Save Image As menu selection.

5. Navigate to the WebSave folder and click the Save button. The image is saved to the hard drive of your computer, using the same name as the image on the Web page. In this case, the file you saved is named cairn.gif. (If you wanted to use a different name, you could type the new filename in the File name box before you clicked Save.)

VISUAL BONUS

Studying the Image Properties Dialog Box

The Image Properties dialog box is composed of three tabbed windows. The Image tab controls the appearance of the image. The Links tab enables you to turn the image into a link to another site or another location on the same page. The Paragraph tab sets the paragraph formatting that's associated with a particular image. Study the Image tab — that's the one you'll use most often.

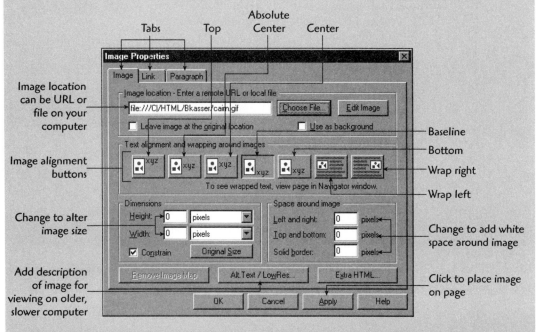

The Image tab controls an image's appearance on a Web page.

Exercise 6: Adding an image to your page

Think back for a moment about a great Web page you visited recently. What part of the page stays in your mind? Was it the clear, concise way in which the text was presented? Or maybe the alignment of the text caught your eye. If you're like most people, the feature that first draws you to a page and then keeps you from forgetting it is the site's graphics. The Web is a visual medium. Although the quality of the text is important, pictures and colors draw people to your page. In this exercise, you add the image of the dog to the Web Guru Page set up in the previous exercises.

1. If the Web Guru Page is not open in Composer and visible on the screen, make it the active Window now.

2. Click the mouse pointer at the top of the page so that the cursor is flashing after the last letter of the sentence, "I'm a Web guru!"

3. Type **and so is my dog** and press Enter.

4. Click Insert → Image. The Image Properties dialog box appears.

5. Click Choose File. Navigate to the WebSave folder, click welcome.gif and then click Open. The filename and its folder location (called a path) appear in the Image location box of the Image Properties dialog box.

6. Click the Absolute center alignment button and then click Apply.

7. Click Close to close the Image Properties dialog box and return to the Composer screen. The cairn terrier appears next to the first sentence.

8. Click the Preview button on the Composer toolbar to see how the page looks in Navigator. Click Yes when you're asked if you want to save the file.

    The page looks all right, but you'll probably agree that it needs some work. (And what about that annoying blinking text? You'll fix this in Exercise 8.)

9. Go back to editing the page by clicking the Composer button on the Windows taskbar. Composer becomes the active window.

10. Position the mouse pointer between the graphic and the first word of the sentence and press Enter. The sentence moves down one line.

11. Click the Preview button to check how the page looks in Navigator. When asked if you want to save the page, click Yes.

    The image is centered at the top of the page and draws your attention.

12. Click the Composer button on the taskbar to continue editing the Web Guru Page.

Exercise 7: Including a list on your page

In this exercise, you create a list on your page. Using lists to present information is an excellent way to grab someone's attention. Before you start this exercise, the Web Guru Page should be visible in the Composer window.

1. Click anywhere on the Web Guru Page. Press Ctrl+End to move the cursor to the bottom of the page.

2. Click Insert → New Line Break. The cursor moves down one line.

TIP

HTML doesn't like multiple line breaks. If you press Enter more than once, you'll see only one line break when you view the page in Navigator (although it will look correct in Composer). If you want the effect of more than one line break, use the New Line Break command for every break desired.

3. A horizontal line sets off a new section of a page. Click Insert → Horizontal Line to add a new visual area to the page.

4. Click Insert → New Line Break. The cursor moves below the horizontal line.

5. Type **Things I've Learned** and press Enter.

6. Click Format → List. Choose Bulletted from the available list types shown in the submenu below. (Even though the correct spelling is Bulleted, the menu displays the word with two t's!)

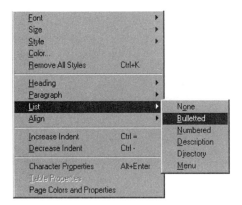

7. A bullet character appears on the next line. Type **How to find Web pages** and press Enter. Notice that the Bullet List button appears pressed on the Format toolbar, and a bullet appears on the next line.

8. Type **How to send and receive e-mail** and press Enter.

9. You've added the names of two sites. Click the Bullet List button on the Format toolbar to turn the feature off. The bullet character on the blank line disappears.

Next, you dress up the list.

10. Highlight "Things I've Learned."

11. Click Format → Heading → 2. The text takes on the Level 2 Heading formatting. Press the right arrow key to deselect the text. Notice that the new format affects the line spacing; the next line moves down to set off the heading.

12. Highlight the two bullet points you typed.

13. Click Format → Size and choose 18 from the font sizes. The items are still selected.

14. Click the Number List button on the toolbar. The bullet characters change to # signs, as shown in the following figure.

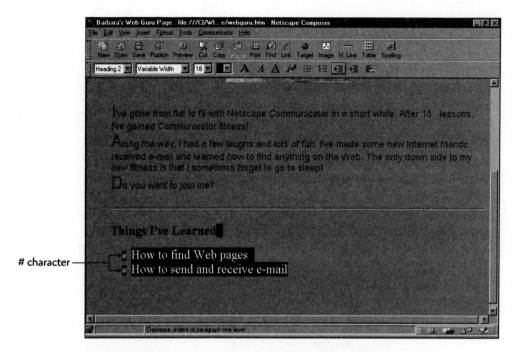

15. Press the right arrow key to deselect the bullet points.

16. Press Enter and then turn off the number list feature by clicking the Number List button on the toolbar.

17. Click the Preview button and click Yes when asked if you want to save the page.

18. The page appears in Navigator. Instead of showing the number symbols, the list points are actually numbered. Click View → Page Source to look at the HTML code. As you see, once you supplied the basic information, Composer added the HTML tags.

19. Close the Source window by clicking the Close button on the title bar.

20. Switch back to Composer so you can make a few more changes.

Great work! Don't quit now — you have a few more changes to make.

FINISHING YOUR PAGE

Your page is almost finished. You've previewed it in Navigator and you know what the finished product will look like. Even though you're excited, you need to make a few more changes. First, you need to edit your page to eliminate the blinking text. Although using many attributes may seem like a good idea as you begin creating your page, too many attributes can distract the viewer. You also need to add a link for easy navigation within your page.

15

Exercise 8: Editing your page

In this exercise, you make some editing changes to your page before publishing it to the Web. Once the page is uploaded to the Web, you need to make any changes on a local copy of the file and then transfer the new file to the Web. Changes you make can be content-related, in which you change the text, or design-related, in which you add or remove page formatting such as colors, alignment, and text attributes. You finally remove the annoying blink in this exercise. You also check your spelling. The Web Guru Page should be on the screen in Composer before you begin.

1. Highlight the sentence, "I'm a Web guru!"

2. Click Format → Style. The Style menu appears with check marks in front of the Bold, Italic, and Blinking attributes.

3. Click the check box next to Blinking to remove that attribute. The check mark disappears from the menu, and the menu closes.

4. Press the right arrow key to deselect the sentence. The page in Composer looks the same.

5. Click the Spelling button. If Composer finds any spelling errors, make the necessary corrections.

6. Click the Preview button to view the page in Navigator. Answer Yes to save the page before Navigator appears.

The blink is gone. You can add, change, or delete any page element. Before you publish the page, however, make sure you view your changes in Navigator so you can see the updated page as others will see it.

Exercise 9: Adding a link on your page

Now, you add a link to your page. Because Web pages have no length limitations, some pages can grow very long. Even though you can use the scroll bar to move from the bottom of the page back up to the top, clicking a link is easier. Once you've mastered the technique, you can add links anywhere in your page.

When you begin this exercise, the Web Guru Page should be visible in the Composer window.

1. Move to the picture of the dog. If necessary, use the scroll bar.

2. Click the picture of the dog to select it. A box appears around the picture.

3. Click Insert → Target. The Target Properties dialog box appears.

4. Type **top** in the text box and click OK. The box closes and you return to the Web Guru Page. A small symbol appears next to the picture of the dog.

5. Press Ctrl+End to move the cursor to the bottom of the page.

6. Click Insert → New Line Break. The cursor moves down one line.

7. Click Insert → Horizontal Line to set off the list section with a horizontal line.

8. Click Insert → New Line Break. The cursor moves below the horizontal line.

9. Type **Return to Top** and press Enter.

10. Highlight the text you just typed and click Insert → Link. The Character Properties dialog box appears with the Link tab selected.

11. The target name Top appears in the second box in the Link section. Click Top to select it and then click Apply.

You could also add a link to another page on the Web, or to a file on your computer, by typing the URL or file location and name in the first box in the Link Section.

12. Click Close to close the Character Properties dialog box and return to your page.

13. Return to Top is still selected. Press the right arrow key to deselect it. Notice that the text is now a link — it's underlined.

GETTING NOTICED

After you've contacted your ISP or network administrator, and followed their directions to get your page published on the Web, you're ready for visitors. With the millions of pages on the Web, what will make people visit yours? After all, you've spent time and energy creating a visual feast to share with the world. How can you attract viewers to your site?

Always tell people about your Web pages. Everyone you meet should know about your pages — especially if the site is business-related. Add your URL to your advertisements, business cards, stationery, and even invoices. People will be curious and will visit your site. Tell your friends and associates that you'll add links to their pages if they add links to yours. Check with the local Chamber of Commerce about adding links to your site from theirs.

You can also publicize yourself by submitting your URL to the search engines. Each of the major search engines has a procedure for submitting your location to their databases. Look for a button or link on their pages to submit registration information. Be aware, however, that it may take several months for your site to appear, because the search engines are barraged with new requests. Companies such as Submit-It (www.submit.com) can submit your information to a group of search engines all at once for a small fee.

However you get your name into cyberspace, don't neglect the page once it's on the Web. Visit your site often and compare it to your competition. If your page contains seasonal information, make sure you update the site in a timely manner. Nothing looks tackier than graphics of Christmas trees and holly boughs around the Fourth of July (unless you sell holiday supplies all through the year).

14. Click the Preview button to view the page in Navigator. Answer Yes to save the page before Navigator appears.

15. Move to the bottom and position the pointer over Return to Top. Because you've made the words into a link, the pointer becomes a hand.

16. Click the link. You move to the dog's picture at the top of your page.

You've done it! You're an amateur Webmaster. When you've perfected your page, it's time to publish it to the Web. If you're an intranet user, talk to your system administrator before you proceed. Many ISPs and online services have policies and procedures about how to publish your pages, so check with them. You may be asked to pay an additional fee for allowing a service to host your Web site.

SKILLS CHALLENGE: BUILDING A RÉSUMÉ

In this Skills Challenge, you build a résumé that you can post on the Web for lots of exposure. (Although you probably feel like you're ready, don't expect to get a new job as a Webmaster just yet!) Take your time. You'll learn a few new skills and brush up on those you've already mastered as you work through the steps of the challenge.

1. (Optional) Sketch out what you want to include on the résumé. If possible, get a copy of your existing résumé to work from.

2. Open Composer. If Composer is already open, go to a blank page by clicking File → New → Blank Page.

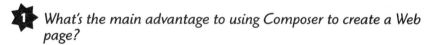

1 *What's the main advantage to using Composer to create a Web page?*

3. Type your name, address, and phone number, pressing Enter after each line.

4. Change the Alignment of the text from left to center.

5. Change the font size used in your name to 24.

6. Change the font size used in your address and phone number to 18.

7. Add a horizontal line.

8. Add a bulleted list showing your professional experience.

9. Turn off the Bullet List feature.

1 *How do you discontinue a bulleted list?*

10. Add a section for Education.

11. Add a section for Interests.

12. Switch to Navigator and view your page.

 Why should you look at the page in Navigator?

13. Change the background color.

TROUBLESHOOTING

Congratulations! You've created and viewed your own Web pages. As you create pages with Composer, you may hit an unexpected snag. Here are some problems you may experience.

Problem	Solution
Help! I was playing around with colors and I hate my new page. Can I get the old colors back?	No problem! With the messed-up page open in Composer, click Format → Colors and Backgrounds. Choose new colors from the dialog box. After you make the changes, view the page in Navigator to make sure it looks the way you want it to.
I created a masterpiece and then I discovered my ISP doesn't host user pages. How can I get my page to the Web?	You have a few options to try. First, think about finding a new ISP to host your site. Or, locate a site on the Web that hosts pages. Some of these sites house personal pages for free. Visit Geocities at www.geocities.com to find out more about their hosting service.
Now that I've learned about Web pages, I want to know more about HTML. Where do I start?	Uh-oh, you've been bitten by the HTML bug! (Relax, you're in good company.) To learn more about HTML, read *Creating Cool HTML 3.2 Web Pages* by Dave Taylor (IDG Books Worldwide, Inc.). You can pick it up at most bookstores or order it from IDG Books Worldwide at www.idgbooks.com. Also, view the page source of every page that you like by clicking View → Page Source.

WRAP UP

Amazing! You've done it — you've gone from Web surfer to Web master. In this lesson, you learned about the following:

- Creating a page with Composer
- Adding graphics to your pages
- Adding links
- Publishing your Web pages

Spend more time designing and editing Web pages. Finish the résumé you started in the Skills Challenge. Create pages for your neighbors, family, and friends. Remember, the more pages you design, the more you learn.

15

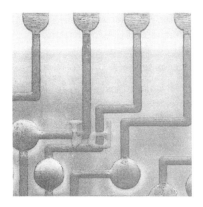

Bonus Questions and Answers

Here are the answers to the questions that appear in the Skills Challenge section of each lesson. The questions are included for easy reference.

Question	Answer
1. What does URL stand for?	Uniform Resource Locator. It is made up of letters, slashes, and periods (usually called *dots*) and represents the unique address of a Web page.
2. What happens when your mouse passes over a link?	The mouse pointer takes the shape of a hand when it passes over a link.
3. How do links appear in Web pages?	The links typically appear as blue, underlined text. Links are purposely programmed by the individual who designed the page.
4. How can you see more of the page than what's currently shown on the screen?	Use the scroll bar or use the Page Up and Page Down keys to move through Web pages.

LESSON 2

Question	Answer
1. Can you describe one way to move to a new Web site?	Type the URL in the Location box on the Location toolbar and press Enter. Another way would be to click a bookmark that you set previously. A third way would be to choose File → Open Page, type the URL, and then click Open.
2. How do you return to a site you've viewed before?	Press the Back button on the Navigation Toolbar to cycle back through the sites you've viewed during the current session. Alternatively, if you typed the URL in the location box, click the down arrow next to the Location box, which shows the last 15 URLs you entered. Select the URL to move to that site.
3. What's the quickest way to create a bookmark to the site that is currently shown on the screen?	Click the right mouse button once. From the resulting shortcut menu, choose Add Bookmark and click the left mouse button.

LESSON 3

Question	Answer
1. Why does this page contain two separate windows?	The page is divided into frames. Frames are separate windows that each have the characteristics of a single Web page.
2. Why didn't the Back button take you back to the site you were viewing before the Miss America site?	When you're working with frames, both the Back and Forward buttons move you to the frame that you viewed before *within* the site, instead of to the previous site.
3. What are two ways to move from field to field in a fill-in form?	Click the mouse in each individual field or press Tab to advance from field to field.
4. What's the fastest way to return to the page that loads when you first open Navigator?	Click the Home button on the toolbar.

LESSON 4

Question	Answer
1. Why does Print Preview show two pages, when there's only one page on the Navigator screen?	Web "pages" aren't pages at all—they're documents of varying lengths and can translate to multiple sheets when they're printed.

LESSON 4 (CONTINUED)

Question	Answer
2. What determines whether headers and footers are included on printed Web pages?	Headers, the information that appears at the top of a printed Web page, and footers, the information that appears at the bottom, are determined in Page Setup, which is accessed from the File menu.
3. What are the two file formats you can use to save Web pages?	You can save the Web page in a text (.TXT) file, which will save only the text. Or you can save the Web page in HyperText Markup Language (.HTML), which saves the text and the formatting.
4. Why can you see the text but not the graphics in a saved Web page?	The graphics are separate elements. Each graphic image needs to be saved separately.

LESSON 5

Question	Answer
1. How do you change the page you see when Navigator opens?	Click Edit → Preferences. Choose Navigator from the Categories on the left side of the dialog box. Click in the Location box of the Home page section and enter the URL of the site you want.
2. What's the difference between your PowerStart page and your home page?	Your PowerStart page is a Navigator feature that you customize with colors, links, and other special elements, while your opening page (sometimes called a home page) is the page you see when Navigator opens. If you wish, however, you can make your PowerStart page your opening page.
3.What is a font?	*Font* is another name for *typeface*. The font you choose in Navigator determines how most Web pages are displayed.
4. What kind of technology is used in Netcaster?	Netcaster uses push technology.

LESSON 6

Question	Answer
1. Name two ways to set up a query so that you include all the words in the search.	Use double quotes around the words, as in "Elvis Presley," or separate the words with AND, as in Elvis AND Presley.

LESSON 6 (CONTINUED)

Question	Answer
2. How you should you structure a search query to find Web documents that contain Elvis Presley but don't mention the word *Graceland*?	The query should read: "Elvis Presley" NOT Graceland.
3. How do search engines build their indexes of Web documents?	Electronic robots, called spiders, worms, or crawlers, roam the Web and index pages they haven't seen before.
4. What is the main difference between Yahoo and HotBot?	HotBot is a search engine, whereas Yahoo is a site directory—more like a master catalog—of Web sites, arranged by categories.

LESSON 7

Question	Answer
1. What are two ways to access the What's New and What's Cool pages.	What's New and What's Cool are available from the Places button on the toolbar, or from the Toolbar folder in your bookmarks.
2. What is SSL?	Secure Sockets Layer (SSL) is a protocol that encrypts the data transmitted back and forth over the Internet.
3. How do you check the security of a site?	To check the security of the site you're viewing, click the Security icon (the lock in the bottom left corner of the page) for information. As a system default, Netscape notifies you if you're about to submit information to a nonsecure source.

LESSON 8

Question	Answer
1. How do you know when a plug-in is loaded?	Most times, the plug-in will integrate seamlessly with Navigator and you won't be aware that it's running. Other times, the plug-in may appear in a small window, as with the Netscape Audio Player plug-in.
2. How do you know when you need a plug-in?	Instead of the page you expected to see, a dialog box appears to inform you that a plug-in is needed.

Question	*Answer*
3. Why do you need to install plug-ins?	The file you downloaded is generally in compressed format and needs to be decompressed before Navigator recognizes it. The installation process takes care of setting up the plug-in to work with Navigator.

Question	*Answer*
1. What are three ways to open the Inbox?	You can open the Inbox by using the Windows Start menu. If another component of Communicator is open, such as Navigator, click the Mailbox icon on the Component toolbar, or choose Communicator → Messenger Mailbox.
2. Can you explain the parts of an e-mail address?	The first part is the user name. The second part, the @ sign, is a separator. The third part shows the unique domain name of your mailhost. An example of an e-mail address is alincoln@union.net.
3. Where does a message go when you schedule it to be sent later?	The message is moved to the Outbox. When you're ready to send it, click Message → Send in Outbox.

Question	*Answer*
1. What are two ways you can sort your messages?	Within the Inbox, click View → Sort and choose an option from the submenu, or click the button you want to sort by at the top of the message list. For example, click the Date button to sort messages in date order.
2. How can you tell if a message is selected?	A selected message appears highlighted.
3. How can you tell if a message has been read?	The envelope icon next to the message appears open.

LESSON 11

Question	Answer
1. How do you create a quick entry to the Address Book?	Within the message, click Message → Add to Address Book.
2. How do nicknames work in the Address Book?	Instead of typing the e-mail address of the recipient, you can type the nickname you set up in the Address Book entry. Messenger substitutes the name and full e-mail address for the nickname, saving you time (and possible errors).
3. Where do messages go after they've been deleted?	Deleted messages are moved to the Trash folder.

LESSON 12

Question	Answer
1. How does Conference identify the computer you're calling?	Conference actually calls the IP (Internet Protocol) number of the computer.
2. Why does the Text Chat tool open in its own window?	Like the Whiteboard, Text Chat is a mini-program. You can close Text Chat without closing Conference.
3. When does your name appear on the Netscape Conference Directory?	Your name appears on the Netscape Conference Directory whenever Conference is open on your computer—provided you didn't uncheck the List my name in phonebook box. If you decide you don't want your name to appear in the directory after you install Conference, click Call → Preferences. Choose the Network tab and uncheck the box. The next time you open Conference, your name will not appear on the directory list.

LESSON 13

Question	Answer
1. What is another term for Internet bulletin board?	Internet bulletin boards are also called discussion groups.
2. What is different about the alt discussion groups?	Alt, which stands for alternative, hosts discussion groups that may be controversial or may contain offensive material. Alt groups are not subject to the same rules and regulations that Usenet groups must follow.

LESSON 13 (CONTINUED)

Question	Answer
3. To whom can you post a reply to a discussion group message?	You can Reply to Sender if you want only the person who posted the message to receive your reply; Reply to Sender and All Recipients if you want all members of the discussion group to receive a reply; Reply to Group to publicly post your reply; or Reply to Discussion Group and Sender if you want your reply sent to both.

A

LESSON 14

Question	Answer
1. Why do you need to save the page?	The Page Wizard uses information that's maintained at the Netscape site. You need to save the page to the hard drive of your computer to make it yours.
2. Why shouldn't you underline text on a Web page?	Underlined text is typically one of the indicators of a link. If you underline text that is not a link, it may be confusing to the people who view your page, especially if you change the text color.
3. Why don't the keywords appear on the page?	They are hidden from view but are included in the HTML code for proper search engine identification.

LESSON 15

Question	Answer
1. What's the main advantage to using Composer to create a Web page?	Composer adds the HTML tags that tell Navigator and other browsers how to format and display your text.
2. How do you discontinue a bullet list?	When you've finished adding list points, click the Bullet List button on the Composer toolbar to turn off the feature.
3. Why should you look at the page in Navigator?	The way the page looks in Navigator is the way the page will look to everyone who views it in Navigator.

Practice Projects

B

After you finish the exercises in this book, use Netscape Communicator every day. Search the Web for anything you want to know. Use the bookmarks that Netscape has set up for you or create your own bookmarks. Visit a chat site to talk with people all over the world. Send e-mail to all your friends and relatives.

I've put together a list of projects and corresponding URLs to help you enhance your Communicator skills. (Keep in mind that because the Web changes daily, some of these sites may not be available when you try to visit them.) Have fun!

Curl up with a good book

On a cold or rainy day, curl up with a good book. In preparation, search for sites that sell books of all types. Look for discount Internet bookstores or sites that offer specialty books about your favorite topic.

Here are a few sites to explore:

- Amazon.com: `www.amazon.com`
- IDG Books Worldwide: `www.idgbooks.com`
- Amuletum Antique Books: `www.tzm.it/amuletum`

Make someone's day

Use the Web to create a dream day for a special someone. Search for sites that feature glorious flowers—real or virtual—and boxes of chocolates. Look for sites that compose and send love letters signed from you. Try the following:

- Chocoholic.com: `www.chocoholic.com`
- The Romantic: `www.a-romantic.com`
- Valentine.com: `www.valentine.com`

Plan a vacation

Plan your dream vacation on the Web. Search for airlines, cruise lines, and special hotel packages.

Here are a few URLs to check out:

- Hotel Reservations Network: `www.180096hotel.com`
- Helmsley Hotels Worldwide: `www.helmsleyhotels.com`
- Around Town Tours: `www.aroundtowntours.com`

Discuss common interests

Do you like sports or politics? Or do you enjoy talking about current events or TV gossip? Find people who share your interests. Use Collabra to join a discussion group. With over 15,000 groups, you're sure to find at least one that appeals to you.

If you're a little nervous or unsure about participating, feel free to "lurk" for a while before you post. You'll find a comprehensive listing of all of the discussion groups at `sunsite.unc.edu:80/usenet-i/groups-html./` on the Web.

Maximize your money

Devise some great investment strategies. Take advantage of the financial sites on the Web as you track the performance of your favorite stocks or mutual funds. Check out the statistics on an up-and-coming company.

Visit these URLs to help you maximize your money:

- Motley Fool: `www.fool.com`
- Charles Schwab & Co. Inc.: `www.schwab.com`
- Quote.com: `www.quote.com`

Improve your golf game

If you want help with your golf game or want the live scores for the tournament of the week, there's a site out on the Web waiting for you. Search for sites that feature the latest golf equipment or mention your favorite tour players.

In your quest for the perfect golf game, visit these sites:

- GolfWeb: www.golfweb.com
- PGA Tour: www.pgatour.com
- Little Silver Pro Shop: www.littlesilvergolf.com

Help kids have fun

Are the kids complaining that they have nothing to do? Many Web sites offer great opportunities for kids. Search for sites that feature children's crafts, cooking, or games.

Use the following sites as a starting point:

- Yahooligans: www.yahooligans.com
- Aunt Annie's Crafts: www.auntannie.com
- Learn 2 Com: www.learn2.com

Be ready for foul weather

Be prepared for tornadoes, hurricanes, and extreme weather. Protect yourself with knowledge! Use the Web to help prepare for any type of weather emergency.

The following sites offer a variety of weather information:

- The Weather Channel: www.weather.com
- National Climatic Data Center: www.ncdc.noaa.gov
- Internet Newspaper Weather Page: www.trib.com/WEATHER

Shop for a car

Time to buy a new car (or at least to dream of one)? The Web abounds with sites that show the latest auto accessories. Read a review of the car you want. Have some fun and visit an interactive site where you build the car of your dreams.

You may want to start with these sites:

- Car and Driver Magazine: www.caranddriver.com
- Edmunds Automobile Buying Service: www.edmunds.com
- Official Cadillac Web Site: www.cadillac.com

B

Find long-lost friends

Use an Internet directory to search for long-lost friends or relatives. When you've found them, send e-mails to say hello. Expect a flood of e-mail in return.

Use these Internet directory sites as a base to begin your search:

- Switchboard People and Business Directory: www.switchboard.com
- Infospace, the Ultimate Directory: www.infospace.com
- Bigfoot: www.bigfoot.com

Expand your horizons

Do some extended research about a topic you find fascinating. For example, maybe you'd like to know more about the rain forest. Or perhaps you want to read up on the latest UFO sightings.

Check out some of these sites to begin your research:

- Yahoo! Reference: www.yahoo.com/reference
- Electric Library: www.elibrary.com
- Discovery Online: www.discovery.com

Enjoy food for thought — and for real

Food, glorious food! Research the best food sites on the Web. Get a recipe for cookies to die for. Go all out and plan a "virtual dinner party" — using only recipes you found on the Web. If you hate to cook, search for restaurant sites and find a new place to enjoy a fabulous dinner.

Here is a sampling of some great food sites:

- The Food Network's CyberKitchen: www.foodtv.com
- Gourmet World: www.gourmetworld.com/
- DineNet Menus Online: www.menusonline.com/

The Accompanying CD-ROM

In addition to all the information you need to successfully run Navigator 4 and Communicator, this book comes with another bonus: a CD-ROM that includes the latest version of Communicator (Version 4.02), complete with Netcaster.

But that's not all: the CD-ROM also includes the EarthLink Network TotalAccess software. This software is very handy if you need a connection to the Internet. The EarthLink Network TotalAccess software enables you to quickly register EarthLink as your Internet service provider and get connected to the Internet.

WHAT YOU NEED FOR INSTALLATION

Before getting into details about the software, let's talk about what you need to install it. The system requirements for installing the CD-ROM are as follows:

- Windows 95
- At least 8MB of RAM (16MB recommended)
- 20MB of free disk space (30MB recommended)
- CD-ROM drive
- 9600Kbps or better modem

Once you've met these requirements, you're ready to run the software that comes on this CD-ROM.

For those of you who already have a connection to the Internet, you can skip ahead to the section entitled "Installing Communicator 4.02."

CONNECTING TO THE INTERNET WITH EARTHLINK NETWORK TOTALACCESS

If you don't have an Internet connection yet, you can use the EarthLink Network TotalAccess software to quickly register EarthLink as your ISP and get an Internet account. This account isn't free, so you'll need to have your credit card ready.

To install the EarthLink Network TotalAccess software and get connected to the Internet, follow these steps:

1. Insert the CD-ROM into your CD-ROM drive and close the door.

2. The CD-ROM comes with an AutoRun feature that makes using the EarthLink Network TotalAccess software easy. Simply return to the desktop (if you're not there already), wait a few moments, and the EarthLink Network TotalAccess splash screen will appear, complete with a cool, moving logo. After a moment, the TotalAccess Installation dialog box shown here appears. Click Next to start the registration process.

If, after waiting a few minutes, the splash screen still does not appear, this may mean that the AutoRun feature on your machine is not enabled. You can still access the software: simply click the Start button, choose Programs → Explorer, and select the CD-ROM drive. Double-click the Win95 folder and then double-click the Setup.exe file. The splash screen appears, and a few moments later, the TotalAccess Installation dialog box appears. Click Next to continue, and go on to Step 3.

3. The next dialog box, as you see in the following figure, tells you that TotalAccess will install the registration software at the default directory of c:\EarthLink, and will guide you through the setup process. You can accept this default location by clicking Next. Otherwise, type into the text box the path of the directory where you want to install the TotalAccess software, and then click Next. TotalAccess will start copying files to the specified directory.

4. As shown in the next figure, a Welcome screen asks if you want to set up a new EarthLink Network account now. Click Yes to accept. If you have another EarthLink Network account and want to use that instead, click No. (If you decide you want to wait until later and exit for now, click Cancel.)

5. If you clicked Yes to set up a new account, the General Information dialog box appears (shown in the following figure), asking for your name, address, phone numbers, and more. Fill in the information requested and then click Next. (If you don't have a second address line or a fax number, you can leave those fields blank.) Another dialog box appears asking for your user name and password.

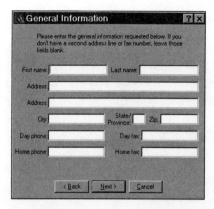

6. The next dialog box (shown in the following figure) enables you to select from two pricing plans: TotalAccess USA or TotalAccess 800. The less expensive option, the TotalAccess USA plan, involves using a local dial-up connection and is available to most areas of the United States. To view local dial-up numbers to see if there's one in your area, click View List. The other option is TotalAccess 800. This option is available for a few dollars more, for users who do not have a local dial-up number available to them. Choose the option that best suits you and click Next.

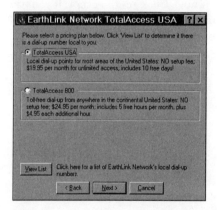

7. Follow the instructions that appear on the rest of the screens to complete the registration process and set up EarthLink as your ISP.

Once you've set up your EarthLink account, you can install the Communicator version 4.02 product included on the CD-ROM. Simply go to Explorer, select the CD-ROM drive, and double-click Nsnav402.exe, the self-extracting file for Communicator 4.02.

You'll get a message asking you to confirm that you want to install Communicator. Click Yes to begin the installation process.

INSTALLING COMMUNICATOR 4.02

If you already have an Internet connection, you can just install Communicator 4.02 to your machine and run it from there. You may still want to check into EarthLink's offer—a little comparison shopping may prove that EarthLink is a better bargain than your current ISP!

The name of the file that contains Communicator 4.02 is a little misleading. It's named Nsnav402.exe, so at first glance, you may think it's just Navigator rather than the full, Standard Edition of Communicator 4.02.

Getting around the splash screen

You've decided that you just want to install Communicator 4.02 on your machine, but when you pop the CD-ROM into your disc drive, the AutoRun feature on the CD-ROM kicks in.

The EarthLink splash screen with a cool, moving logo automatically appears onscreen, prompting you to register an account with EarthLink. What do you do?

It takes an extra step or two, but you can still install Communicator 4.02 to your machine without signing up for a new account with EarthLink. Follow these steps:

1. When the first TotalAccess Installation dialog box appears automatically after the splash screen finishes running, and asks if you want to register an account, click Cancel. You'll be returned to your desktop.

2. Click the Start button.

3. Select Programs → Windows Explorer.

4. In Explorer, scroll down to your CD-ROM drive and select it.

5. Double-click Nsnav402.exe. The file is self-extracting, so when you double-click it, you'll get a message asking you to confirm that you want to install Communicator. Click Yes to start the installation process. The program is automatically installed.

The screens that appear next take you through the installation process step-by-step. See the section entitled "The rest of the installation process" for more information.

If the splash screen doesn't appear

Even if the EarthLink splash screen does not come up automatically after you pop the CD-ROM into your CD-ROM drive and close the door, or if you've already set up the EarthLink account, you can install Communicator 4.02 fairly easily.

Follow these steps:

1. Click the Start button and select Programs → Windows Explorer.

2. Select your CD-ROM drive.

3. Double-click Nsnav402.exe, the self-extracting file for Communicator 4.02.

4. A message appears, asking you to confirm that you want to install Communicator 4.02. Click Yes to begin the installation process. The program is automatically installed.

The screens that appear next take you through the installation process step-by-step.

The rest of the installation process

A short time after you click Yes to begin the installation process, a Welcome dialog box appears. When it does, follow these steps:

1. The Welcome dialog box asks if you'd like to begin installing. Click Next.

2. In the next screen that appears—the Setup Type dialog box—you can select the type of installation you want to perform. The Typical installation installs the components that the "typical" Communicator user needs (which, to Netscape, means *all* of them). A Custom installation enables you to choose only certain components if you don't require some of Communicator's accessory features, such as Conference. If you know you need everything, leave the Typical option selected; otherwise, select the Custom option.

3. If you've never installed a Netscape brand product, then the default directory that InstallShield uses as Communicator's home directory will be a subdirectory of \Program Files. If you've used Netscape Navigator before—even if you uninstalled it—the default directory will be the same as that of your previous Netscape product. If you need to change the directory location, you can do so now (or you can wait to change it). Type the directory path in the Destination Directory field, or click the Browse button to choose the directory location from Windows' File Open dialog box. Click Next to continue.

Follow the instructions in the dialog boxes that appear next to complete your installation.

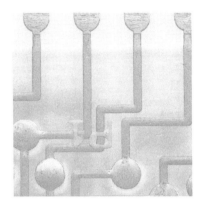

Index

SYMBOLS

- (minus sign) in Preferences dialog box, 31
+ (plus sign)
   in Collabra, 233
   in Preferences dialog box, 31
" (quotation marks) in searches, 107

A

About Plug-ins Netscape page, 151, 152
about:global location, 133
about:jwz location, 133
about:mozilla location, 133
Acrobat Reader, 147
Add User dialog box, 197-198
Address Book, 196-203
   adding entries manually, 197-198
   adding entries quickly, 196-197
   with Conference, 215
   deleting entries, 199

   editing entries, 198-199
   mailing lists, 199-201
   opening, 197
   overview, 196
   searching for people, 202-203
   sorting entries, 200-201, 207
   using, 201-202
addresses
   domain names, 18-19
   e-mail addresses, 163, 174
   See also Address Book; history feature; URLs
advTHANKSance, 167
aliases for bookmarks, 41-42
alt discussion groups, 231
Always use my colors check box, 32, 95
anchor of links, 30
AND in searches, 107
AOL Netfind, 106
Appearance preferences
   Colors sheet, 31-32, 95

my2cents.idgbooks.com

IDG BOOKS WORLDWIDE, INC.

END-USER <u>LICENSE AGREEMENT</u>

<u>**Read This**</u>. **You should carefully read these terms and conditions before opening the software packet(s) included with this book ("Book"). This is a license agreement ("Agreement") between you and IDG Books Worldwide, Inc. ("IDGB"). By opening the accompanying software packet(s), you acknowledge that you have read and accept the following terms and conditions. If you do not agree and do not want to be bound by such terms and conditions, promptly return the Book and the unopened software packet(s) to the place you obtained them for a full refund.**

1. <u>**License Grant**</u>. IDGB grants to you (either an individual or entity) a nonexclusive license to use one copy of the enclosed software program(s) (collectively, the "Software") solely for your own personal or business purposes on a single computer (whether a standard computer or a workstation component of a multiuser network). The Software is in use on a computer when it is loaded into temporary memory (i.e., RAM) or installed into permanent memory (e.g., hard disk, CD-ROM, or other storage device). IDGB reserves all rights not expressly granted herein.

2. <u>**Ownership**</u>. IDGB is the owner of all right, title, and interest, including copyright, in and to the compilation of the Software recorded on the disk(s)/CD-ROM. Copyright to the individual programs on the disk(s)/CD-ROM is owned by the author or other authorized copyright owner of each program. Ownership of the Software and all proprietary rights relating thereto remain with IDGB and its licensors.

3. <u>**Restrictions on Use and Transfer.**</u>

   (a) You may only (i) make one copy of the Software for backup or archival purposes, or (ii) transfer the Software to a single hard disk, provided that you keep the original for backup or archival purposes. You may not (i) rent or lease the Software, (ii) copy or reproduce the Software through a LAN or other network system or through any computer subscriber system or bulletin-board system, or (iii) modify, adapt, or create derivative works based on the Software.

   (b) You may not reverse engineer, decompile, or disassemble the Software. You may transfer the Software and user documentation on a permanent basis, provided that the transferee agrees to accept the terms and conditions of this Agreement and you retain no copies. If the Software is an update or has been updated, any transfer must include the most recent update and all prior versions.

4. Restrictions on Use of Individual Programs. You must follow the individual requirements and restrictions detailed for each individual program in Appendix C: The Accompanying CD-ROM of this Book. These limitations are contained in the individual license agreements recorded on the disk(s)/CD-ROM. These restrictions may include a requirement that after using the program for the period of time specified in its text, the user must pay a registration fee or discontinue use. By opening the Software packet(s), you will be agreeing to abide by the licenses and restrictions for these individual programs. None of the material on this disk(s) or listed in this Book may ever be distributed, in original or modified form, for commercial purposes.

5. Limited Warranty.

(a) IDGB warrants that the Software and disk(s)/CD-ROM are free from defects in materials and workmanship under normal use for a period of sixty (60) days from the date of purchase of this Book. If IDGB receives notification within the warranty period of defects in materials or workmanship, IDGB will replace the defective disk(s)/CD-ROM.

(b) IDGB AND THE AUTHOR OF THE BOOK DISCLAIM ALL OTHER WARRANTIES, EXPRESS OR IMPLIED, INCLUDING WITHOUT LIMITATION IMPLIED WARRANTIES OF MERCHANTABILITY AND FITNESS FOR A PARTICULAR PURPOSE, WITH RESPECT TO THE SOFTWARE, THE PROGRAMS, THE SOURCE CODE CONTAINED THEREIN, AND/OR THE TECHNIQUES DESCRIBED IN THIS BOOK. IDGB DOES NOT WARRANT THAT THE FUNCTIONS CONTAINED IN THE SOFTWARE WILL MEET YOUR REQUIREMENTS OR THAT THE OPERATION OF THE SOFTWARE WILL BE ERROR FREE.

(c) This limited warranty gives you specific legal rights, and you may have other rights which vary from jurisdiction to jurisdiction.

6. Remedies.

(a) IDGB's entire liability and your exclusive remedy for defects in materials and workmanship shall be limited to replacement of the Software, which may be returned to IDGB with a copy of your receipt at the following address: Disk Fulfillment Department, Attn: Netscape Navigator 4 Browsing and Beyond, IDG Books Worldwide, Inc., 7260 Shadeland Station, Ste. 100, Indianapolis, IN 46256, or call 1-800-762-2974. Please allow 3-4 weeks for delivery. This Limited Warranty is void if failure of the Software has resulted from accident, abuse, or misapplication. Any replacement Software will be warranted for the remainder of the original warranty period or thirty (30) days, whichever is longer.

(b) In no event shall IDGB or the author be liable for any damages whatsoever (including without limitation damages for loss of business profits, business interruption, loss of business information, or any other pecuniary loss) arising from the use of or inability to use the Book or the Software, even if IDGB has been advised of the possibility of such damages.

(c) Because some jurisdictions do not allow the exclusion or limitation of liability for consequential or incidental damages, the above limitation or exclusion may not apply to you.

7. **U.S. Government Restricted Rights.** Use, duplication, or disclosure of the Software by the U.S. Government is subject to restrictions stated in paragraph (c) (1) (ii) of the Rights in Technical Data and Computer Software clause of DFARS 252.227-7013, and in subparagraphs (a) through (d) of the Commercial Computer—Restricted Rights clause at FAR 52.227-19, and in similar clauses in the NASA FAR supplement, when applicable.

8. **General.** This Agreement constitutes the entire understanding of the parties and revokes and supersedes all prior agreements, oral or written, between them and may not be modified or amended except in a writing signed by both parties hereto which specifically refers to this Agreement. This Agreement shall take precedence over any other documents that may be in conflict herewith. If any one or more provisions contained in this Agreement are held by any court or tribunal to be invalid, illegal, or otherwise unenforceable, each and every other provision shall remain in full force and effect.

CD-ROM INSTALLATION INSTRUCTIONS

The CD-ROM that accompanies this book contains Version 4.02 of Communicator as well as the cool EarthLink Network TotalAccess software for setting up an ISP account. To install the CD-ROM, follow these steps:

1. Insert the CD-ROM into your CD-ROM drive and close the door.

2. The CD-ROM comes with an AutoRun feature that makes installing the EarthLink Network TotalAccess software easy. Simply return to the desktop (if you're not there already) and wait a few moments while the EarthLink Network TotalAccess splash screen appears. After a moment, the TotalAccess Installation dialog box appears.

3. Do one of the following:

- Click Next to start the registration process and set up an EarthLink account. Then, follow the onscreen instructions to complete the registration. (See Appendix C for more details.)

- If you don't want to set up an EarthLink account, but do want to install version 4.02 of Communicator from the CD-ROM, click Cancel. Then, click the Start button, choose Programs → Explorer, select the CD-ROM drive, and double-click Nsnav402.exe, the self-extracting file for Communicator. Follow the instructions in Appendix C to finish the installation.

Appendix C provides more information about what you need to run the CD-ROM and install the software on it. It also provides alternative instructions for installing the software on the CD-ROM in case the EarthLink splash screen does not appear automatically after you place the CD-ROM in the CD-ROM drive.